Fourth Workshop on Intelligent and Interactive Writing Assistants (In2Writing 2025)

Albuquerque, New Mexico, USA
4 May 2025

ISBN: 979-8-3313-1918-2

Printed from e-media with permission by:

Curran Associates, Inc.
57 Morehouse Lane
Red Hook, NY 12571

Some format issues inherent in the e-media version may also appear in this print version.

Printed with permission by Curran Associates, Inc. (2026)

For permission requests, please contact the Association for Computational Linguistics
at the address below.

Association for Computational Linguistics
209 N. Eighth Street
Stroudsburg, Pennsylvania 18360

Phone: 1-570-476-8006
Fax: 1-570-476-0860

acl@aclweb.org

Additional copies of this publication are available from:

Curran Associates, Inc.
57 Morehouse Lane
Red Hook, NY 12571 USA
Phone: 845-758-0400
Fax: 845-758-2633
Email: curran@proceedings.com
Web: www.proceedings.com

In2Writing 2025

Fourth Workshop on Intelligent and Interactive Writing Assistants

Proceedings of the Workshop

May 4, 2025

The In2Writing organizers gratefully acknowledge the support from the following sponsors.

grammarly

Order copies of this and other ACL proceedings from:

Association for Computational Linguistics (ACL)
317 Sidney Baker St. S
Suite 400 - 134
Kerrville, TX 78028
USA
Tel: +1-855-225-1962
acl@aclweb.org

Introduction

We are excited to welcome you to the Fourth Workshop on Intelligent and Interactive Writing Assistants (In2Writing 2025). The workshop is being held in-person on May 4th 2025 in conjunction with NAACL 2025 in Albuquerque, New Mexico.

The purpose of this interdisciplinary workshop is to facilitate discussion around writing assistants, thereby enhancing our understanding of their usage in writing process and predicting the consequences. To this end, we strive to bring together researchers from the human-computer interaction (HCI) and natural language processing (NLP) communities by alternating our workshop venue between HCI and NLP venues. Previous editions of the workshop were held during ACL 2022, CHI 2023 and CHI 2024.

Our call for papers this year focused on answering the question: How can we develop technology that appropriately supports diverse writing tasks? With the increased influx and adoption of tools for computational writing assistence, it is an opportune moment to discuss research on methods for development of tools more aligned with user needs and the impacts of the long-term use of these tools on individuals, communities, and language as a whole. We invited regular short (4-page) and long (8-page) paper submissions as well as system demos (4-page). Authors were asked to indicate of they wanted their submissions to be archival or non-archival. We received 17 submissions in total, each of which received two reviews and a meta review. We sincerely thank our Program Committee for their efforts during the review period. We accepted 12 submissions in total - 10 of which were archival and included in these Proceedings. We are thankful for all the authors for choosing our workshop to showcase their work.

At the workshop, in addition to poster and oral presentations of the papers, we have an exciting series of talks. Our keynote speaker is N Katherine Hayles (Distinguished Research Professor of English at the University of California, Los Angeles and the James B. Duke Professor of Literature Emerita at Duke University as well as a Member of the American Academy of Arts and Science). We will also have invited talks from Carly Schnitzler (Author of Crafting What We Cannot Live Without: How Creative Computational Communities Generate Social Change, and Writing Program Faculty at Johns Hopkins University), Max Kreminski (Director, Storytelling Lab at Midjourney) and Wei Xu (Associate Professor, College of Computing, Georgia Institute of Technology). We will also have an interactive panel discussion with our speakers. We thank them for helping us make our workshop a vibrant and diverse place for stimulating discussions on a variety of relevant topics.

We would like to thank our sponsors, Grammarly and Midjourney for their support.

We are grateful for our advisors for helping shape the direction of the workshop, Vipul Raheja (Grammarly), Dongyeop Kang (University of Minnesota) and Mina Lee (University of Chicago).

Finally, it is our great pleasure to welcome you in-person to the workshop. We hope that you will have an enjoyable and productive time and leave with fond memories of In2Writing 2025!

- Katy Ilonka Gero, John Joon Young Chung, David Zhou, Ting-Hao Kenneth Huang, Vishakh Padmakumar, Thiemo Wambsganss, Sarah Sterman

Organizing Committee

Program Chairs

John Joon Young Chung, Midjourney
Katy Ilonka Gero, Harvard University
Ting-Hao Kenneth Huang, Pennsylvania State University
Vishakh Padmakumar, New York University
Sarah Sterman, University of Illinois Urbana-Champaign
Thiemo Wambsganss, BFH - Bern University of Applied Sciences
David Zhou, University of Illinois Urbana-Champaign

Advisors

Vipul Raheja, Grammarly
Dongyeop Kang, University of Minnesota
Mina Lee, University of Chicago

Program Committee

Reviewers

Kenneth C. Arnold, Calvin University
Karim Benharrak
Avinash Bhat
Daniel Buschek, University of Bayreuth
Alex Calderwood
Yuexi Chen
John Joon Young Chung, Midjourney
Debarati Das
Paramveer Dhillon, University of Michigan
Wanyu Du, Amazon
Senjuti Dutta
Aidan Z. Fitzsimons, Northwestern University
Katy Ilonka Gero, School of Engineering and Applied Sciences, Harvard University
Alicia Guo, University of Washington
Shirley Anugrah Hayati, University of Minnesota - Twin Cities
Xinyu Hua, Bloomberg
Chieh-Yang Huang, MetaMetrics
Ting-Hao Kenneth Huang, Pennsylvania State University
Andrew Jelson, Virginia Polytechnic Institute and State University
Ashvini Kumar Jindal, LinkedIn
Dayeon Ki, University of Maryland, College Park
Yewon Kim
Dae Hyun Kim, Yonsei University
Zae Myung Kim, University of Minnesota - Twin Cities
Taewook Kim, Northwestern University, Northwestern University
Simon Knight, University of Technology Sydney
Max Kreminski, Midjourney
Yoonjoo Lee, Korea Advanced Institute of Science & Technology
Minhwa Lee, University of Minnesota - Twin Cities
Seyed Parsa Neshaei
Risako Owan, University of Minnesota - Twin Cities
Vishakh Padmakumar, New York University
Jane Pan, New York University
Melissa Roemmele, Midjourney
Agnia Sergeyuk, JetBrains Research
Shannon Zejiang Shen
Antonette Shibani, University of Technology Sydney
Melanie Subbiah, Columbia University
Thiemo Wambsganss, BFH - Bern University of Applied Sciences
Ruyuan Wan, Pennsylvania State University
Yadi Wang
Sitong Wang, Columbia University
Azmine Toushik Wasi
Fangyuan Xu, New York University
David Zhou, University of Illinois Urbana-Champaign
Tim Zindulka, Universität Bayreuth

Table of Contents

Understanding Writing Assistants for Scientific Figure Captions: A Thematic Analysis
Ho Yin Sam Ng, Ting-Yao Hsu, Jiyoo Min, Sungchul Kim, Ryan A. Rossi, Tong Yu, Hyunggu Jung and Ting-Hao Kenneth Huang 1

ARWI: Arabic Write and Improve
Kirill Chirkunov, Bashar Alhafni, Chatrine Qwaider, Nizar Habash and Ted Briscoe 11

ReadCtrl: Personalizing text generation with readability-controlled instruction learning
Hieu Tran, Zonghai Yao, Lingxi Li and Hong yu 19

AI Writing Assistants in Tanzanian Universities: Adoption Trends, Challenges, and Opportunities
Alfred Malengo Kondoro 37

From Crafting Text to Crafting Thought: Grounding Intelligent Writing Support to Writing Center Pedagogy
Yijun Liu and Tal August 47

Interaction-Required Suggestions for Control, Ownership, and Awareness in Human-AI Co-Writing
Kenneth C. Arnold and Jiho Kim 62

Voice Interaction With Conversational AI Could Facilitate Thoughtful Reflection and Substantive Revision in Writing
Jiho Kim, Philippe Laban, Xiang Chen and Kenneth C. Arnold 69

RONA: Pragmatically Diverse Image Captioning with Coherence Relations
Aashish Anantha Ramakrishnan, Aadarsh Anantha Ramakrishnan and Dongwon Lee 74

Multi-Agent Based Character Simulation for Story Writing
Tian Yu, Ken Shi, Zixin Zhao and Gerald Penn 87

An Analysis of Scoring Methods for Reranking in Large Language Model Story Generation
Megan Deering and Gerald Penn 109

Program

Sunday, May 4, 2025

09:00 - 09:10	*Welcome Session*
09:10 - 10:00	*Key Note Speaker*
10:00 - 10:20	*Invited Talk 1*
10:20 - 10:40	*Invited Talk 2*
10:40 - 11:00	*Invited Talk 3*
11:00 - 12:00	*Panel Discussion*
12:00 - 13:30	*Lunch Break*
13:30 - 14:30	*Poster Session*
14:30 - 15:30	*Oral Presentations*
15:30 - 17:00	*Closing Session and Social*

Designing Writing Assistants for Scientific Figure Captions: A Thematic Analysis

Ho Yin (Sam) Ng[1], Ting-Yao Hsu[1], Jiyoo Min[2], Sungchul Kim[3], Ryan A. Rossi[3], Tong Yu[3], Hyunggu Jung[4], Ting-Hao 'Kenneth' Huang[1],

[1]Pennsylvania State University, [2]University of Seoul, [3]Adobe Research, [4]Seoul National University

Correspondence: sam.ng@psu.edu

Abstract

Scientific figure captions are essential for communicating complex data but are often overlooked, leading to unclear or redundant descriptions. While many studies focus on generating captions as an 'output', little attention has been given to the writer's process of crafting captions for scientific figures. This study examines how researchers use AI-generated captions to support caption writing. Through thematic analysis of interviews and video recordings with 18 participants from diverse disciplines, we identified four key themes: (1) integrating captions with figures and text, (2) bridging gaps between language proficiency and domain expertise, (3) leveraging multiple AI-generated suggestions, and (4) adapting to diverse writing norms. These findings provide actionable design insights for developing AI writing assistants that better support researchers in creating effective scientific figure captions.

1 Introduction and Backgrounds

Scientific figures communicate complex data and concepts to readers in research papers (Durbin Jr, 2004). These figures are accompanied by captions, providing essential context and explanations to enhance the reader's understanding of the presented information (Qian et al., 2021). Writing figure captions may seem straightforward, but many researchers overlook them, resulting in unclear explanations that confuse readers (Jambor et al., 2021; Huang et al., 2023). Crafting a good caption demands clarity, brevity, and alignment with the figure's purpose, making it more challenging than it appears. It requires specialized language and detailed explanations to effectively communicate abstract and complex scientific concepts (Gomez-Perez and Ortega, 2019). The difficulty of this task has contributed to the prevalence of low-quality captions in scientific literature (Huang et al., 2023), highlighting the need for improved approaches to caption writing.

Meanwhile, artificial intelligence (AI), especially large language models (LLMs), offers seemingly promising solutions for producing reasonable quality captions (Anagnostopoulou et al., 2024; Liew and Mueller, 2022; Rotstein et al., 2024; Gopu et al., 2023). For example, the SCICAP project (Hsu et al., 2021) compiled a large dataset of scientific figures and captions from arXiv papers to develop models for generating high-quality captions for scientific figures. Many caption-generation models have been proposed for scientific figures (Rojas and Carranza, 2024; Cao and Liu, 2024; Singh et al., 2023; Wu et al., 2024). Despite these advancements, there remains a limited understanding of how AI-generated captions benefit writers of scholarly papers. While prior research has demonstrated that AI-generated captions are effective from a reader's perspective, as shown through human evaluation methods (Zhang et al., 2024; Aguirre et al., 2023; Hsu et al., 2023), their utility for writers has been underexplored from a Human-Computer Interaction (HCI) perspective. Prior studies often only focused on readers' perspectives—having people evaluate AI-generated captions by providing ratings or feedback—rather than examining the writing process itself from the writers' perspective. Recent efforts have started to address this gap. For instance, SCICAPENTER showed that AI-generated captions can reduce cognitive load for writers (Hsu et al., 2024), and another study investigated how different configurations and inputs improve caption generation to assist writers (Ng et al.). However, these efforts emphasize quantitative measures, such as cognitive load or usability of AI outputs, and fall short of capturing qualitative, higher-level insights from practitioners engaged in the caption-writing process, which can guide the design of future writing assistants.

This paper seeks to address this gap by examining how scholarly paper writers interact with

Proceedings of the Fourth Workshop on Intelligent and Interactive Writing Assistants (In2Writing 2025), pages 1–10
May 4, 2025

AI-generated captions during the writing process through a *qualitative* lens. We analyzed video recordings and transcripts from a think-aloud study (Ng et al.) in which participants rewrote figure captions for their previously published papers, as well as their post-study interview responses. Using thematic analysis (Clarke and Braun, 2017), guided by a design space for writing assistants proposed by Lee *et al.* (Lee et al., 2024), we tailored the framework to the unique context of scientific figure captions. We identified four main themes in the study data: *(i)* the multimodal and complex context inherent in figure caption writing, *(ii)* the gaps between domain-specific knowledge and linguistic expression, especially in describing complex scientific concepts in English, *(iii)* the diverse ways participants utilized AI-generated suggestions, and *(iv)* the variations in norms and conventions for figure captions across different academic disciplines. By identifying these challenges and insights, this paper seeks to bridge the gap between current AI capabilities and the specific needs of scientific writers, contributing to the advancement of more effective and intuitive writing assistance technologies.

2 Methods

2.1 Data

We acquired the video recordings and transcripts collected in a prior study by Ng *et al.* (Ng et al.), which involved 18 participants from diverse research fields. The participant pool included researchers from Computer Science/Informatics (28%), Human-Computer Interaction (22%), Artificial Intelligence/Robotics (17%), and other fields such as Energy and Minerals Engineering, Mechanical Engineering, Environmental Engineering, Chemistry/Biochemistry, Materials Science, and Cybersecurity (6% each). Participants were aged 22 to 44, with the majority (78%) between 26 and 29 years old. 72% of participants reported that English was not their first language. We briefly outline their study protocol below.

Original Study: Caption Re-Writing Study and Interview. The original study used a mixed-methods approach that combined writing tasks, think-aloud protocols, and semi-structured interviews (Ng et al.). Sessions were conducted via Zoom and lasted approximately one hour. The procedure consists of three main steps: **(1) Pre-task Interview**, participants described their typical caption-writing process, figure creation methods, and characteristics of effective captions.

(2) Writing Task, participants received a Google Doc link to rewrite two captions from their previously published works. They were provided with three configurations of AI-generated captions using GPT-4o, which varied by input type and output length:

1. UNLIMITED: Figure image and reference paragraphs as input, with no output length restrictions.

2. 30-WORD: Same inputs as UNLIMITED, but output limited to 30 words.

3. TEXT-ONLY: Reference paragraphs only as input (no image), with unlimited output length.

An example of these caption generation configurations is provided in Appendix A (Fig. 2). Participants could use these AI-generated captions in any way they found helpful while completing their task. Throughout the process, participants verbalized their thoughts using a think-aloud protocol.

(3) Post-task Interview, participants reflected on the AI-generated options, suggested improvements for AI tools, and compared their rewritten captions to the originals.

2.2 Analysis Approach

We conducted a qualitative analysis to explore how participants interact with AI-generated captions, how they write captions, and how they view AI use for scientific figures.

We adopted an existing design space for intelligent writing assistants by Lee *et al.* (Lee et al., 2024) as our deductive framework, applying its five *aspects*, *i.e.*, Task, User, Technology, Interaction, and Ecosystem, to organize and interpret the data. We used thematic analysis (Clarke and Braun, 2017) on interview transcripts and video recordings as follows: First, the first author of this paper reviewed all the transcripts and manually annotated text spans relevant to the five aspects. Then, these annotation were then grouped into specific codes (Fig. 1). Finally, the codes were synthesized into higher-level themes, capturing areas of agreement and divergence among participants. As a result, we identified four main themes from the data, which we describe in the section below.

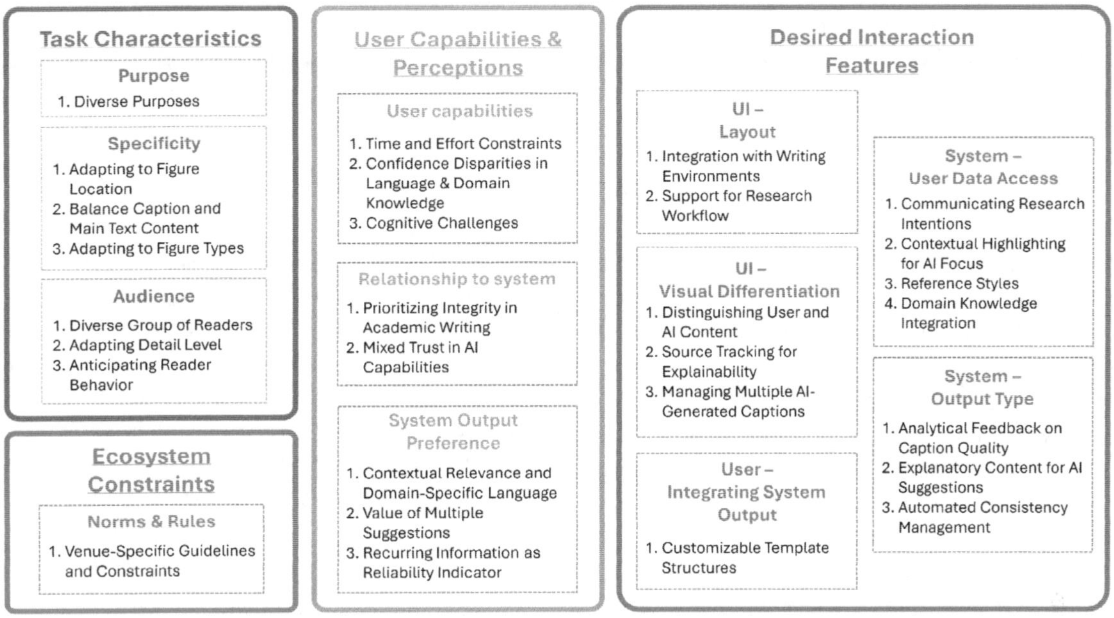

Figure 1: Codes developed for qualitative analysis of researchers' interactions with AI-generated captions, categorized under Lee *et al.* (Lee et al., 2024)'s design space aspects: TASK, USER, INTERACTION, and ECOSYSTEM.

3 Findings

Our analysis identified four key themes regarding researchers' experiences with AI-generated captions for scientific figure caption writing. These themes corresponded to the **TASK, USER, INTERACTION, AND ECOSYSTEM** aspects of the guiding design space (Lee et al., 2024), while the TECHNOLOGY aspect was less prominent in participants' concerns. Below, we detail the four themes that emerged from our thematic analysis, noting their alignment with the relevant design space aspects. In the following, we used the participant labels (P1, P2, P3, etc.) from the original interview study. Keeping these labels maintains consistency between our analysis and the prior work.

3.1 Considering Figures, Captions, and Text in a Multi-modal Context (TASK)

Our findings reveal a strong connection between figures, captions, and main text in research papers. Participants stressed the need for AI-generated captions to align with each figure and its context (P2, P3, P7, P8, P11, P12). For example, P2 highlighted the importance of context awareness: "*It depends on the figures in different sections of the research papers. If it is in the results section or the methods section, we will use the precise [caption].*" Moreover, our findings highlight the importance of treating captions, figures, and main text as an interconnected whole (P1, P2, P3, P7, P11, P15, P16). As P15 explained: "*It depends on the situation or context of the paragraph. Sometimes I write text first and then add the captions and images [figures]. But sometimes, if I already have images [figures], I make sentences around them.*"

Many participants also emphasized the importance of avoiding redundancy among figures, captions, and the main text (P7, P9, P11, P14, P16, P17). As P11 noted: "*Add details and data in captions or under figures that you didn't mention in the text of your paper... if you have described or mentioned some of the details that is [sic] visible in the figure, there is no need to repeat that information over and over again in the caption.*"

3.2 Gaps in Confidence Across Language and Domain Knowledge (USER)

Our findings indicate a clear contrast in participants' confidence regarding language proficiency versus technical or domain expertise. Many participants, especially non-native English speakers, reported lower confidence in writing captions due to language concerns (P4, P5, P8, P10, P15). As P8 noted: "*Difficult to write these long captions because for me it's hard to construct nice and beautiful sentences.*" By contrast, participants generally felt more assured in their domain knowledge (P1, P11, P15, P16, P18). Several even believed their expertise surpassed the capabilities of AI. For example, P1 remarked: "*I feel like I know best. And so I would do what I think is best. I feel like I might know better than AI on how to caption the figure on my paper.*"

This theme highlights a key challenge in caption writing: many researchers, especially non-native English speakers, struggle with language despite their technical and domain expertise. For captions specifically, this language barrier is significant because captions must clearly communicate complex visual information independently.

AI captioning tools can address this gap by complementing researchers' domain knowledge with language support: Researchers verify scientific accuracy, while AI improves linguistic clarity. This collaboration directly addresses the unique demands of figure captions, helping researchers create clear, accessible visual explanations for diverse scientific audiences.

3.3 Leveraging Multiple (AI) Suggestions and Perspectives (INTERACTION)

In the original study, participants were presented with multiple AI suggestions generated by different approaches. Our analysis shows that offering multiple perspectives—despite being generated by AI instead of humans—can be beneficial, as it could inspire paper writers. Paper writers can explore different angles instead of relying on a single solution, thereby enhancing creativity and decision-making. We further break it down into two types of usages:

3.3.1 Inspiration Through Diversity of Suggestions

Participants valued AI's ability to present multiple approaches to caption writing, often using these ideas as inspiration rather than direct answers. Many participants (P2, P3, P4, P6, P9, P10, P11, P13, P14, P15, P16, P17, P18) incorporated multiple suggestions into their work, finding it helpful to compare options and select the most useful elements for their final captions. P3 offered an insightful analogy: "*[It] feels like having three extra collaborators write captions for me and then I'm like cherry picking different parts to write my caption.*" This collaborative view highlights how AI can supplement, rather than replace, human creativity in scientific writing.

3.3.2 Trust Through Repetition of Suggestions

A notable finding emerged on how participants handled multiple AI-generated suggestions. Participants often used a comparative approach, trusting elements that appeared consistently across different outputs. As P10 noted: "*I will read all the suggestions and think about what is [sic] the common things in the captions, so which means that kind of information is important.*" Several participants (P6, P10, P14) observed that seeing similar content across AI suggestions influenced their own writing, guiding them to adopt particular phrasings or details. This observation reveals a potential cognitive bias in AI writing assistants, where repetition across suggestions may inadvertently shape researchers' perceptions of what is important or accurate. Recognizing this effect is essential for designing AI tools that support, rather than unduly influence, scientific communication.

3.4 Adapting to Diverse Norms in Scientific Writing (ECOSYSTEM)

Our analysis identified significant variations in caption writing practices across scientific disciplines and publication venues, shaped by explicit venue-specific requirements and implicit discipline-specific styles. It highlights the complex challenges researchers face when crafting captions. These challenges involve balancing formal guidelines with unwritten conventions:

3.4.1 Explicit Venue-Specific Requirements

Participants stressed the importance of following explicit guidelines set by conferences and journals, highlighting a need for flexible AI writing assistants. Several participants (P4, P6, P10, P11, P12, P18) noted challenges related to page or word limits and specific formatting rules. As P10 explained: "*A lot of conference and journal have different limits. Sometimes I want to write more information, but I have to cut down some of it.*" This tension between providing comprehensive captions and adhering to publication constraints suggests that AI tools should be capable of tailoring output to specific venue requirements, such as word count or formatting rules.

3.4.2 Implicit Discipline-Specific Styles

Beyond explicit guidelines, variations in caption styles across disciplines presented a more implicit challenge. Many participants (P2, P5, P7, P8, P9, P11, P12, P15) reported relying on examples from their field to guide their caption writing. As P15 described: "*If I make the captions for the [figure], then first I refer to other papers because there are a lot of papers about with the same or similar topics.*". This reliance on field-specific examples highlights the influence of unwritten disciplinary norms on caption writing. These norms are often understood within the community but not explicitly documented. Some participants also noted highly specific conventions unique to their fields. For instance, P9 remarked: "*I don't know other majors and other research papers, how they arrange their papers. But I think for data science area, it is not professional to include numbers [in captions].*"

These findings reveal a wide range of implicit writing styles across disciplines that researchers learn through exposure and practice rather than formal guidelines.

4 Discussion

Our analysis identifies four key themes that can guide the development of more effective writing assistants for scientific figure captions: (1) integrating captions with figures and text, (2) addressing gaps between language proficiency and domain expertise, (3) utilizing multiple AI-generated suggestions, and (4) accommodating diverse writing norms. In this section, we propose practical design recommendations for future caption-writing tools, using two illustrative examples to highlight strengths and limitations: SciCapenter (Hsu et al., 2024), which generates captions with quality ratings and contextual information to aid refinement (see Appendix B, Fig. 3), and FigurA11y (Singh et al., 2024), which focuses on accessibility by creating alt text drafts and offering interactive revision tools (see Appendix C, Fig. 4). By analyzing these systems, we identify gaps in current approaches and offer insights to guide the development of more versatile and user-centered AI writing assistants.

4.1 Design Suggestions

4.1.1 Integrating Captions with Figure and Text

Our study showed that writers often struggle to maintain consistency between captions, figures, and main text. While SciCapenter partially addresses this need by displaying related figure-mentioning paragraphs alongside captions, providing useful context during caption editing. However, it lacks deeper integration between captions and the broader manuscript structure for the writer to tracing the connection easily.

Recommendation. Future AI caption writing tools could enable interactive linking between captions, figures, and text to improve consistency and reduce redundancy:

1. **Interactive Linking and Visualization**: Create clickable, color-coded links between figure components, captions, and related text sections, allowing researchers to easily trace relationships between different elements of their manuscript, enhancing overall coherence.

2. **Automated Consistency Checking**: Implement automated checks to flag discrepancies in terminology or data representations, prompting researchers to review and refine content for improved accuracy and coherence throughout their manuscripts.

4.1.2 Bridging Language Gaps While Incorporating Domain Expertise

AI tools excel at generating linguistically coherent captions but often struggle with nuanced domain-specific knowledge. While systems like FigurA11y demonstrate the potential of human-AI collaboration, they still have limitations in understanding complex domain-specific relationships.

Recommendation. Future AI caption writing tools could combine AI language capabilities with user domain expertise:

1. **Domain Knowledge Input Interface**: Allow researchers to input key domain concepts or terminology, guiding AI outputs to ensure captions are tailored to specific disciplines or venues. This could involve developing an interface where users can upload custom glossaries or select from a searchable ontology of domain-specific terms, which would help the AI model generate more accurate and relevant captions.

2. **AI Confidence Highlighting and Output Refinement**: Develop AI models that assess their confidence in generated content, highlighting areas of low confidence for user refinement, thus leveraging human expertise to ensure scientific accuracy.

4.1.3 Leveraging Multiple AI Suggestions

Our study revealed that diverse AI suggestions inspire creativity. SciCapenter generates multiple options with quality ratings, but lacks diversity in focusing on different aspects of the figure (e.g., methods vs. results).

Recommendation. Future AI caption writing tools could generate and combine diverse suggestions:

1. **Multi-prompt Generation**: Implement parallel prompting strategies using different instruction sets (e.g., focusing on visual elements, data relationships, or research implications).

2. **Interactive combination interface**: Provide a modular editing environment where users can combine elements from multiple suggestions, such as drag-and-drop paragraph components.

4.1.4 Adapting to Diverse Writing Norms

Participants noted that caption styles vary across disciplines and venues. While existing systems like SciCapenter provide general-purpose solutions, they lack customization for specific norms. For example, it does not allow users to tailor captions to discipline-specific styles or venue requirements.

Recommendation. Future AI caption writing tools could adapt to different writing contexts:

1. **Venue-Specific Template**: Offer preconfigured templates based on common guidelines from major journals to ensure compliance with submission standards (e.g. word limits, formatting conventions).

2. **Exemplar-Based Learning**: Analyze captions from similar publications within a discipline to generate outputs aligned with established norms, using visually or contextually similar figures as guides.

4.2 Limitations

Our study provides valuable insights into how researchers interact with AI-generated captions for scientific figures, but it has limitations that should be addressed in future research. First, the original study's controlled environment, where participants rewrote captions for their previously published papers, may not fully capture the complexities of real-world scientific writing scenarios. Typically, paper authors write captions for works in progress rather than published papers, which presents different challenges and considerations. Second, while we refer to SciCapenter and FigurA11y as examples to illustrate design suggestions, these systems differ significantly from the original study setup. In the study, participants received AI-generated captions through Google Docs in a one-way interaction—they could not prompt the AI for refinements or engage in iterative feedback. This contrasts with SciCapenter and FigurA11y, which offer interactive caption refinement capabilities. Our work provides foundational insights into researchers' needs that could enhance these and future systems.

5 Conclusion and Future Work

This study explored how researchers interact with AI-generated captions to improve scientific figure caption writing. By conducting thematic analysis of interviews and video recordings, we identified four key themes: (1) integrating captions with figures and text, (2) bridging gaps between language proficiency and domain expertise, (3) leveraging multiple AI-generated suggestions, and (4) adapting to diverse writing norms. These themes highlight the unique challenges of caption writing and provide actionable insights for designing AI writing assistants. By focusing on the writer's process rather than just the output, this research contributes to a deeper understanding of how AI can assist researchers in crafting effective figure captions. These insights lay the groundwork for developing more effective and intuitive AI tools that enhance scientific communication.

Building on these insights, future research should focus on developing and testing AI tools for scientific caption writing in real-world scenarios. Such evaluations will reveal their effectiveness and usability while providing deeper insights into researchers' needs and challenges. Observations of authentic writing practices will guide refinements, ensuring that AI systems address the complexities of caption writing across disciplines. This work will lead to more adaptable, user-centered AI solutions that enhance both the writing process and the quality of scientific communication.

References

Carlos Aguirre, Shiye Cao, Amama Mahmood, and Chien-Ming Huang. 2023. Crowdsourcing thumbnail captions: Data collection and validation. *ACM Transactions on Interactive Intelligent Systems*, 13(3):1–28.

Aliki Anagnostopoulou, Thiago Gouvea, and Daniel Sonntag. 2024. Enhancing journalism with ai: A study of contextualized image captioning for news articles using llms and lmms. *arXiv preprint arXiv:2408.04331*.

Stanley Cao and Kevin Liu. 2024. Figuring out figures: Using textual references to caption scientific figures. *arXiv preprint arXiv:2407.11008*.

Victoria Clarke and Virginia Braun. 2017. Thematic analysis. *The journal of positive psychology*, 12(3):297–298.

Charles G Durbin Jr. 2004. Effective use of tables and figures in abstracts, presentations, and papers. *Respiratory care*, 49(10):1233–1237.

Jose Manuel Gomez-Perez and Raul Ortega. 2019. Look, read and enrich-learning from scientific figures and their captions. In *Proceedings of the 10th International Conference on Knowledge Capture*, pages 101–108.

Arunkumar Gopu, Pratyush Nishchal, Vishesh Mittal, and Kuna Srinidhi. 2023. Image captioning using deep learning techniques. In *2023 IEEE International Conference on Contemporary Computing and Communications (InC4)*, volume 1, pages 1–5. IEEE.

Ting-Yao Hsu, C Lee Giles, and Ting-Hao Huang. 2021. Scicap: Generating captions for scientific figures. In *Findings of the Association for Computational Linguistics: EMNLP 2021*, pages 3258–3264.

Ting-Yao Hsu, Chieh-Yang Huang, Shih-Hong Huang, Ryan Rossi, Sungchul Kim, Tong Yu, C Lee Giles, and Ting-Hao Kenneth Huang. 2024. Scicapenter: Supporting caption composition for scientific figures with machine-generated captions and ratings. In *Extended Abstracts of the CHI Conference on Human Factors in Computing Systems*, pages 1–9.

Ting-Yao Hsu, Chieh-Yang Huang, Ryan Rossi, Sungchul Kim, C Lee Giles, and Ting-Hao K Huang. 2023. Gpt-4 as an effective zero-shot evaluator for scientific figure captions. *arXiv preprint arXiv:2310.15405*.

Chieh-Yang Huang, Ting-Yao Hsu, Ryan Rossi, Ani Nenkova, Sungchul Kim, Gromit Yeuk-Yin Chan, Eunyee Koh, Clyde Lee Giles, and Ting-Hao'Kenneth' Huang. 2023. Summaries as captions: Generating figure captions for scientific documents with automated text summarization. *arXiv preprint arXiv:2302.12324*.

Helena Jambor, Alberto Antonietti, Bradly Alicea, Tracy L Audisio, Susann Auer, Vivek Bhardwaj, Steven J Burgess, Iuliia Ferling, Małgorzata Anna Gazda, Luke H Hoeppner, et al. 2021. Creating clear and informative image-based figures for scientific publications. *PLoS biology*, 19(3):e3001161.

Mina Lee, Katy Ilonka Gero, John Joon Young Chung, Simon Buckingham Shum, Vipul Raheja, Hua Shen, Subhashini Venugopalan, Thiemo Wambsganss, David Zhou, Emad A Alghamdi, et al. 2024. A design space for intelligent and interactive writing assistants. In *Proceedings of the CHI Conference on Human Factors in Computing Systems*, pages 1–35.

Ashley Liew and Klaus Mueller. 2022. Using large language models to generate engaging captions for data visualizations. *arXiv preprint arXiv:2212.14047*.

Ho Yin Sam Ng, Ting-Yao Hsu, Jiyoo Min, Sungchul Kim, Ryan A Rossi, Tong Yu, Hyunggu Jung, and Ting-Hao Kenneth Huang. Understanding how paper writers use ai-generated captions in figure caption writing. In *2nd AI4Research Workshop: Towards a Knowledge-grounded Scientific Research Lifecycle*.

Xin Qian, Eunyee Koh, Fan Du, Sungchul Kim, Joel Chan, Ryan A Rossi, Sana Malik, and Tak Yeon Lee. 2021. Generating accurate caption units for figure captioning. In *Proceedings of the Web Conference 2021*, pages 2792–2804.

Mateo Alejandro Rojas and Rafael Carranza. 2024. Enhancing scientific figure captioning through cross-modal learning. *arXiv preprint arXiv:2406.17047*.

Noam Rotstein, David Bensaïd, Shaked Brody, Roy Ganz, and Ron Kimmel. 2024. Fusecap: Leveraging large language models for enriched fused image captions. In *Proceedings of the IEEE/CVF Winter Conference on Applications of Computer Vision*, pages 5689–5700.

Ashish Singh, Prateek Agarwal, Zixuan Huang, Arpita Singh, Tong Yu, Sungchul Kim, Victor Bursztyn, Nikos Vlassis, and Ryan A Rossi. 2023. Figcaps-hf: A figure-to-caption generative framework and benchmark with human feedback. *arXiv preprint arXiv:2307.10867*.

Nikhil Singh, Lucy Lu Wang, and Jonathan Bragg. 2024. Figura11y: Ai assistance for writing scientific alt text. In *Proceedings of the 29th International Conference on Intelligent User Interfaces*, pages 886–906.

Jian Wu, Börje F Karlsson, and Manabu Okumura. 2024. Caption alignment and structure-aware attention for scientific table-to-text generation. *IEEE Access*.

Jifan Zhang, Lalit Jain, Yang Guo, Jiayi Chen, Kuan Lok Zhou, Siddharth Suresh, Andrew Wagenmaker, Scott Sievert, Timothy Rogers, Kevin Jamieson, et al. 2024. Humor in ai: Massive scale crowd-sourced preferences and benchmarks for cartoon captioning. *arXiv preprint arXiv:2406.10522*.

A AI-Generated Caption Example

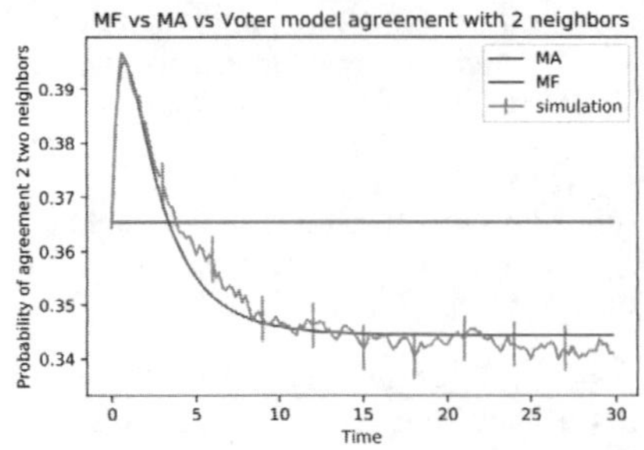

Model	Generated Caption
IMG+TEXT (30-WORD)	Comparison of mean-field (MF) and Markovian approximation (MA) models with simulation for voter model agreement probability on a 3-regular tree, showing improved accuracy of the Markovian approach.
TEXT-ONLY (UNLIMITED)	Comparison of the ad hoc Markovianized local equation and the original local equation for the voter model on a 3-regular tree truncated after 9 generations, demonstrating improved accuracy in predicting the probability of root agreement with two neighbors.
IMG+TEXT (UNLIMITED)	Comparison of Mean-Field (MF), Markovian Approximation (MA), and simulation results for the probability of agreement with two neighbors in a voter model on a 3-regular tree.

Figure 2: GPT-4o generated captions in three different configurations: (i) GPT-4o (image+text) with a 30-word limit, (ii) GPT-4o (text-only) with unlimited length, and (iii) GPT-4o (image+text) with unlimited length. Reprinted From (Ng et al.).

B Design of SCICAPENTER

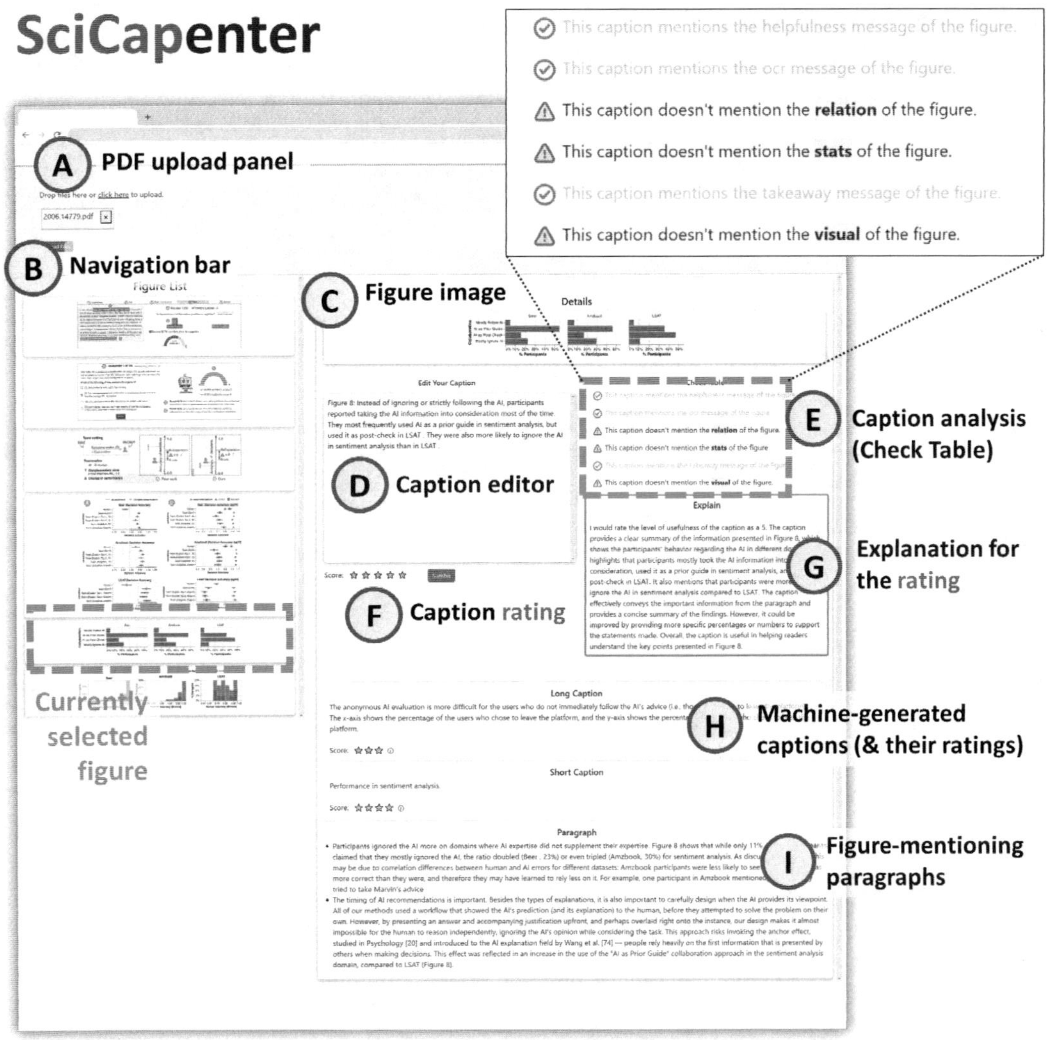

[This image shows the interface of the SCICAPENTER system, which includes several key components for document and caption management.]

Figure 3: Overview of SCICAPENTER system interface. **PDF Upload Panel (A):** A drag-and-drop interface for uploading PDF files. **Navigation Bar (B):** A horizontal bar showing a list of figures extracted from the uploaded document. **Figure Image (C):** The main area displaying the image of the selected figure. **Caption Editor (D):** A text box for editing the caption of the selected figure. **Caption Rating (F):** A feedback system that allows GPT to rate the quality of the caption, represented by a star rating. **Caption Analysis (Check Table) (E):** Icons indicating the presence or absence of key elements in the caption, such as helpfulness or takeaway message. **Explanation for the Rating (G):** A textual explanation providing insight into why a particular star rating was given to the caption. **Machine-generated Captions & Their Ratings (H):** This section includes long and short captions generated by AI models, each accompanied by their respective star ratings. **Figure-mentioning Paragraphs (I):** Paragraphs in the document that mention the target figure, providing context or additional information.

C Design of FIGURA11Y

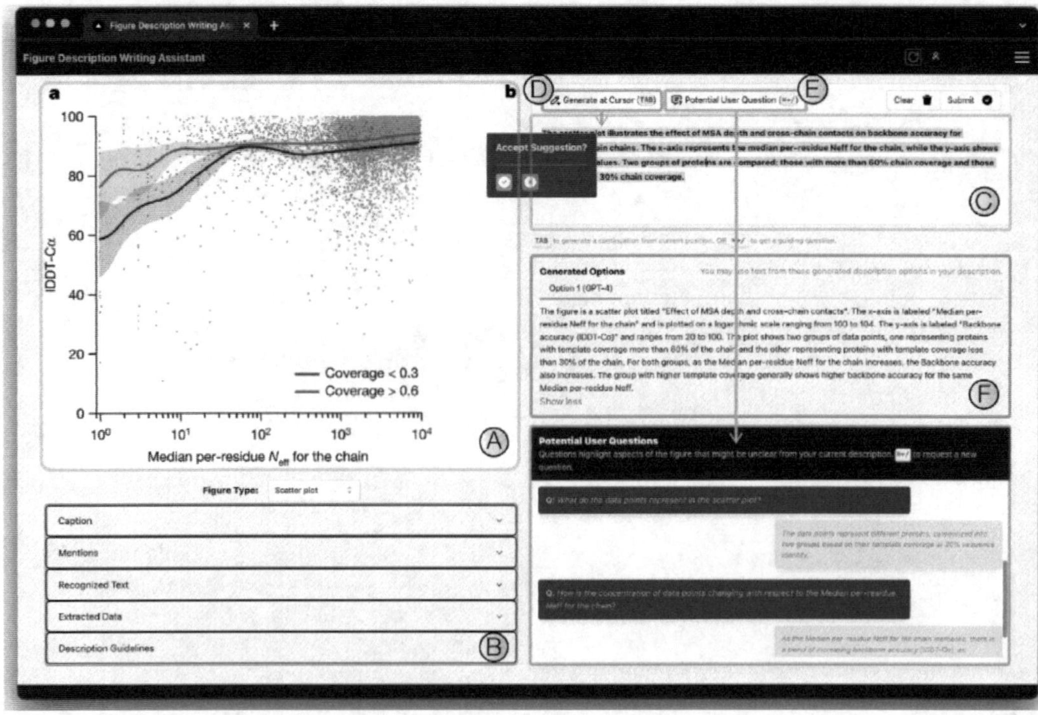

[This image shows the interface of the FIGURA11Y system, which includes several key components for document and caption management.]

Figure 4: Overview of FIGURA11Y system interface. On the left, it shows (A) the figure and (B) extracted metadata. On the right, it shows (C) the description authoring field, (D) the *Generate at Cursor* feature with generated initial text below, (E) the *Potential User Questions* request button and results, and (F) a pre-generated draft description.

ARWI: Arabic Write and Improve

Kirill Chirkunov,[1] Bashar Alhafni,[1,2] Chatrine Qwaider,[1]
Nizar Habash,[1,2] Ted Briscoe[1]
[1]MBZUAI, [2]New York University Abu Dhabi
{kirill.chirkunov,chatrine.qwaider,ted.briscoe}@mbzuai.ac.ae
{alhafni,nizar.habash}@nyu.edu

Abstract

Although Arabic is spoken by over 400 million people, advanced Arabic writing assistance tools remain limited. To address this gap, we present ARWI, a new writing assistant that helps learners improve essay writing in Modern Standard Arabic. ARWI is the first publicly available[1] Arabic writing assistant to include a prompt database for different proficiency levels, an Arabic text editor, state-of-the-art grammatical error detection and correction, and automated essay scoring aligned with the Common European Framework of Reference standards for language attainment. Moreover, ARWI can be used to gather a growing auto-annotated corpus, facilitating further research on Arabic grammar correction and essay scoring, as well as profiling patterns of errors made by native speakers and non-native learners. A preliminary user study shows that ARWI provides actionable feedback, helping learners identify grammatical gaps, assess language proficiency, and guide improvement.

1 Introduction

Arabic is the national language of over 400 million people and one of the UN's six official languages (Ryding and Wilmsen, 2021; United Nations, 2024). Yet, Arabic writing assistance tools remain severely underdeveloped. Unlike English, which has numerous competitive writing assistants and CEFR-benchmarked grading systems (Council of Europe, 2001), Arabic tools are limited to a few commercial error-correction systems with no objective public evaluation. Enhanced writing assistants could benefit millions of Arabic writers and aid corpus collection, advancing Arabic NLP.

The development of Arabic writing assistants faces major challenges, with one of the most significant being the lack of a diverse Arabic corpus that captures the wide range of writing variations, including grammatical errors made by both native speakers and second language learners. Having such a comprehensive corpus would enable the creation of writing assistants that not only provide accurate error detection and correction suggestions but also motivate learners to continuously enhance their Arabic writing skills. Additionally, these assistants would contribute to ongoing data collection while actively supporting users in refining their writing abilities.

In response to these challenges, we introduce **ARWI**, a writing assistant tool specifically designed to help MSA writers improve their essay-writing skills. **ARWI** features an intuitive interface and user experience based on the following core components:

- **Essay Prompt Database**: A library of writing topics across CEFR levels.
- **Arabic Text Editor**: Highlights errors, aids structuring, and supports iterative drafting.
- **Grammar Error Detection & Correction (GED/C)**: Identifies errors (e.g., orthography, morphology) and offers feedback.
- **Automated Essay Scoring (AES)**: Assesses grammar, vocabulary, and errors to estimate CEFR levels (A1-C2).
- **Progress Tracking**: Stores revisions and visualizes improvement.
- **User Profiling**: Allows learners to specify dialect, native language, and proficiency.
- **Auto-Annotated Corpora**: A growing repository of diverse, auto-annotated essay samples.

Section 2 presents related work; and Section 3 presents a description of the ARWI system. We discuss a preliminary user experiment in Section 4, and our conclusions and outlook in Section 5.

[1]https://arwi.mbzuai.ac.ae/

Proceedings of the Fourth Workshop on Intelligent and Interactive Writing Assistants (In2Writing 2025), pages 11–18
May 4, 2025 ©2025 Association for Computational Linguistics

2 Related Work

2.1 Existing datasets for writing improvement

Prominent English datasets include the CoNLL-2014 corpus (Ng et al., 2014)–derived from the NUCLE (Dahlmeier et al., 2013) release with approximately 1.2 million words–along with WI-LOCNESS (Bryant et al., 2019; Granger, 1998) which offers 3,000 annotated essays (628K words) grouped by CEFR levels. More recently, the Write & Improve annotated corpus (Nicholls et al., 2024) has provided a large resource of 23,000 annotated essays with detailed CEFR annotations, supporting both Grammatical Error Detection/Correction (GED/C) and Automatic Essay Scoring (AES) tasks. In addition, several English GED/C datasets such as GMEG-Yahoo and GMEG-Wiki (Napoles et al., 2019) extend the scope by covering different business domains as well as formal and informal speech registers. The JFLEG dataset (Napoles et al., 2017) further complements these resources by focusing on fluency as opposed to minimal meaning-preserving edits.

Arabic datasets are limited in both size and diversity. The QALB-2014 corpus (Mohit et al., 2014) contains around 1.2 million words across 21,396 sentences from online commentaries on Al Jazeera articles, each paired with a corrected version to facilitate GED/C research. QALB-2015 (Rozovskaya et al., 2015) adds another layer by offering 622 annotated essay sentences (approximately 140K words) from both native and non-native writers. Complementing these, the ZAEBUC corpus (Habash and Palfreyman, 2022) comprises 214 annotated Arabic essays (about 33.3K words) with CEFR grades, thus addressing both GED/C and AES tasks. However, even combined, these Arabic resources lack the extensive genre, topic and proficiency-level stratification of their English counterparts.

2.2 Arabic Writing Assistance Tools

In contrast to numerous English writing assistants like Write&Improve,[2] Grammarly, and others (Sanz-Valdivieso, 2024), which assess fluency and grammar, Arabic tools (e.g., Sahehly,[3] Qalam[4]) focus on common errors but lack overall writing quality feedback. They show good performance in identifying and correcting common errors, such as Hamza placement or confusion between Ha, Ta, and Ta-Marbuta, but lack the capability to detect and correct more nuanced error types, such as merge/split errors or issues related to the shortening of long vowels, as outlined in comprehensive error taxonomies (Alfaifi and Atwell, 2012; Alfaifi et al., 2013).

2.3 LLMs as Arabic Writing Assistants

The advent of large language models (LLMs) has led to the development of writing assistants based on zero-shot or few-shot prompt engineering (Fitria, 2023; Yancey et al., 2023; Pack et al., 2024; Kim et al., 2024), as seen in multilingual (ChatGPT, Gemini, etc.) and Arabic-centric LLMs (Jais Chat (Sengupta et al., 2023) and Fanar (Team et al., 2025)). Despite their strong baseline performance, these models tend to fall short when compared to specialized systems focused on GED/C and AES (Wu et al., 2023; Alhafni and Habash, 2025).

Recent fine-tuning experiments on English GED/C and AES datasets have yielded promising results, demonstrating that pretrained LLMs can achieve state-of-the-art performance in GEC (Omelianchuk et al., 2024) if used within ensemble models. This observation underscores the potential benefits of creating a rich, diverse corpus of annotated Arabic texts, which would facilitate the fine-tuning of LLMs specifically for MSA writing assistance.

3 System Description

3.1 Overview of ARWI

ARWI functions as a web application, integrating a front-end user interface with a backend of specialized REST API services and data collection infrastructure. The system includes an Arabic text editor with diacritics support, GED/C auto-annotation, AES module, and progress tracking that displays learning trajectories and revision improvements. ARWI delivers personalized, actionable feedback to help users continuously enhance their writing skills. Screenshots of the system are provided in Figure 1 to illustrate ARWI's current UI/UX and typical pattern of use. Figure 2 in Appendix A shows the English version of the interface.

3.2 Core Components

3.2.1 Collection of Essay Prompts

We develop an expandable database of essay prompts to provide targeted writing tasks for all

[2] https://writeandimprove.com/
[3] https://sahehly.com/
[4] https://qalam.ai/

Figure 1: A before-and-after example of using ARWI's Arabic interface. In (a) the text receives a B1 CEFR and a large number of errors marked with red underlining; in (b) the results shows improved writing and is raised to B2 CEFR. See Appendix A for the English version of the interface.

CEFR levels. Each prompt covers a specific topic across various domains, aligning with Arabic cultural sensitivities and supporting both formal and informal genres. ARWI enforces a minimum word count: 50 words for beginners (A1-A2), 100 for intermediate writers (B1-B2), and 200+ for advanced learners (C1-C2).

Beginner prompts focus on descriptive writing (e.g., favorite animals, family traditions). Intermediate learners engage with reflective or argumentative topics (e.g., pros and cons of wearing uniforms), while advanced writers tackle analytical discussions (e.g., AI ethics, environmental sustainability). Additionally, some prompts include optional media elements, such as images, to support descriptive tasks involving processes, interior spaces, or graphical representations.

Many Arabic proficiency exams, including CIMA[5] and ALPT[6], require writing tasks. Our essay prompt design draws inspiration from these exams, aligning with their task types. By mapping prompts to the CEFR scale, we ensure appropriate difficulty levels and help learners prepare for CEFR-benchmarked Arabic proficiency tests.

3.2.2 Arabic Text Editor

The editor disables *real-time* spell-checking and auto-corrections, instead providing actionable feedback from the GED/C module upon submission. This approach encourages users to review and apply changes manually, reinforcing learning and improving retention. See Figure 1.

3.2.3 GED/C Module

For GED, we adopt a two-stage token-level classification approach, similar to (Alhafni et al., 2023), by fine-tuning CAMeLBERT-MSA (Inoue et al., 2021). The first classifier performs binary GED, identifying whether a token is erroneous, while the second classifier provides a more fine-grained analysis, categorizing errors based on the ARETA taxonomy (Belkebir and Habash, 2021). These classifiers are applied sequentially: the binary classifier runs first, followed by the fine-grained classifier. This cascaded setup ensures high precision in our GED module.

For GEC, we develop a text-editing system that predicts character-level edits for each input token, generating the corrected text when applied (Alhafni and Habash, 2025). Both GED/C models are fine-tuned on a combination of QALB-2014 and ZAEBUC.

3.2.4 AES Module

The AES module leverages a fine-tuned version of CAMeLBERT-MSA to predict the CEFR levels of MSA essays. We fine-tune CAMeLBERT-MSA was on the ZAEBUC dataset and a larger synthetic dataset with topic, genre and level diversity for essay scoring (Qwaider et al., 2025).

[5] https://www.imarabe.org/

[6] https://www.arabacademy.com/alpt/

3.2.5 User Progress Tracking System

The User Progress Tracking System provides writers with clear and measurable feedback, recording CEFR scores and tracking error reduction over time. This historical data is presented through a linear graph that dynamically illustrates the user's learning trajectory.

3.2.6 User Profiling

Users who register have the option to input their native language or Arabic dialect and estimated proficiency level. This metadata enables more targeted prompting and feedback. It also supports further annotation of the auto-annotated essays collected to create, for example, (non-)native, dialect, or CEFR level specific profiles of users.

4 Preliminary User Experiment

Our goal is to determine if ARWI's feedback leads to measurable improvements in text quality such as reduction in grammatical errors or increased CEFR scores, and whether users find the UI/UX intuitive.

4.1 Experimental Setup

A total of 34 non-native mixed-gender undergraduate Arabic learners organized into four groups participated with proficiency levels ranging from A1-B1. Five essay prompts were offered tailored to the participants' CEFR level. Topics included Family and Friends, Sports and Hobbies, Spring Break, Travel Experience, and Weekly Schedule, with each essay suggested to be 120-500 words. A user survey was designed for UI and UX assessment, using a 5-point Likert scale with one-choice answers, along with two open-ended questions regarding the most and least useful features. Participants had 20 minutes for writing, 10 for corrections, and 10 for a user survey. A1 participants prepared texts in advance, allowing more time for correction.

Out of 112 total submissions, where users clicked the Check button and received feedback, 67 submissions were selected, representing the work of 12 different users, because they provided multiple submissions to incremental improvements to a single essay. 8 of these users reduced errors in their essay. One user submission contained only 3 errors in a 212-word initial draft but 4 errors in the final version, but with high CEFR scores suggesting this participant focused on content rather than error correction. The remaining submissions were by A1-B1 learners, where submissions typically contained tens of grammar errors.

Criteria	Avg. Score	Std. Dev
Clear navigation	3.68	0.90
User-friendly	3.71	0.89
Intuitive	3.59	1.09
Visually Appealing	3.03	1.03
Overall Satisfaction	3.65	0.58

Table 1: User feedback survey ratings regarding the UI experience. Ratings are on a 5-point Likert scale, with 5 being strongly positive, 3 neutral, and 1 strongly negative.

No instances of overall CEFR score improvement were observed during the 30-minute writing sessions. Significant score improvements on this relatively course-grained scale would likely require a much longer learning period.

The survey results shown in Table 1 indicate that the overall user experience of the system is moderately positive (see Appendix B for more details). Criteria such as "*Clear navigation*", "*User-friendly*", and "*Overall Satisfaction*" all received average scores around 3.65 to 3.71, suggesting that users generally find ARWI easy to navigate and use. However, the "*Visually Appealing*" criterion received a lower average score of 3.03, indicating room for improvement in visual design. Standard deviations (0.58 to 1.09) show a moderate degree of variability in users' perceptions, with the "Intuitive" rating exhibiting slightly higher deviation. This suggests that while many users appreciate the UI's intuitiveness, there is a subset for whom it is less clear. When asked whether they would recommend the system to others, approximately 85% of users responded affirmatively.

5 Conclusions and Outlook

By integrating a collection of essay prompts, a text editor, grammar error detection, correction suggestions, and automated essay scoring modules, ARWI provides targeted, iterative, actionable feedback that allows users to improve their writing and see improvements in their writing quality over time. We make ARWI publicly available at: `https://arwi.mbzuai.ac.ae/`.

Our preliminary experiment suggests the system is useful, but improvements are needed to the UI, a more fine-grained representation of progress would be useful, and more intuitive error correction hints are needed. We intend to incrementally improve the system based on further user experimentation, feedback, and analytics.

Limitations

Several aspects of ARWI require further refinement. The user interface needs adjustments based on user study feedback, including font size and screen real estate optimization. Error detection, classification, and correction suggestions require improved accuracy. Additionally, a larger study with a more diverse pool of native and non-native students across age groups, along with teacher feedback, is essential for a more comprehensive evaluation.

Ethical Considerations

The study parameters were approved by the internal review board (IRB) of our university. All user study participants were volunteers, and the purpose of the study was explained to them directly.

We recognize that AI assessment systems can make errors that may impact the student learning process and could be misused. This is not our intention. ARWI is designed to serve as a support tool for teachers and learners, not as a standalone evaluator.

References

A. Alfaifi, E. Atwell, and G. Abuhakema. 2013. Error annotation of the Arabic learner corpus. In *Language Processing and Knowledge in the Web*, volume 8105 of *Lecture Notes in Computer Science*. Springer, Berlin, Heidelberg.

Abdullah Alfaifi and Eric Atwell. 2012. Arabic learner corpora (alc): A taxonomy of coding errors. In *The 8th International Computing Conference in Arabic*.

Bashar Alhafni and Nizar Habash. 2025. Enhancing text editing for grammatical error correction: Arabic as a case study. *Preprint*, arXiv:2503.00985.

Bashar Alhafni, Go Inoue, Christian Khairallah, and Nizar Habash. 2023. Advancements in Arabic grammatical error detection and correction: An empirical investigation. In *Proceedings of the 2023 Conference on Empirical Methods in Natural Language Processing*, pages 6430–6448, Singapore. Association for Computational Linguistics.

Riadh Belkebir and Nizar Habash. 2021. Automatic error type annotation for Arabic. In *Proceedings of the 25th Conference on Computational Natural Language Learning*, pages 596–606, Online. Association for Computational Linguistics.

Christopher Bryant, Mariano Felice, Øistein E. Andersen, and Ted Briscoe. 2019. The BEA-2019 shared task on grammatical error correction. In *Proceedings of the Fourteenth Workshop on Innovative Use of NLP for Building Educational Applications*, pages 52–75, Florence, Italy. Association for Computational Linguistics.

C. o. E. Council of Europe. 2001. Common european framework of reference for languages: learning, teaching, assessment.

Daniel Dahlmeier, Hwee Tou Ng, and Siew Mei Wu. 2013. Building a large annotated corpus of learner English: The NUS corpus of learner English. In *Proceedings of the Eighth Workshop on Innovative Use of NLP for Building Educational Applications*, pages 22–31, Atlanta, Georgia. Association for Computational Linguistics.

Tira Nur Fitria. 2023. Artificial intelligence (ai) technology in openai chatgpt application: A review of chatgpt in writing English essay. In *ELT Forum: Journal of English Language Teaching*, volume 12, pages 44–58.

Sylviane Granger. 1998. The computer learner corpus: A versatile new source of data for sla research. In Sylviane Granger, editor, *Learner English on Computer*, pages 3–18. Addison Wesley Longman, London & New York.

Nizar Habash and David Palfreyman. 2022. ZAEBUC: An annotated Arabic-English bilingual writer corpus. In *Proceedings of the Thirteenth Language Resources and Evaluation Conference*, pages 79–88, Marseille, France. European Language Resources Association.

Go Inoue, Bashar Alhafni, Nurpeiis Baimukan, Houda Bouamor, and Nizar Habash. 2021. The interplay of variant, size, and task type in Arabic pre-trained language models. In *Proceedings of the Sixth Arabic Natural Language Processing Workshop*, pages 92–104, Kyiv, Ukraine (Virtual). Association for Computational Linguistics.

Minsun Kim, SeonGyeom Kim, Suyoun Lee, Yoosang Yoon, Junho Myung, Haneul Yoo, Hyunseung Lim, Jieun Han, Yoonsu Kim, So-Yeon Ahn, Juho Kim, Alice Oh, Hwajung Hong, and Tak Yeon Lee. 2024. Designing prompt analytics dashboards to analyze student-chatgpt interactions in efl writing. *Preprint*, arXiv:2405.19691.

Behrang Mohit, Alla Rozovskaya, Nizar Habash, Wajdi Zaghouani, and Ossama Obeid. 2014. The first QALB shared task on automatic text correction for Arabic. In *Proceedings of the EMNLP 2014 Workshop on Arabic Natural Language Processing (ANLP)*, pages 39–47, Doha, Qatar. Association for Computational Linguistics.

Courtney Napoles, Maria Nădejde, and Joel Tetreault. 2019. Enabling robust grammatical error correction in new domains: Data sets, metrics, and analyses. *Transactions of the Association for Computational Linguistics*, 7:551–566.

Courtney Napoles, Keisuke Sakaguchi, and Joel Tetreault. 2017. Jfleg: A fluency corpus and benchmark for grammatical error correction. In *Proceedings of the 15th Conference of the European Chapter of the Association for Computational Linguistics: Volume 2, Short Papers*, pages 229–234, Valencia, Spain. Association for Computational Linguistics.

Hwee Tou Ng, Siew Mei Wu, Ted Briscoe, Christian Hadiwinoto, Raymond Hendy Susanto, and Christopher Bryant. 2014. The CoNLL-2014 shared task on grammatical error correction. In *Proceedings of the Eighteenth Conference on Computational Natural Language Learning: Shared Task*, pages 1–14, Baltimore, Maryland. Association for Computational Linguistics.

Diane Nicholls, Andrew Caines, and Paula Buttery. 2024. The Write & Improve Corpus 2024: Error-annotated and CEFR-labelled essays by learners of English. *Research Outputs*.

Kostiantyn Omelianchuk, Andrii Liubonko, Oleksandr Skurzhanskyi, Artem Chernodub, Oleksandr Korniienko, and Igor Samokhin. 2024. Pillars of grammatical error correction: Comprehensive inspection of contemporary approaches in the era of large language models. *Preprint*, arXiv:2404.14914.

Austin Pack, Alex Barrett, and Juan Escalante. 2024. Large language models and automated essay scoring of English language learner writing: Insights into validity and reliability. *Computers and Education: Artificial Intelligence*, 6:100234.

Chatrine Qwaider, Bashar Alhafni, Kirill Chirkunov, Nizar Habash, and Ted Briscoe. 2025. Enhancing arabic automated essay scoring with synthetic data and error injection. *Preprint*, arXiv:2503.17739.

Alla Rozovskaya, Houda Bouamor, Nizar Habash, Wajdi Zaghouani, Ossama Obeid, and Behrang Mohit. 2015. The second QALB shared task on automatic text correction for Arabic. In *Proceedings of the Second Workshop on Arabic Natural Language Processing*, pages 26–35, Beijing, China. Association for Computational Linguistics.

Karin Ryding and David Wilmsen, editors. 2021. *The Cambridge Handbook of Arabic Linguistics*. Cambridge Handbooks in Language and Linguistics. Cambridge University Press.

Lucía Sanz-Valdivieso. 2024. Technology-powered multilingual professional and technical writing: An integrative literature review of landmark and the latest writing assistance tools. *IEEE Transactions on Professional Communication*, 67(3):301–315.

Neha Sengupta, Sunil Kumar Sahu, Bokang Jia, and et al. 2023. Jais and jais-chat: Arabic-centric foundation and instruction-tuned open generative large language models. *Preprint*, arXiv:2308.16149.

Fanar Team, Ummar Abbas, Mohammad Shahmeer Ahmad, and et al. 2025. Fanar: An arabic-centric multimodal generative ai platform. *arXiv preprint arXiv:2501.13944*.

United Nations. 2024. Arabic language and AI: Advancing innovation while preserving cultural heritage. Accessed: 2025-02-28.

Haoran Wu, Wenxuan Wang, Yuxuan Wan, Wenxiang Jiao, and Michael Lyu. 2023. Chatgpt or grammarly? evaluating chatgpt on grammatical error correction benchmark. *Preprint*, arXiv:2303.13648.

K. Yancey, Geoffrey T. LaFlair, Anthony Verardi, and Jill Burstein. 2023. Rating short l2 essays on the cefr scale with gpt-4. In *Workshop on Innovative Use of NLP for Building Educational Applications*.

A ARWI Interface

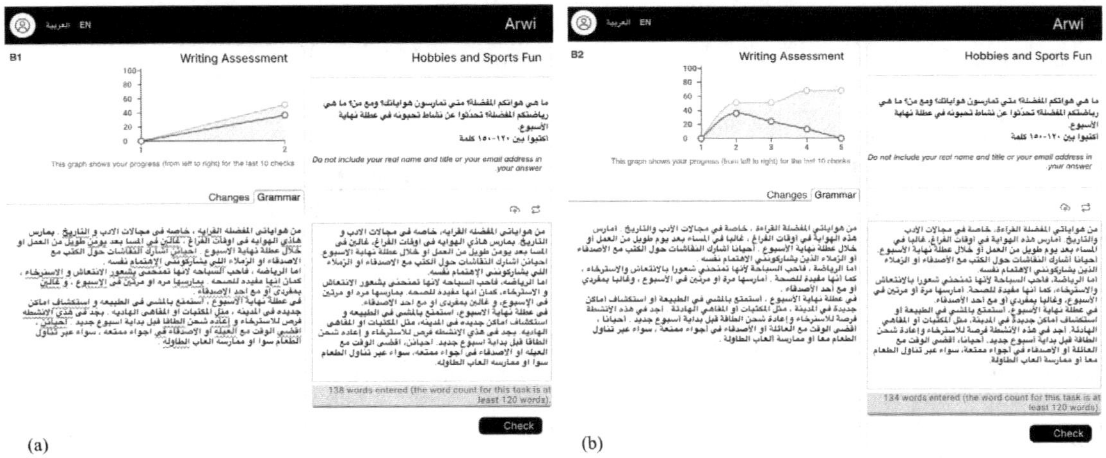

Figure 2: A before-and-after example of using ARWI's English interface. In (a) the text receives a B1 CEFR and a large number of errors marked with red underlining; in (b) the results shows improved writing and is raised to B2 CEFR. The **essay prompt** can be translated as "*What are your favorite hobbies? When do you practice your hobbies? And with whom? What is your favorite sport? Talk about an activity you enjoy on the weekend. Write between 120-150 words.*" The **written essay** can be translated as: "*One of my favorite hobbies is reading, especially in the fields of literature and history. I engage in this hobby during my free time, often in the evening after a long day of work or during the weekend. Sometimes, I participate in book discussions with friends or colleagues who share the same interest. As for sports, I enjoy swimming because it gives me a sense of refreshment and relaxation, and it is also beneficial for my health. I practice it once or twice a week, often alone or with a friend. During the weekend, I enjoy walking in nature or exploring new places in the city, such as libraries or quiet cafés. I find these activities to be an opportunity to relax and recharge before the start of a new week. Sometimes, I spend time with family or friends in a fun atmosphere, whether by sharing a meal together or playing board games.*"

B User Feedback Survey

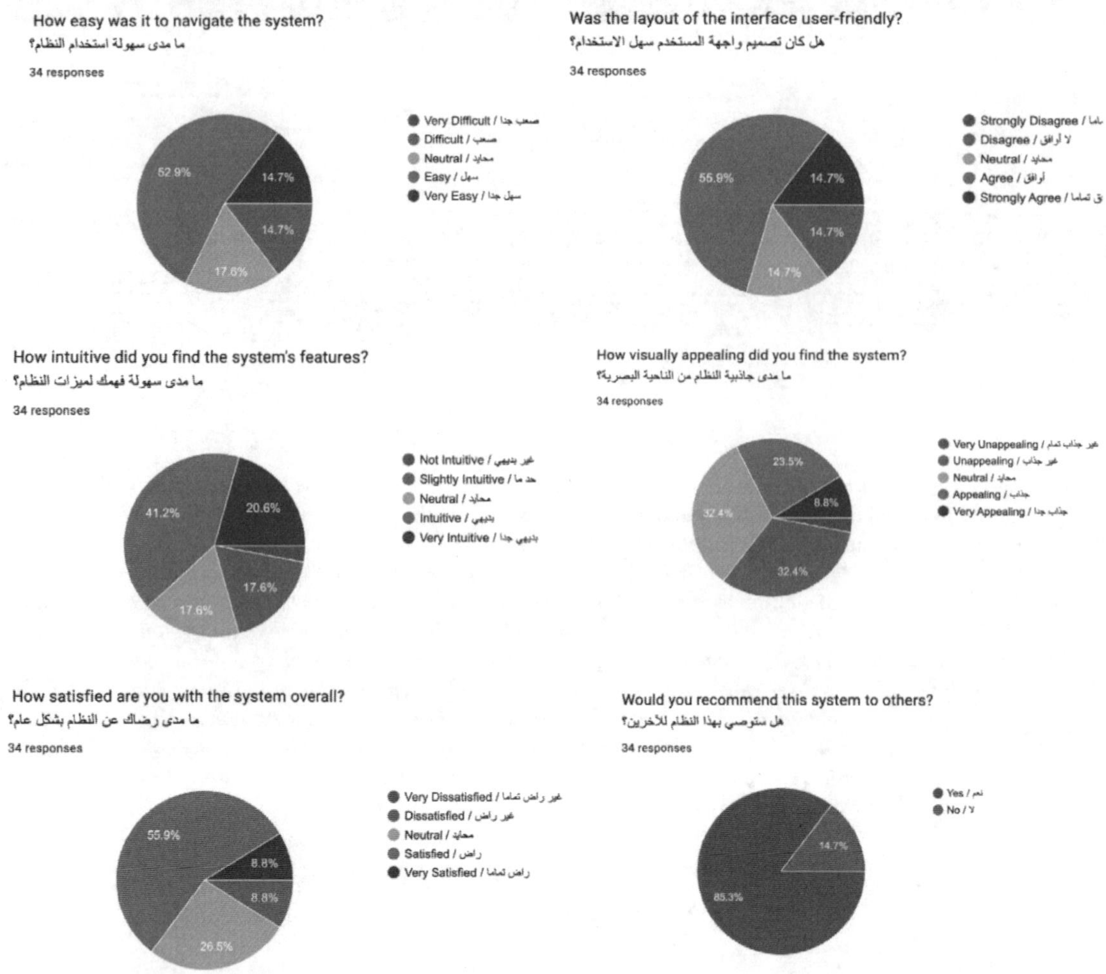

Figure 3: Qualitative feedback collected from 34 users who participated in the preliminary experiments with Arwi. The survey comprised five one-choice questions rated on a 5-point Likert scale and one binary question. The results highlight that certain aspects of the user interface–specifically its intuitiveness and visual appeal–require further refinement. Overall, users provided moderately positive feedback regarding their experience of usage.

ReadCtrl: Personalizing text generation with readability-controlled instruction learning

Hieu Tran [*1], **Zonghai Yao** [*1], **Lingxi Li** [1], **Hong Yu** [1,2]
[1] Manning College of Information and Computer Sciences, UMass Amherst, MA, USA
[2] Miner School of Computer and Information Sciences, UMass Lowell, MA, USA
{hieutran, zonghaiyao}@umass.edu

Abstract

Content generation conditioning on users' readability is an important application for personalization. In an era of large language models (LLMs), readability-controlled text generation based on LLMs has become increasingly important. This paper introduces a novel methodology called "Readability-Controlled Instruction Learning (ReadCtrl)," which aims to instruction-tune LLMs to tailor users' readability levels. Unlike the traditional methods, which primarily focused on categorical readability adjustments—typically classified as high, medium, and low or expert and layperson levels—with limited success, ReadCtrl introduces a dynamic framework that enables LLMs to generate content at various (near continuous level) complexity levels, thereby enhancing their versatility across different applications. Our results show that the ReadCtrl-Mistral-7b models significantly outperformed strong baseline models such as GPT-4 and Claude-3, with a win rate of 52.1%:35.7% against GPT-4 in human evaluations. Furthermore, ReadCtrl has shown significant improvements in automatic evaluations, as evidenced by better readability metrics (e.g., FOG, FKGL) and generation quality metrics (e.g., BLEU, SARI, SummaC-Factuality, UniEval-Consistency and Coherence). These results underscore ReadCtrl's effectiveness and tenacity in producing high-quality, contextually appropriate outputs that closely align with targeted readability levels, marking a significant advancement in personalized content generation using LLMs [1].

1 Introduction

Existing personalization methods mainly focus on the semantics of the content that individuals need, such as retrieving information based on individuals' search queries (Chen et al., 2023; Kirk et al., 2024; Shanahan et al., 2023) and summarization based on content representation (Richardson et al., 2023). However, one important aspect of personalization that has not been widely explored is readability-controlled content generation, which is particularly relevant for writers and readers with varying expertise levels(Vajjala, 2021). This involves tailoring content to match individuals' readability levels, which can vary widely due to differences in education, domain familiarity, and writing proficiency(Ribeiro et al., 2023). The emergence of large language models (LLMs) has further advanced this field, ushering in a transformative era of

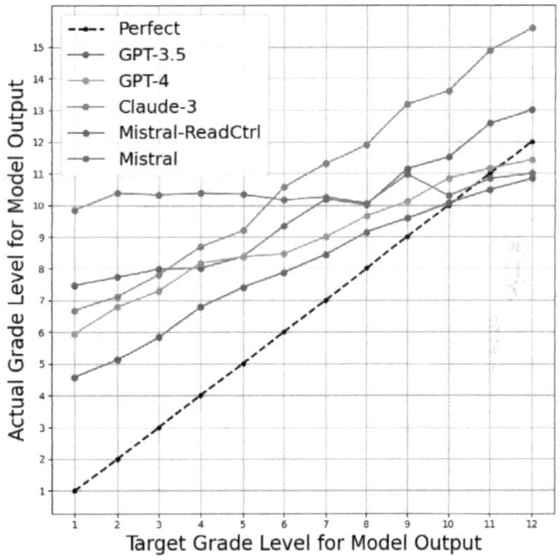

Figure 1: ReadCtrl instruction following ability. While current SOTA LLMs such as GPT and Claude (under the few-shot setting) show an upward trend in aligning their output with the target grade level, they fall significantly short of the 'perfect' adherence curve. Other weaker LLMs like Mistral-7b demonstrate little to no capacity to adjust to ReadCtrl instructions, as indicated by the flat line parallel to the x-axis. Notably, Mistral-ReadCtrl's performance closely approaches 'perfect', showcasing its advanced capability to tailor output to the specified readability level as set out by ReadCtrl instructions.

* indicates equal contribution

[1]Our code and data will be released at https://github.com/bio-nlp/ReadCtrl

Proceedings of the Fourth Workshop on Intelligent and Interactive Writing Assistants (In2Writing 2025), pages 19–36
May 4, 2025 ©2025 Association for Computational Linguistics

personalized writing assistance(Pu and Demberg, 2023). It is crucial for content generated by these models to be not only accurate and relevant but also adaptable to the stylistic and cognitive preferences of different users (e.g., writers and readers). The emphasis on customized content creation underscores the critical role of LLM alignment methods in digital interactions, especially in environments where users may require varying levels of guidance and editorial control(Zhou et al., 2023; Sun et al., 2023; Qin et al., 2024). At the heart of this innovative area are the principles of readability control instructions, designed to dynamically adapt the output vocabulary distribution to the specific context of each interaction. This can be achieved by analyzing chat history, interpreting user profiles, or responding to direct interaction requests, significantly enhancing LLMs' versatility (Huang et al., 2023).

Previous efforts in the domain of controllable text generation have primarily centered on binary readability adjustments, typically categorized into tasks of simplification, complication, or sibling style transfer (Goldsack et al., 2022; Guo et al., 2021; Luo et al., 2022). Despite their objectives, these approaches often fail to fully address the diverse personalization needs due to the limited variety in training data and a concentrated emphasis on readability. In traditional supervised finetuning scenarios, designing multiple readability-level ground truths for training data to facilitate readability control is not scalable. As a result, models may not have sufficient exposure to varied text complexities, limiting their ability to adjust content according to user-specific readability needs accurately. In response, the field of artificial intelligence is shifting towards more dynamic systems that can adapt outputs to meet users' unique preferences and requirements (Kirk et al., 2024). This shift is heralding a new era of personalized content creation that extends beyond standard domains like information retrieval to specialized areas, enhancing user engagement and satisfaction through tailored content.

This paper addresses these challenges by introducing a novel methodology termed "readability-controlled instruction learning (ReadCtrl)." Our findings demonstrate that ReadCtrl can empower LLMs to transform input text into content with controlled readability accurately. As illustrated in Figure 1, our investigation across a range of state-of-the-art LLMs shows varying degrees of compliance with readability-controlled instructions. Mainstream models like GPT (Achiam et al., 2023) and Claude (Anthropic, 2024), despite demonstrating an Upward trend, fall significantly short of the ideal 'perfect' adherence curve—they show a tendency towards compliance but lack precise output control. In contrast, models that previously struggled with readability control, such as Mistral-7b (Jiang et al., 2023)—illustrated almost as a horizontal line in the figure—have shown significant enhancement with the integration of ReadCtrl, such as Mistral-ReadCtrl. These models now nearly meet the ideal performance curve, showcasing their improved ability to customize outputs to specific readability demands. Specifically, ReadCtrl incorporates explicit instruction tuning based on readability and is rigorously tested through tasks designed to evaluate the model's ability to adjust output complexity. These tasks include text simplification, which aims to reduce the output's readability relative to the input; paraphrase generation, which maintains the input's readability; and semantic entailment generation, which adjusts the output's readability, potentially increasing or decreasing it in relation to the input. By employing a clear instruction—"*Given an input text, please output an entailment with a readability score around {target readability score}*"—models like Mistral-ReadCtrl demonstrate the efficacy of ReadCtrl in generating content that is not only semantically coherent but also finely adjusted to meet diverse comprehension needs and preferences.

In our initial experiments, we evaluated the model's performance in a "seen setting," where models were tested using datasets on which they were trained, such as ASSET (Alva-Manchego et al., 2020) for text simplification, PAWS (Zhang et al., 2019) for paraphrase generation, and SNLI (Bowman et al., 2015) for semantic entailment. This setting established a baseline for instruction tuning, confirming that the models could effectively adhere to readability instructions in familiar contexts. Subsequent experiments involved an "unseen setting," testing the models against new datasets they had not encountered during training, such as WikiSmall (Zhu et al., 2010) for text simplification, MRPC (Dolan and Brockett, 2005) for paraphrase generation, and MultiNLI (Williams et al., 2017) for semantic entailment. This phase was critical for assessing the models' adaptability and accuracy in novel contexts, reflecting their generalizability and real-world applicability. We utilized several readability assessment metrics, including the Gunning Fog Index (Gunning, 1952) and Flesch-Kincaid Grade Level (Kincaid et al., 1975), to quantitatively evaluate the complexity of the generated texts. Additionally, we employed a range of automatic generation metrics for generation quality evaluation, such as BLEU (Papineni et al., 2002), SARI (Xu et al., 2016), Factuality (Laban et al., 2022), Consistency and Coherence (Zhong et al., 2022), to assess the quality of the generated texts, aiming to balance readability, information retention, factuality, consistency, and coherence during evaluation.

These evaluations confirmed the effectiveness of our ReadCtrl methodology across a diverse range of tasks and datasets. Particularly, Mistral-ReadCtrl excelled in both seen and unseen settings, showcasing robust performance metrics. For instance, in the unseen MRPC dataset, Mistral ReadCtrl achieved the lowest readability gap (1.66), the highest factuality (0.8184), and excellent BLEU (0.3798) and SARI (44.4327) scores, significantly outperforming competitors like GPT-4 and Claude-3. In the WikiSmall dataset, it recorded a readability gap of just 2.09, the highest coherence score (0.9763), and a strong SARI score of 42.1033. Furthermore, detailed human and LLM-as-a-judge (Lan et al., 2024) evaluations were conducted to compare Mistral-ReadCtrl with GPT-4 across different tasks and readability requirements. Mistral-ReadCtrl demonstrated superior performance, achieving a win rate of 52.1% in human evaluations and 58.3% in AI assessments, compared to GPT-4's 35.7% and 38.4%, respectively. Notably strong results were observed in tasks involving WikiSmall (62.5% in Human Eval, 67.7% in AI Eval) and SNLI (66.7% in Human Eval).

2 Methodology

2.1 Task Overview

Our methodology is designed to evaluate the effectiveness of instruction tuning conditional on readability across a suite of tasks, specifically focusing on text simplifications, paraphrase generation, and semantic entailment generation. These tasks are strategically chosen to test the model's capability in adjusting the complexity of its output to match specified readability levels. They serve a broad spectrum of applications, from enhancing educational material accessibility to refining technical documentation for diverse audiences.

- **Text Simplifications:** Here, the aim is to reduce the readability level of the given input text, making it more accessible to a wider audience or readers with varying comprehension skills. This task challenges the model to simplify complex text while preserving its essential content and meaning, demonstrating the ability to decrease textual complexity upon demand.
- **Paraphrase Generation:** In this task, the model is tasked with rewording the given text to produce a paraphrase that maintains the original's readability level. This requires a nuanced understanding of language to ensure the output remains true to the input's complexity and style, facilitating content reformulation without altering its accessibility.
- **Semantic Entailment Generation:** This involves creating text that semantically follows from the given input, with the flexibility to increase or decrease the readability level. The model must grasp the underlying meaning of the input text and generate output that logically entails the input, demonstrating versatility in producing content with adjustable complexity levels.

We employ the instruction tuning approach conditional on readability for all these tasks. This method provides explicit instructions to the model to control the output text's readability score, ensuring that the generated content aligns with the intended complexity level for the target audience. This approach underlines our belief that these tasks can all contribute to readability control generation, where, depending on the task—be it text simplification, paraphrase generation, or semantic entailment generation—the model is calibrated to generate output with the desired readability level. In text simplification, the goal is to lower the readability of the output relative to the input, while in paraphrase generation, the output's readability should mirror the input's. For the semantic entailment generation task, the output's readability may vary, being either higher or lower than the input's, thereby offering a versatile tool for adjusting text complexity across a wide range of contexts.

2.2 Instruction Design for Readability Control

To achieve the desired readability level across various tasks, we employ straightforward and singular

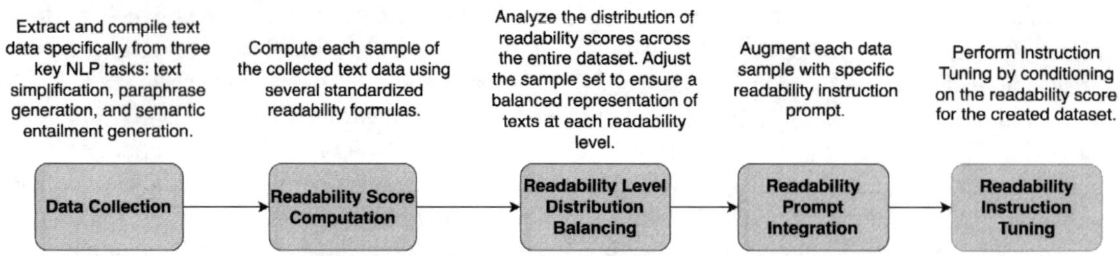

Figure 2: Overview of ReadCtrl data construction.

instruction. This approach emphasizes the model's ability to tailor its output to meet specific readability goals, demonstrating its versatility and effectiveness in readability control. The instruction is as follows:

"Given an input text, please output an entailment with a readability score around target readability score."

This concise instruction mandates the model to generate content that not only semantically follows from the given input but also aligns with a specified readability level, showcasing the model's capacity to produce targeted outputs that cater to diverse comprehension needs and preferences.

2.3 Implementation and Readability Scoring

The readability of the generated text is quantitatively evaluated using a suite of established readability metrics. We calculate the following readability scores [2]:

- **Gunning Fog Index:** Estimates the years of formal education required to understand the text on the first reading (Gunning, 1952).
- **Flesch-Kincaid Grade Level:** Translates the US grade level needed to comprehend the text (Kincaid et al., 1975).
- **Automated Readability Index:** Outputs a score correlating to the US grade level necessary for understanding (Senter and Smith, 1967).
- **Coleman-Liau Index:** Estimates the US grade level needed to comprehend the text using letter count instead of syllable count (Coleman and Liau, 1975).

These metrics are selected for their diverse approaches to assessing text complexity, offering a comprehensive understanding of the text's readability. Subsequently, an average Reading Grade Level (RGL) is derived from these scores to represent the text's overall readability. The integration of these readability assessments into our methodology allows a nuanced approach to generating text that meets the specified readability criteria. By adjusting the instruction based on the target RGL, we can fine-tune the complexity of the output, making our approach adaptable to a wide range of applications, from educational content to technical documentation. This process underscores the importance of readability in tailoring content to specific audience needs, a critical factor in communication effectiveness across various domains.

3 Experiments

3.1 Dataset

Our experimental framework is designed to assess the model's performance across various tasks, specifically focusing on text simplification, paraphrase generation, and semantic entailment generation. To facilitate a comprehensive evaluation, we utilize six distinct datasets, two for each task, which enables us to explore the model's capabilities in both seen and unseen settings. The datasets employed in our experiments are outlined as follows:

- **Text Simplification:** For this task, we use the ASSET (Alva-Manchego et al., 2020) and WikiSmall (Zhu et al., 2010) datasets. ASSET is a diverse corpus for automatic sentence simplification, providing high-quality simplifications with multiple references per source sentence, making it ideal for instruction tuning and evaluation in seen settings. WikiSmall serves as an additional dataset for evaluating performance in an unseen setting, offering a different collection of simplified sentences derived from Wikipedia articles.
- **Paraphrase Generation:** We utilize the PAWS (Zhang et al., 2019) (Paraphrase Adversaries from Word Scrambling) and MRPC (Microsoft Research Paraphrase Corpus) (Dolan and Brockett, 2005) datasets. PAWS contains pairs of sentences paraphrasing each other, including those

[2] More details can be found in Appendix A.

constructed through controlled word scrambling, making it suitable for training and the seen setting evaluations. MRPC offers a collection of sentence pairs labeled as paraphrases or not, sourced from online news sources, to test the model's paraphrasing ability in unseen settings.

- **Semantic Entailment Generation:** For this task, the SNLI (Stanford Natural Language Inference) (Bowman et al., 2015) and MultiNLI (Multi-Genre Natural Language Inference) (Williams et al., 2017) datasets are employed. SNLI is a large collection of sentence pairs annotated with textual entailment information, used for instruction tuning and seen setting evaluation. MultiNLI extends this to a broader range of genres and contexts, providing a robust challenge for the model in unseen settings.

In our experimental setup, instruction tuning is performed on the training sets of ASSET, PAWS, and SNLI to align the model's output with specific readability goals. The effectiveness of this approach is then evaluated in two distinct settings: a *seen setting*, using the test sets of ASSET, PAWS, and SNLI, and an *unseen setting*, using the test sets of WikiSmall, MRPC, and MultiNLI. This methodology allows us to not only measure the model's immediate response to the instruction tuning but also its generalizability and adaptability to different textual contexts and tasks.

3.2 Evaluation Metrics

To comprehensively evaluate the model's performance across the different tasks, we employ a multifaceted set of metrics that assess various aspects of the generated texts. These metrics enable us to gauge the model's effectiveness in adjusting readability, maintaining factual accuracy, and ensuring textual coherence and consistency. The following metrics are used:

- **Average Readability Score:** This metric calculates the average readability level of the generated texts, providing insight into the overall accessibility of the content produced by the model.
- **Readability Gap (Delta):** The readability gap is measured as the difference between the requested readability level and the actual readability level of the generated text. This metric assesses the model's precision in hitting target readability levels.
- **Factuality:** Factuality is evaluated based on the methodology from the SummaC (Laban et al., 2022) work, which offers a means to assess the factual alignment of the generated text with the source content or input.
- **Consistency and Coherence:** These aspects are measured using criteria from the UniEval (Zhong et al., 2022) framework, which provides standardized metrics for evaluating the logical consistency and coherence of the text, ensuring that the generated content is not only readable but also logically structured and coherent.
- **SARI:** The SARI (System output Against References and the Input sentence) (Xu et al., 2016) metric is utilized to assess the quality of text simplification. It measures the model's ability to produce simplified text that is both accurate and helpful, comparing the generated output against both the original text and reference simplifications.
- **BLEU:** The BLEU (Bilingual Evaluation Understudy) (Papineni et al., 2002) metric is applied to evaluate paraphrase generation and semantic entailment tasks. It quantifies the linguistic similarity between the generated texts and reference texts, indicating the model's capability to produce coherent and contextually appropriate content.

These metrics collectively offer a robust framework for assessing the nuanced performance of the model across various dimensions of text generation, readability adjustment, and content quality.

3.3 Evaluated Models

In our study, we evaluate a diverse set of models to understand their efficacy in handling tasks related to term definition generation, text simplification, and text complication, particularly focusing on adjusting text complexity according to specified readability levels. The models include:

- **GPT-3.5:** As a precursor to GPT-4, GPT-3.5 has demonstrated substantial capabilities in generating human-like text across various tasks. It serves as a baseline to understand the incremental improvements brought about by its successors and other models.
- **GPT-4:** The latest iteration from OpenAI's GPT series at the time of our study, GPT-4, represents a significant leap in language model performance, offering improved comprehension and generation capabilities over its predecessors.
- **Claude-3:** As a model known for its understanding and generation abilities, Claude-3 has been in-

Models	Readability Gap↓	Factuality↑	Consistency↑	Coherence↑	BLEU↑	SARI↑
ASSET (seen) | WikiSmall (unseen) - Text Simplification						
Claude-3	3.6323 | 4.53	0.5221 | 0.4612	0.9301 | 0.9391	0.934 | 0.9396	0.1874 | 0.1606	40.6964 | 32.9996
GPT-3.5	2.8635 | 3.12	0.7231 | 0.6721	0.9641 | 0.9401	0.9648 | 0.9231	0.2739 | 0.194	41.0061 | 33.9842
GPT-4	2.7465 | 2.69	0.6547 | 0.5892	**0.9688** | **0.9556**	**0.9687** | 0.949	0.2061 | 0.1666	39.7319 | 31.4657
Mistral-ReadCtrl	**1.8384** | **2.09**	**0.7687** | **0.7168**	0.9423 | 0.9477	0.9653 | **0.9763**	**0.4317** | **0.4321**	**49.3521** | **42.1033**
SNLI (seen) | MultiNLI (unseen) - Semantic Entailment Generation						
Claude-3	4.6433 | 5.64	0.5102 | 0.3904	0.919 | 0.8292	0.9331 | 0.8346	0.0446 | 0.0303	48.3281 | 44.4344
GPT-3.5	2.8333 | 6.7	0.5176 | 0.3967	0.9049 | 0.8829	0.8982 | 0.896	0.0875 | 0.0378	51.0201 | 44.0607
GPT-4	2.4733 | 3.36	0.5632 | 0.5167	0.9488 | **0.8961**	0.9382 | 0.8879	0.105 | 0.0562	**52.1153** | **46.4204**
Mistral-ReadCtrl	**1.8733** | **2.21**	**0.7406** | **0.6542**	**0.9491** | 0.8804	**0.9437** | **0.9122**	**0.183** | **0.1137**	51.6644 | 43.8289
PAWS (seen) | MRPC (unseen) - Paraphrase Generation						
Claude-3	2.4333 | 2.61	0.5141 | 0.4736	0.921 | 0.9154	0.9183 | 0.9012	0.2393 | 0.1679	38.3459 | 36.7783
GPT-3.5	1.5433 | 2.64	0.7443 | 0.5868	0.9761 | **0.9683**	0.9746 | 0.9679	0.3873 | 0.2059	37.9808 | 37.3417
GPT-4	1.4467 | 2.19	0.7085 | 0.5203	**0.979** | 0.9635	**0.978** | 0.9639	0.3122 | 0.153	34.3525 | 34.8477
Mistral-ReadCtrl	**0.6367** | **1.66**	**0.7871** | **0.8184**	0.9677 | 0.9669	0.9735 | **0.9769**	**0.6649** | **0.3798**	**60.5332** | **44.4327**

Table 1: Main results for seen | unseen tasks in ReadCtrl.

cluded as a baseline for its efficiency in handling various NLP tasks and its purported adaptability to instruction-based prompts, making it a relevant comparison for our instruction-tuned model.

- **Mistral 7B ReadCtrl:** Our proposed model has been instruction-tuned to adjust the readability level of generated texts based on explicit instructions. Mistral 7B is designed to excel in the specific tasks of text simplification, paraphrase generation, and semantic entailment generation, leveraging instruction tuning to achieve precise control over the readability of its outputs.

Each of these models brings unique strengths and capabilities to the table, allowing us to conduct a comprehensive comparison that not only highlights Mistral 7B's advancements in controlling readability but also situates these achievements within the broader context of current NLP technologies. By evaluating Mistral 7B against these established models, we aim to demonstrate its efficacy and potential applications in enhancing readability control in automatic text generation.

3.4 Results

3.4.1 Performance on seen tasks

Table 1 presents a performance comparison of Claude-3, GPT-3.5, GPT-4, and our model, Mistral-ReadCtrl, on seen tasks involving three datasets where instruction tuning was implemented: ASSET, SNLI, and PAWS. Regarding the Readability Gap, Mistral-ReadCtrl demonstrates superior precision in adhering to target readability levels, achieving the lowest scores across all datasets, indicating effective control over text readability. Factuality scores, which assess the accuracy of content compared to the original, show that Mistral-ReadCtrl maintains higher factual consistency than its counterparts. When evaluating Consistency and Coherence, which measure the logical flow and structural soundness of texts, Mistral-ReadCtrl performs robustly, though it is slightly outperformed by GPT-4 in the PAWS dataset. For BLEU and SARI metrics, critical for evaluating the linguistic and contextual appropriateness of text simplification and paraphrase generation, Mistral-ReadCtrl again posts the highest scores, showcasing its efficacy in producing high-quality, contextually appropriate responses.

3.4.2 Performance on unseen tasks

Table 1 illustrates the performance of four models — Claude-3, GPT-3.5, GPT-4, and Mistral-ReadCtrl — on unseen tasks, using the datasets WikiSmall for text simplification, MultiNLI for semantic entailment generation, and MRPC for paraphrase generation. These results are crucial for assessing each model's ability to generalize beyond the data types encountered during training.

In the WikiSmall dataset, Mistral-ReadCtrl outperforms other models with the lowest readability gap of 2.09, suggesting superior control aligning with the target readability levels. It also achieves the highest factuality and coherence scores and significantly outstrips the competition in BLEU and SARI scores, indicating its effectiveness in maintaining content quality in text simplification tasks.

Mistral-ReadCtrl again shows notable performance for the MultiNLI dataset, which focuses on semantic entailment generation, with the lowest readability gap of 2.21 and the highest factuality and coherence scores among the models. However, while its BLEU score is the highest, it slightly trails

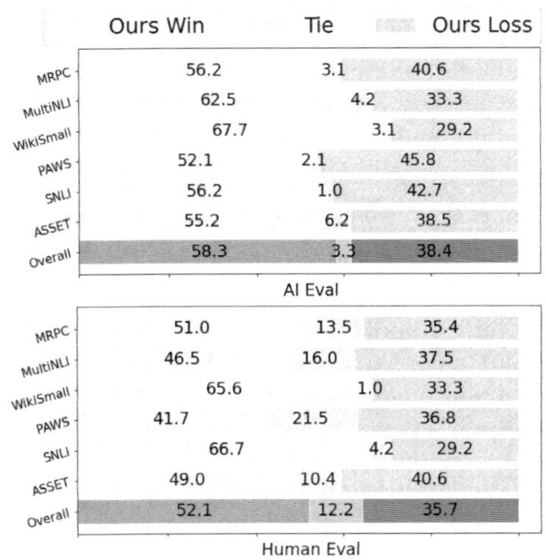

Figure 3: Win rate (%) for Mistral-ReadCtril vs GPT-4 (3 shots) using AI (Claude3 and GPT3.5) and Human evaluation.

behind GPT-4 in SARI, demonstrating strong but not leading performance in generating entailments that are semantically aligned with the input.

In the MRPC dataset, which tests the model's ability to generate paraphrases, Mistral-ReadCtrl leads to a readability gap of 1.66, the highest factuality and coherence scores, and the best BLEU and SARI scores. This highlights its exceptional ability to generate paraphrases that not only adhere closely to the desired readability level but also maintain high levels of linguistic and contextual integrity.

Overall, the data from the unseen tasks confirm Mistral-ReadCtrl's robust generalization capabilities across different types of text generation tasks, demonstrating its potential as a versatile tool in NLP applications where adapting to varied content types and maintaining consistent quality is critical.

4 Human Evaluation

4.1 Human Evaluation settings

Our human evaluation was conducted by 5 human evaluators and 1 expert evaluator [3]. We randomly sampled 6 data from the test datasets of 6 data sets, and a total of 36 data appeared in the human evaluation. We give detailed instructions to the annotators: "*You are evaluating two systems, both of which are trying to convert inputs to specific readability requirements to produce output suitable for the user. I will show you the input and output of the two systems on grade 2/5/8/11, respectively. Tell me which system's output you prefer by specifying system 1 or system 2 or tie if the quality is the same. Please explain the reason for your preference.*". And they worked using our evaluation system to select preference; see Figure 4 (left). Each time, we randomly shuffle the outputs of two systems (Mistral-ReadCtrl and GPT-4), and they can choose the one that better meets the readability requirements and has higher output quality. If they think the outputs of the two systems are tied, they can choose both. After we get judgments from multiple people per instance, we do not aggregate their labels before calculating the win rate but count them individually. We also used a similar setting of our human preference evaluation for AI evaluation with claude-3-opus-20240229 and gpt-3.5-turbo-0125 as the judge [4].

Grade 2	
Employ short, straightforward sentence structures	100%
Focus only on essential details, omitting unnecessary complexity	85.7%
Use very simple vocabulary and avoid complex words	76.2%
Break down information into clear sequential steps	35.7%
Grade 5	
Introduce some more varied and content-specific vocabulary	71.4%
Use longer sentences with conjunctions to combine ideas	57.1%
Provide additional context and relevant details	28.6%
Explain concepts more directly instead of narratives	23.8%
Grade 8	
Use complex sentence structures like passive voice	66.7%
Employ richer descriptive language and vivid details	54.8%
Incorporate academic and technical terminology	47.6%
Establish clear logical connections between ideas	21.4%
Grade 11	
Construct elaborate compound-complex sentences	42.9%
Use sophisticated vocabulary from all domains	40.5%
Write with consistent formality and academic tone	33.3%
Employ advanced stylistic techniques like figurative language	23.8%

Table 2: Readability control strategies for Mistral 7B ReadCtrl. The number represents what proportion of the system output in the corresponding grade level uses the corresponding method to adjust the readability.

After preference evaluation, we then worked with one Linguistics expert for the readability control strategies annotation. We summarized 4 different reasons for each grade level (see Table 2) and then asked the expert to use our evaluation system for readability control strategies annotation; see Figure 4 (right). Each time, the expert needed to select all qualified control strategies for the output of our system (Mistral 7B ReadCtrl), where multiple selections are allowed.

[3]More details can be found on Appendix B.

[4]More details can be found on Appendix C

4.2 Human Evaluation Results

As shown in Figure 3, the human evaluation prefers Mistral-ReadCtrl with an overall win rate of 49.4% as opposed to GPT-4, while AI evaluation gave us a broader win rate of 58.3%. Specifically, both seen settings (ASSET, SNLI, PAWS) and unseen settings (WikiSmall, MultiNLI, MRPC) exhibit consistent results across human evaluation and AI evaluation. Among these, the lead in WikiSmall and SNLI is most pronounced. Delving further, human annotations shed light on the operational tactics of Mistral-ReadCtrl. For example, when catering to Grade 2 readability, it implemented straightforward sentence structures with 100% adherence, focused on essential details 85.7% of the time, and employed very simple vocabulary in 76.2% of instances. For more advanced Grade 5 and 8 requirements, it adeptly introduced content-specific vocabulary (71.4% for Grade 5) and complex sentence structures (66.7% for Grade 8), illustrating the model's dexterity in scaling complexity according to the readability demands.

5 Related Work

Early efforts for readability control in natural language generation (NLG) included microplanning steps to tailor the text to match different target reading levels (Moraes et al., 2016; Agrawal and Carpuat, 2019; Marchisio et al., 2019). More recent studies, such as those by Luo et al. (2022), have investigated controllable abstractive and extractive approaches for generating summaries tailored for layman and expert audiences from biomedical documents. Concurrently, recent work Pu and Demberg (2023); Rao and Tetreault (2018); Yao and Yu (2021) examined the ability of the language models to adapt its outputs to different target audiences and writing styles, ranging from formal to informal, whereas Imperial (2022) highlighted that GPT2 models struggle with preserving the linguistic complexity of input prompts. Significant developments have also been made in models for Plain Language Summarization (PLS) from scientific papers (Devaraj et al., 2021; Goldsack et al., 2023; Guo et al., 2023), focusing on generating simplified texts that retain the original content's meaning.

Text Simplification aims to enhance the readability of sentences by reducing their linguistic complexity, with various important societal applications, such as increasing accessibility for those with cognitive disabilities and also for patient education, non-native speakers, and children with reading difficulties (Martin et al., 2020; Cao et al., 2020). Various aspects of simplified outputs have been addressed, including adapting to specific levels (Nishihara et al., 2019), incorporating edit operations (Kumar et al., 2020; Mallinson et al., 2020), enforcing lexical and syntactic constraints (Martin et al., 2019), applying linguistically motivated syntactic rules (Maddela et al., 2020), and integrating complex span extraction and lay language generation (Chen et al., 2018; Kwon et al., 2022; Jiang and Xu, 2024; Yao et al., 2023) into the simplification process. In contrast to traditional text simplification, which primarily focuses on controlling the extent of paraphrasing, our approaches are designed to produce succinct and informative output for various tasks in both seen and unseen settings, while maintaining different fine-grained levels of desired readability.

Finally, our work follows the instruction tuning technique (Zhang et al., 2023a) to help LLMs learn to follow readability-controlled instructions. Traditional supervised fine-tuning (SFT) techniques often struggle with fine-grained readability control, as they depend on manual annotation or synthetic data generation for enriching readability data, followed by model fine-tuning. This method requires considerable financial and time resources, with repeated tasks for each domain-specific application. Alternatively, recent advances in instruction learning offer a more generalized approach, as highlighted in several studies (Wei et al., 2021; Wang et al., 2022; Honovich et al., 2022; Zhang et al., 2023b; Tran et al., 2023). Instruction learning operates on the premise that the model already possesses the necessary knowledge and skills to perform the target task but requires instructional data to learn how to follow the instructions effectively. By using a FLAN-style Instruction Fine-Tuning method (Wei et al., 2021), we gathered task-specific instructions for ReadCtrl and conducted fine-tuning. Our evaluations, both automatic and human, on seen and unseen tasks, confirm ReadCtrl's effectiveness, simplifying the adaptation process and broadening application scope with minimal data needs.

6 Conclusion

The ReadCtrl approach enhances the adaptability of LLMs by dynamically adjusting content complexity to bridge the gap between writers and readers with diverse expertise. By outperforming mainstream models like GPT-4 in evaluations, Mistral-ReadCtrl demonstrates its capability to generate nuanced, high-quality outputs, highlighting its potential in enabling personalized writing and reading experiences.

7 Limitations

In this paper, we propose a new instruction-learning approach to enhance the controllability of readability levels. While this adjustment is not specific to any particular language, we conducted all of our experiments and analysis exclusively on English-language summarization datasets. Additionally, due to the resource limitation, our analysis was limited to Text Simplification (ASSET and WikiSmall datasets), Paraphrase Generation (PAWS and MRPC datasets), and Semantic Entailment Generation (SNLI and MultiNLI datasets), reflecting their prevalent application in NLG studies. Consequently, this paper does not extend to exploring style variations in non-English and other relevant tasks and datasets, such as some mentioned text-to-text generation datasets in the tutorial at ACL 2024 (Dou et al., 2023). Thus, the scope of this study is confined, and the results may not be universally applicable across different linguistic and stylistic contexts. For readability evaluation, studies have shown that readability formulas may not be ideal for medical text (Zheng and Yu, 2017) because short texts (e.g., abbreviations and fragmented texts rather than complete sentences) are common in EHR notes. In future work, we may explore machine-learning-based approaches (Zheng et al., 2018) for readability in subdomains. Finally, due to resource constraints, we were unable to have actual grade 2, 5, 8, and 11 students provide pairwise preference feedback during our human evaluation. In the future, we plan to collect human evaluation feedback from more appropriate target groups to enhance the reliability of our results further.

8 Ethics Statement

While Mistral-ReadCtrl has demonstrated a high level of readability controllability on several NLG datasets dataset, this does not imply their use as general controllable interactive models (like some chatbot systems). These models should be thoroughly evaluated before being used in different settings to ensure reliability.

References

Josh Achiam, Steven Adler, Sandhini Agarwal, Lama Ahmad, Ilge Akkaya, Florencia Leoni Aleman, Diogo Almeida, Janko Altenschmidt, Sam Altman, Shyamal Anadkat, et al. 2023. Gpt-4 technical report. *arXiv preprint arXiv:2303.08774*.

Sweta Agrawal and Marine Carpuat. 2019. Controlling text complexity in neural machine translation. *arXiv preprint arXiv:1911.00835*.

Fernando Alva-Manchego, Louis Martin, Antoine Bordes, Carolina Scarton, Benoît Sagot, and Lucia Specia. 2020. Asset: A dataset for tuning and evaluation of sentence simplification models with multiple rewriting transformations. *arXiv preprint arXiv:2005.00481*.

Anthropic. 2024. The claude 3 model family: Opus, sonnet, haiku.

Samuel R Bowman, Gabor Angeli, Christopher Potts, and Christopher D Manning. 2015. A large annotated corpus for learning natural language inference. *arXiv preprint arXiv:1508.05326*.

Yixin Cao, Ruihao Shui, Liangming Pan, Min-Yen Kan, Zhiyuan Liu, and Tat-Seng Chua. 2020. Expertise style transfer: A new task towards better communication between experts and laymen. *arXiv preprint arXiv:2005.00701*.

Jin Chen, Zheng Liu, Xunpeng Huang, Chenwang Wu, Qi Liu, Gangwei Jiang, Yuanhao Pu, Yuxuan Lei, Xiaolong Chen, Xingmei Wang, Defu Lian, and Enhong Chen. 2023. When large language models meet personalization: Perspectives of challenges and opportunities. *ArXiv*, abs/2307.16376.

Jinying Chen, Emily Druhl, Balaji Polepalli Ramesh, Thomas K Houston, Cynthia A Brandt, Donna M Zulman, Varsha G Vimalananda, Samir Malkani, and Hong Yu. 2018. A natural language processing system that links medical terms in electronic health record notes to lay definitions: system development using physician reviews. *Journal of medical Internet research*, 20(1):e26.

Meri Coleman and Ta Lin Liau. 1975. A computer readability formula designed for machine scoring. *Journal of Applied Psychology*, 60(2):283.

Ashwin Devaraj, Byron C Wallace, Iain J Marshall, and Junyi Jessy Li. 2021. Paragraph-level simplification of medical texts. In *Proceedings of the conference. Association for Computational Linguistics. North American Chapter. Meeting*, volume 2021, page 4972. NIH Public Access.

Bill Dolan and Chris Brockett. 2005. Automatically constructing a corpus of sentential paraphrases. In *Third international workshop on paraphrasing (IWP2005)*.

Yao Dou, Philippe Laban, Claire Gardent, and Wei Xu. 2023. Automatic and human-ai interactive text generation. *arXiv preprint arXiv:2310.03878*.

Tomas Goldsack, Zhihao Zhang, Chenghua Lin, and Carolina Scarton. 2022. Making science simple: Corpora for the lay summarisation of scientific literature. *arXiv preprint arXiv:2210.09932*.

Tomas Goldsack, Zhihao Zhang, Chenghua Lin, and Carolina Scarton. 2023. Domain-driven and discourse-guided scientific summarisation. In *European Conference on Information Retrieval*, pages 361–376. Springer.

Robert Gunning. 1952. The technique of clear writing. *(No Title)*.

Yue Guo, Tal August, Gondy Leroy, Trevor Cohen, and Lucy Lu Wang. 2023. Appls: A meta-evaluation testbed for plain language summarization. *arXiv preprint arXiv:2305.14341*.

Yue Guo, Wei Qiu, Yizhong Wang, and Trevor Cohen. 2021. Automated lay language summarization of biomedical scientific reviews. In *Proceedings of the AAAI Conference on Artificial Intelligence*, volume 35, pages 160–168.

Or Honovich, Thomas Scialom, Omer Levy, and Timo Schick. 2022. Unnatural instructions: Tuning language models with (almost) no human labor. *arXiv preprint arXiv:2212.09689*.

Xu Huang, Jianxun Lian, Yuxuan Lei, Jing Yao, Defu Lian, and Xing Xie. 2023. Recommender ai agent: Integrating large language models for interactive recommendations. *arXiv preprint arXiv:2308.16505*.

Joseph Marvin Imperial. 2022. Uniform complexity for text generation. *arXiv preprint arXiv:2204.05185*.

Albert Q Jiang, Alexandre Sablayrolles, Arthur Mensch, Chris Bamford, Devendra Singh Chaplot, Diego de las Casas, Florian Bressand, Gianna Lengyel, Guillaume Lample, Lucile Saulnier, et al. 2023. Mistral 7b. *arXiv preprint arXiv:2310.06825*.

Chao Jiang and Wei Xu. 2024. Medreadme: A systematic study for fine-grained sentence readability in medical domain. *arXiv preprint arXiv:2405.02144*.

J Peter Kincaid, Robert P Fishburne Jr, Richard L Rogers, and Brad S Chissom. 1975. Derivation of new readability formulas (automated readability index, fog count and flesch reading ease formula) for navy enlisted personnel.

Hannah Rose Kirk, Bertie Vidgen, Paul Röttger, and Scott A Hale. 2024. The benefits, risks and bounds of personalizing the alignment of large language models to individuals. *Nature Machine Intelligence*, pages 1–10.

Dhruv Kumar, Lili Mou, Lukasz Golab, and Olga Vechtomova. 2020. Iterative edit-based unsupervised sentence simplification. *arXiv preprint arXiv:2006.09639*.

Sunjae Kwon, Zonghai Yao, Harmon S Jordan, David A Levy, Brian Corner, and Hong Yu. 2022. Medjex: A medical jargon extraction model with wiki's hyperlink span and contextualized masked language model score. *arXiv preprint arXiv:2210.05875*.

Philippe Laban, Tobias Schnabel, Paul N Bennett, and Marti A Hearst. 2022. Summac: Re-visiting nli-based models for inconsistency detection in summarization. *Transactions of the Association for Computational Linguistics*, 10:163–177.

Tian Lan, Wenwei Zhang, Chen Xu, Heyan Huang, Dahua Lin, Kai Chen, and Xian-ling Mao. 2024. Criticbench: Evaluating large language models as critic. *arXiv preprint arXiv:2402.13764*.

Zheheng Luo, Qianqian Xie, and Sophia Ananiadou. 2022. Readability controllable biomedical document summarization. *arXiv preprint arXiv:2210.04705*.

Mounica Maddela, Fernando Alva-Manchego, and Wei Xu. 2020. Controllable text simplification with explicit paraphrasing. *arXiv preprint arXiv:2010.11004*.

Jonathan Mallinson, Aliaksei Severyn, Eric Malmi, and Guillermo Garrido. 2020. Felix: Flexible text editing through tagging and insertion. *arXiv preprint arXiv:2003.10687*.

Kelly Marchisio, Jialiang Guo, Cheng-I Lai, and Philipp Koehn. 2019. Controlling the reading level of machine translation output. In *Proceedings of Machine Translation Summit XVII: Research Track*, pages 193–203.

Louis Martin, Angela Fan, Éric De La Clergerie, Antoine Bordes, and Benoît Sagot. 2020. Muss: Multilingual unsupervised sentence simplification by mining paraphrases. *arXiv preprint arXiv:2005.00352*.

Louis Martin, Benoît Sagot, Eric de la Clergerie, and Antoine Bordes. 2019. Controllable sentence simplification. *arXiv preprint arXiv:1910.02677*.

Priscilla Moraes, Kathleen F McCoy, and Sandra Carberry. 2016. Enabling text readability awareness during the micro planning phase of nlg applications. In *Proceedings of the 9th International Natural Language Generation conference*, pages 121–131.

Daiki Nishihara, Tomoyuki Kajiwara, and Yuki Arase. 2019. Controllable text simplification with lexical constraint loss. In *Proceedings of the 57th annual meeting of the association for computational linguistics: Student research workshop*, pages 260–266.

Kishore Papineni, Salim Roukos, Todd Ward, and Wei-Jing Zhu. 2002. Bleu: a method for automatic evaluation of machine translation. In *Proceedings of the*

40th annual meeting of the Association for Computational Linguistics, pages 311–318.

Dongqi Pu and Vera Demberg. 2023. Chatgpt vs human-authored text: Insights into controllable text summarization and sentence style transfer. *arXiv preprint arXiv:2306.07799*.

Yiwei Qin, Kaiqiang Song, Yebowen Hu, Wenlin Yao, Sangwoo Cho, Xiaoyang Wang, Xuansheng Wu, Fei Liu, Pengfei Liu, and Dong Yu. 2024. Infobench: Evaluating instruction following ability in large language models. *arXiv preprint arXiv:2401.03601*.

Sudha Rao and Joel Tetreault. 2018. Dear sir or madam, may i introduce the gyafc dataset: Corpus, benchmarks and metrics for formality style transfer. *arXiv preprint arXiv:1803.06535*.

Leonardo FR Ribeiro, Mohit Bansal, and Markus Dreyer. 2023. Generating summaries with controllable readability levels. *arXiv preprint arXiv:2310.10623*.

Chris Richardson, Yao Zhang, Kellen Gillespie, Sudipta Kar, Arshdeep Singh, Zeynab Raeesy, Omar Zia Khan, and Abhinav Sethy. 2023. Integrating summarization and retrieval for enhanced personalization via large language models. *arXiv preprint arXiv:2310.20081*.

RJ Senter and Edgar A Smith. 1967. Automated readability index. Technical report, Technical report, DTIC document.

Murray Shanahan, Kyle McDonell, and Laria Reynolds. 2023. Role play with large language models. *Nature*, pages 1–6.

Jiao Sun, Yufei Tian, Wangchunshu Zhou, Nan Xu, Qian Hu, Rahul Gupta, John Frederick Wieting, Nanyun Peng, and Xuezhe Ma. 2023. Evaluating large language models on controlled generation tasks. *arXiv preprint arXiv:2310.14542*.

Hieu Tran, Zhichao Yang, Zonghai Yao, and Hong Yu. 2023. Bioinstruct: Instruction tuning of large language models for biomedical natural language processing. *arXiv preprint arXiv:2310.19975*.

Sowmya Vajjala. 2021. Trends, limitations and open challenges in automatic readability assessment research. *arXiv preprint arXiv:2105.00973*.

Peiyi Wang, Lei Li, Liang Chen, Dawei Zhu, Binghuai Lin, Yunbo Cao, Qi Liu, Tianyu Liu, and Zhifang Sui. 2023. Large language models are not fair evaluators. *arXiv preprint arXiv:2305.17926*.

Yizhong Wang, Yeganeh Kordi, Swaroop Mishra, Alisa Liu, Noah A Smith, Daniel Khashabi, and Hannaneh Hajishirzi. 2022. Self-instruct: Aligning language models with self-generated instructions. *arXiv preprint arXiv:2212.10560*.

Jason Wei, Maarten Bosma, Vincent Y Zhao, Kelvin Guu, Adams Wei Yu, Brian Lester, Nan Du, Andrew M Dai, and Quoc V Le. 2021. Finetuned language models are zero-shot learners. *arXiv preprint arXiv:2109.01652*.

Adina Williams, Nikita Nangia, and Samuel R Bowman. 2017. A broad-coverage challenge corpus for sentence understanding through inference. *arXiv preprint arXiv:1704.05426*.

Wei Xu, Courtney Napoles, Ellie Pavlick, Quanze Chen, and Chris Callison-Burch. 2016. Optimizing statistical machine translation for text simplification. *Transactions of the Association for Computational Linguistics*, 4:401–415.

Zonghai Yao, Nandyala Siddharth Kantu, Guanghao Wei, Hieu Tran, Zhangqi Duan, Sunjae Kwon, Zhichao Yang, Hong Yu, et al. 2023. Readme: Bridging medical jargon and lay understanding for patient education through data-centric nlp. *arXiv preprint arXiv:2312.15561*.

Zonghai Yao and Hong Yu. 2021. Improving formality style transfer with context-aware rule injection. *arXiv preprint arXiv:2106.00210*.

Zhiyuan Zeng, Jiatong Yu, Tianyu Gao, Yu Meng, Tanya Goyal, and Danqi Chen. 2023. Evaluating large language models at evaluating instruction following. *arXiv preprint arXiv:2310.07641*.

Shengyu Zhang, Linfeng Dong, Xiaoya Li, Sen Zhang, Xiaofei Sun, Shuhe Wang, Jiwei Li, Runyi Hu, Tianwei Zhang, Fei Wu, et al. 2023a. Instruction tuning for large language models: A survey. *arXiv preprint arXiv:2308.10792*.

Xinlu Zhang, Chenxin Tian, Xianjun Yang, Lichang Chen, Zekun Li, and Linda Ruth Petzold. 2023b. Alpacare: Instruction-tuned large language models for medical application. *arXiv preprint arXiv:2310.14558*.

Yuan Zhang, Jason Baldridge, and Luheng He. 2019. Paws: Paraphrase adversaries from word scrambling. *arXiv preprint arXiv:1904.01130*.

Jiaping Zheng and Hong Yu. 2017. Readability formulas and user perceptions of electronic health records difficulty: a corpus study. *Journal of medical Internet research*, 19(3):e59.

Jiaping Zheng, Hong Yu, et al. 2018. Assessing the readability of medical documents: a ranking approach. *JMIR medical informatics*, 6(1):e8611.

Lianmin Zheng, Wei-Lin Chiang, Ying Sheng, Siyuan Zhuang, Zhanghao Wu, Yonghao Zhuang, Zi Lin, Zhuohan Li, Dacheng Li, Eric Xing, et al. 2024. Judging llm-as-a-judge with mt-bench and chatbot arena. *Advances in Neural Information Processing Systems*, 36.

Ming Zhong, Yang Liu, Da Yin, Yuning Mao, Yizhu Jiao, Pengfei Liu, Chenguang Zhu, Heng Ji, and Jiawei Han. 2022. Towards a unified multi-dimensional evaluator for text generation. *arXiv preprint arXiv:2210.07197*.

Jeffrey Zhou, Tianjian Lu, Swaroop Mishra, Siddhartha Brahma, Sujoy Basu, Yi Luan, Denny Zhou, and Le Hou. 2023. Instruction-following evaluation for large language models. *arXiv preprint arXiv:2311.07911*.

Zhemin Zhu, Delphine Bernhard, and Iryna Gurevych. 2010. A monolingual tree-based translation model for sentence simplification. In *Proceedings of the 23rd International Conference on Computational Linguistics (Coling 2010)*, pages 1353–1361.

A Readability Metrics

Developed by Kincaid et al. (1975), the **Flesch-Kincaid Grade Level(FKGL)** score is a metric that assigns higher scores to texts that are easier to read. It is calculated using the formula:

$$\text{FKGL} = 206.835 - 1.015\left(\frac{\text{totalWords}}{\text{totalSentences}}\right) - 84.6\left(\frac{\text{totalSyllables}}{\text{totalWords}}\right)$$

The **Gunning Fog Index (GFI)**, proposed by Gunning (1952), quantifies the level of formal education required to comprehend a text upon first reading. It is computed as:

$$GFI = 0.4\left(\frac{\text{totalWords}}{\text{totalSentences}} + 100\frac{\text{longWords}}{\text{totalWords}}\right)$$

where *longWords* are defined as words containing more than seven characters. Higher values indicate lower readability.

The **Automated Readability Index (ARI)**, developed by Senter and Smith (1967), correlates to the U.S. school grade level needed to understand the text. It uses the formula:

$$ARI = 4.71\left(\frac{\text{totalCharacters}}{\text{totalWords}}\right) + 0.5\left(\frac{\text{totalWords}}{\text{totalSentences}}\right) - 21.43$$

Developed by Coleman and Liau (1975), the **Coleman-Liau Index (CLI)** focuses on characters rather than syllables to assess text readability. The formula for CLI is:

$$CLI = 0.0588L - 0.296S - 15.8$$

where L is the average number of letters per 100 words, and S is the average number of sentences per 100 words. This metric provides an estimate of the grade level required to understand the text.

B More details about human evaluation

We provide additional details on our human evaluation setup. Human preference annotators are 5 students who have completed a bachelor's degree or above from an American university and are fluent in English. We add some tasks with known answers (i.e., cases where the most/least readable and good/bad quality text should be clear), enabling us to estimate the accuracy of annotators who work on these. Annotators with low accuracy on tasks with known answers are automatically removed from our worker pool. Only the annotators who passed these final tests were accepted to work on the human preference in this paper. We gave annotators fair compensation (20$/hrs).

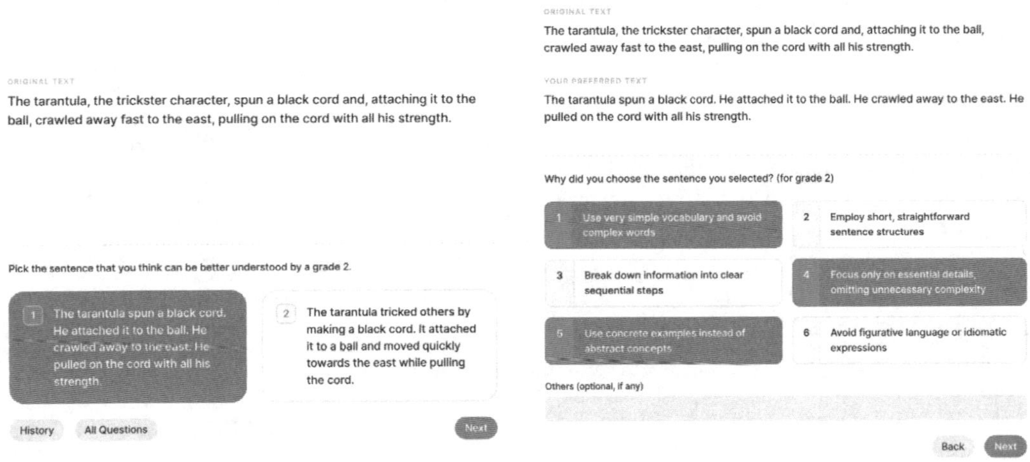

Figure 4: Screenshot of the human evaluation.

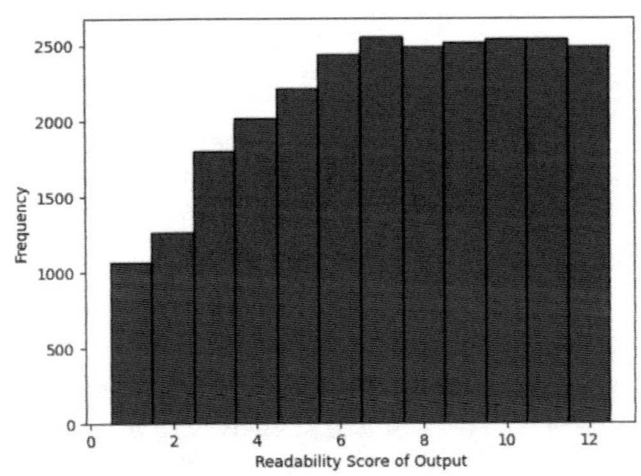

Figure 5: Distribution of examples readability scores from instruction tuning datasets

C More details about LLM evaluation

To reduce the heavy human evaluation and make the evaluation easier to reproduce, we use a similar setting of our human preference evaluation for AI evaluation. Comparison-based feedback evaluation assesses the accuracy of LLM in deciding preferences between two responses. However, it is widely acknowledged that current LLMs exhibit significant **positional bias** (Lan et al., 2024; Wang et al., 2023; Zheng et al., 2024; Zeng et al., 2023), i.e., LLMs tend to prefer responses based on their specific position in the prompt. We implement a rigorous verification process to mitigate the effects of positional bias to evaluate the real capability. Specifically, given responses R_a and R_b to be compared, we obtain the comparison based on two orders, noted as $F_a^c = F_c(R_a, R_b)$ and $F_b^c = F_c(R_b, R_a)$. The objective scores are computed by:

$$s = \frac{1}{N}\sum_{i=1}^{N} \mathbb{1}(L(F_{a,i}^c, F_{b,i}^c))$$

where $L(F_a^c, F_b^c)$ is true if and only if $F_a^c \neq F_b^c$ and F_a^c, F_b^c align with ground-truth preference label. N is the number of test samples. The prompts we used for LLM-as-a-judge (claude-3-opus-20240229 and gpt-3.5-turbo-0125) evaluation can be found in Table 4.

Parameter	Value
Computing Infrastructure	40GB NVIDIA A100 GPU
Optimizer	Adam
Optimizer Params	$\beta = (0.9, 0.999), \epsilon = 10^{-8}$
Learning rate	3×10^{-4}
Learning Rate Decay	Linear
Weight Decay	0
Warmup Steps	200
Batch size	128
Epoch	5

Table 3: Hyperparameter settings for Mistral 7B ReadCtrl.

D Hyper-parameter Settings

The experiments were executed using the version 4.37.1 of the transformers library released by Hugging Face. In Table 3, we report the hyperparameters used to train the models on our combined dataset. We use the Adam optimizer and employ a linearly decreasing learning rate schedule with warm-up step is 200. In this section, we detail our experimental setup, the datasets employed, and the evaluation strategy adopted for assessing the performance of our instruction-tuned LLMs in various BioNLP tasks. Furthermore, all experiments were conducted using two Nvidia A100 GPUs, each with 40 GB of memory. The CPU used was an Intel Xeon Gold 6230 processor, and the system was equipped with 192 GB of RAM.

E Experiments with GPT3.5, GPT4, Claude-3

All of our experiments were conducted on the version of GPT3.5, GPT4 and Claude 3 between 25 March 2023 and 13 April 2024 by using the OpenAI's API.10 We set temperature = 1, top_p=1, frequency penalty = 0, and presence penalty = 0.

F ReadCtrl instruction following evaluation setting

We have plotted Figures 1, 6, 7, 8, 9, 10, and 11 by calculating the readability scores or reading levels of the outputs generated in response to prompts that request specific reading levels ranging from 1 to 12. These calculations were performed across all test sets of the six datasets mentioned in the Experiment section. Additionally, we calculated the standard deviation of the readability scores across these test sets to assess the consistency of the output's readability.

G Examples of output generated by Mistral-ReadCtrl and GPT4 during ReadCtrl instruction following evaluation

Tables 4 present distinct levels of output generated by the Mistral-ReadCtrl and GPT4 and their readability scores given by Flesch-Kincaid Grade Level (FKG), Gunning fog index (GFI), and Coleman-Liau index (CLI) metrics.

We will delve into the observed discrepancies between the Readability Gap and the performance curves in our evaluation, as demonstrated by our results for the PAWS and MultiNLI datasets. The Readability Gap, calculated as the average difference between the actual readability score of the output and the requested readability score across all samples, shows intriguing variations in behavior across different datasets.

For the PAWS dataset, although the Readability Gap appears almost perfect in Table 1, the corresponding curve does not exhibit as favorable performance. This anomaly can be attributed to the output readability distribution of PAWS, which is somewhat concentrated within a specific range (typically between 4-8). While this concentration allows for excellent performance within this median range, it leads to a less generalized performance across the full spectrum of readability levels (from 1-12). Therefore, even a small Readability Gap in numerical terms may not accurately reflect an evenly distributed ability to target all requested readability levels.

Conversely, the MultiNLI dataset exhibits a larger Readability Gap in Table 1, yet the performance curve approaches perfection. This suggests that while the average gap is larger, the outputs are more uniformly distributed across the entire range of readability levels, allowing for closer adherence to the target levels across a broader spectrum. This indicates a more generalized and adaptable performance despite the numerically larger gap.

This analysis underscores the importance of considering both the Readability Gap and the distribution of output readability scores when assessing model performance. A low Readability Gap might suggest excellent average performance but could conceal poor adaptability across a range of readability levels. Conversely, a higher Readability Gap might indicate a more uniform distribution of performance across all levels, suggesting a different kind of effectiveness.

Further investigation into these patterns for all six datasets employed in our study reveals similar trends.

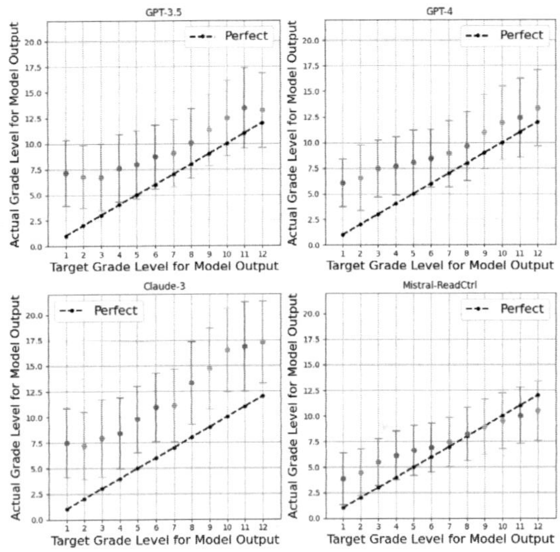

Figure 6: ReadCtrl instruction following ability evaluation on ASSET.

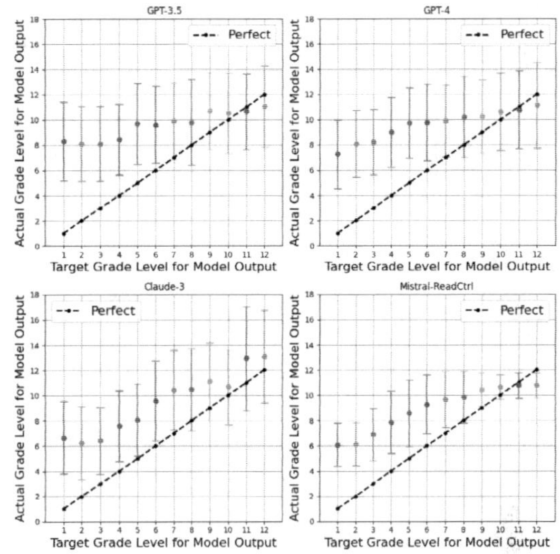

Figure 8: ReadCtrl instruction following ability evaluation on PAWS

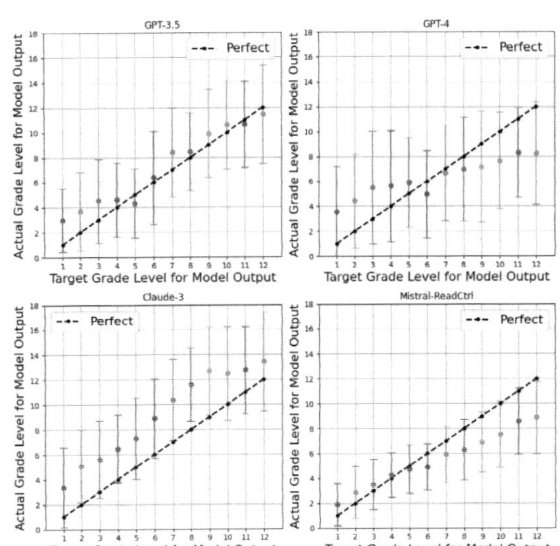

Figure 7: ReadCtrl instruction following ability evaluation on SNLI

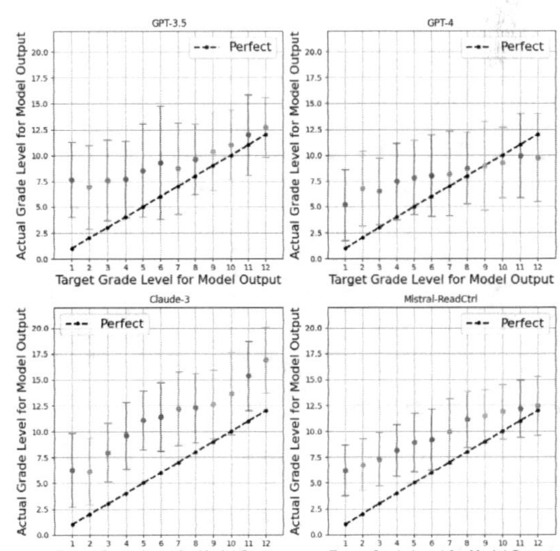

Figure 9: ReadCtrl instruction following ability evaluation on WikiSmall

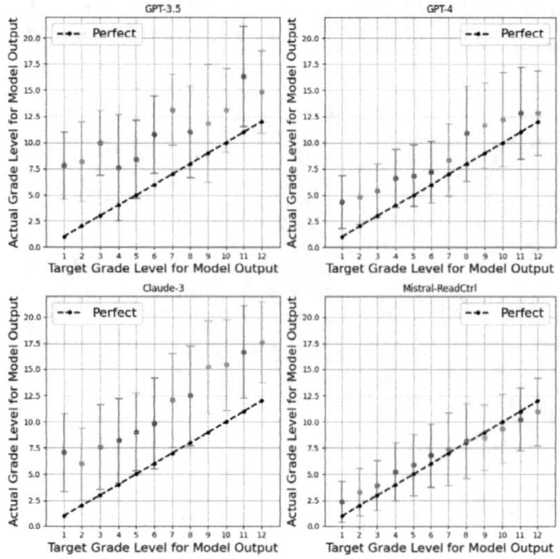

Figure 10: ReadCtrl instruction following ability evaluation on MultiNLI

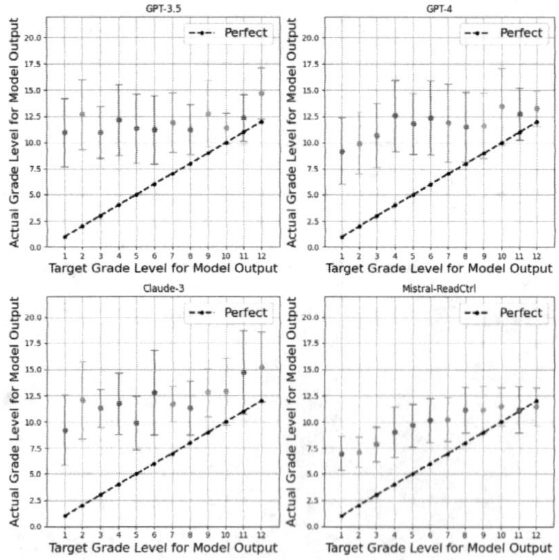

Figure 11: ReadCtrl instruction following ability evaluation on MRPC

H Prompts

Type	Prompt
AI Evaluation	You are evaluating two systems, both of which are trying to convert inputs to specific readability requirements to produce output suitable for the user. I will show you the input and output of the two systems on grade 2/5/8/11, respectively. Tell me which system's output you prefer by specify system 1 or system 2 or tie if the quality is the same. Please explain the reason for your preference. Input: {input} System 1 output: grade 2: {system1_2} grade 5: {system1_5} grade 8: {system1_8} grade 11: {system1_11} System 2 output: grade2: {system2_2} grade 5: {system2_5} grade 8: {system2_8} grade 11: {system2_11} Please use the following json format for your output: 'grade 2 preference': xxxx, 'grade 2 preference reasons': xxxx, 'grade 5 preference': xxxx, 'grade 5 preference reasons': xxxx, 'grade 8 preference': xxxx, 'grade 8 preference reasons': xxxx, 'grade 11 preference': xxxx, 'grade 11 preference reasons': xxxx Please only output your response following the required format, and do not output any other content. Now tell me your preference and reasons:
Readability Control Generation Prompt	Below is an instruction that describes a task. Write a response that appropriately completes the request. ### Instruction: please output an entailment at a {grade}-reading level. ### Input: {input} ### Response:

All prompts used in our work.

Document	FKG	GFI	CLI
The tarantula, the trickster character, spun a black cord and, attaching it to the ball, crawled away fast to the east, pulling on the cord with all his strength.	9.9	15.74	14.8
Requested level: second-grade reading level(Mistral ReadCtrl)			
The tarantula spun a black cord. He attached it to the ball. He crawled away to the east. He pulled on the cord with all his strength.	0.0	4.2	0.8
Requested level: second-grade reading level(GPT-4)			
The tarantula tricked others by making a black cord. It attached it to a ball and moved quickly towards the east while pulling the cord.	4.6	6.6	5.9
Requested level: fifth-grade reading level(Mistral ReadCtrl)			
The tarantula, the trickster character, spun a black cord. He attached it to the ball and crawled away fast to the east. He pulled on the cord with all his strength.	2.6	6.7	4.2
Requested level: fifth-grade reading level(GPT-4)			
The tarantula, who is known for playing tricks, made a black cord. He attached it to the ball and quickly crawled east, pulling the cord as hard as he could.	4.4	7.33	6.2
Requested level: eighth-grade reading level(Mistral ReadCtrl)			
The tarantula, the trickster character, spun a black cord and attached it to the ball. He crawled away fast to the east, pulling on the cord with all his strength.	4.4	8.67	7.1
Requested level: eighth-grade reading level(GPT-4)			
The tarantula, the sneaky character, made a black cord and tied it to the ball. It quickly moved east, pulling the cord strongly.	4.2	8.08	6.2
Requested level: eleventh-grade reading level(Mistral ReadCtrl)			
The tarantula, the trickster character, spun a black cord and attached it to the ball before crawling away to the east, pulling on the cord with all his strength.	11.1	14.36	14.8
Requested level: eleventh-grade reading level(GPT-4)			
The character of the tarantula, known for trickery, spun a black cord. He attached this cord to the ball and rapidly scuttled eastward, tugging at the cord with maximum force.	6.8	10.0	9.0

Table 4: Examples of generated summaries for different readability levels measured using FKG, GFI and CLI metrics.

AI Writing Assistants in Tanzanian Universities: Adoption Trends, Challenges, and Opportunities

Alfred Malengo Kondoro
Hanyang University
Seoul, Republic of Korea
alfr3do@hanyang.ac.kr

Abstract

This study examines the adoption, challenges, and impact of AI writing assistants in Tanzanian universities, with a focus on their role in supporting academic writing, enhancing accessibility, and accommodating low-resource languages such as Swahili. Through a structured survey of 1,005 university students, we analyze AI usage patterns, key barriers to adoption, and the improvements needed to make AI writing assistants more inclusive and effective. Findings reveal that limited Swahili integration, affordability constraints, and ethical concerns hinder AI adoption, disproportionately affecting students in resource-constrained settings. To address these challenges, we propose strategies for adapting AI models to diverse linguistic, academic, and infrastructural contexts, emphasizing Swahili-language support, AI literacy initiatives, and accessibility-focused AI development. By bridging these gaps, this study contributes to the development of AI-driven educational tools that are more equitable, contextually relevant, and effective for students in Tanzania and beyond.

1 Introduction

AI-powered writing assistants are increasingly used in higher education to enhance academic writing, research, and content generation by improving grammar, coherence, and fluency (Rahmi et al., 2024; Widiati et al., 2023; Song and Song, 2023). While these tools are highly effective in high-resource languages such as English, French, and Mandarin, they perform poorly in low-resource languages like Swahili due to a lack of linguistic datasets. This often results in AI-generated content that is inaccurate or contextually irrelevant for Swahili-speaking users (Shikali and Mokhosi, 2020; Wanjawa and Muchemi, 2020; Murindanyi et al., 2023; Mathayo and Kondoro, 2024).

Wanjawa et al. (2022) noted that AI models trained predominantly on English struggle with Swahili's morphological complexity, syntax, and academic vocabulary, making them less effective for formal academic writing in Tanzanian universities.

Despite the global rise in AI writing assistant adoption, there is limited research on their effectiveness in non-Western academic settings, particularly among Swahili-speaking students in Tanzania. Maginga et al. (2024) demonstrate the importance of localized Swahili-language AI training in improving contextual understanding and communication, showing how general AI models often fail to account for linguistic and cultural nuances relevant to Swahili-speaking users. In addition to linguistic limitations, students face infrastructural barriers, affordability constraints, and ethical concerns that hinder effective use of AI writing tools (Carroll, 2018; Voss et al., 2023). These challenges disproportionately impact students who rely on Swahili for academic communication and coursework, thereby limiting equitable access to AI-driven educational support.

Tanzania's language policy further complicates the adoption of AI writing tools. While Swahili serves as the medium of instruction in primary and secondary education, English takes over at the university level, creating a linguistic divide that students must learn to navigate (Tibategeza and du Plessis, 2012). This transition often places Swahili-speaking students at a disadvantage, particularly when using AI tools that are optimized for English-language input and academic conventions. As Mwansoko (2003) explains, Swahili has developed its own formal academic register, characterized by distinct syntactic, lexical, and morphological features; yet these are frequently overlooked by AI models primarily trained on English, limiting the relevance and accuracy of AI-generated academic content for Tanzanian users.

Given these challenges, it is critical to explore how AI writing assistants can be adapted to bet-

Proceedings of the Fourth Workshop on Intelligent and Interactive Writing Assistants (In2Writing 2025), pages 37–46

ter serve students who use low-resource languages in resource-constrained environments. This study addresses this gap through three central research questions:

1. **How can AI writing assistants support student learning and academic outcomes, particularly for Tanzanian university students?**

2. **How can AI tools be improved to better serve low-resource languages such as Swahili?**

3. **What strategies can enhance AI writing assistant accessibility and inclusivity in resource-constrained settings?**

These questions are vital as AI continues to shape academic learning globally, yet its limitations for low-resourced languages users remain underexplored. By understanding the experiences of Swahili-speaking students, we aim to develop more inclusive AI tools that address linguistic and infrastructural inequities.

To investigate these questions, we conducted a structured survey involving 1,005 university students across Tanzania. The goal was to assess their adoption patterns, challenges, and expectations regarding AI writing assistants. Moussa and Belhiah (2024) and Yu and Canton (2023) highlight that university students are key users of digital learning tools and play a pivotal role in shaping institutional adoption trends. Similarly, Shibani and Shum (2024) argues that students' experiences with AI can influence policy, curriculum development, and workforce readiness.

Findings from this study will contribute practical recommendations to improve AI writing assistants for Swahili speakers, while also addressing issues of accessibility, equity, and linguistic inclusiveness in AI-powered education (Lee, 2024; Vassel et al., 2024; Sabharwal and Sahni, 2024).

2 Related Works

AI-powered writing assistants have been widely adopted in higher education for improving grammar, fluency, coherence, and overall academic writing quality, particularly in high-resource languages such as English (Rahmi et al., 2024; Syarifah and Fakhruddin, 2024; Zhao, 2022). These tools support personalized feedback, scaffold writing support, and structure planning. However, concerns persist about misinformation, over-reliance, academic dishonesty, and loss of critical thinking (Negeri et al., 2024; Pramjeeth and Ramgovind, 2024).

Studies from Tanzania have highlighted both enthusiasm and caution in AI adoption: while students find AI tools helpful, faculty members express skepticism, citing concerns over academic integrity, job security, and data misuse (Mambile and Mwogosi, 2025). These findings echo trends in South African institutions, where AI adoption is increasing but still hindered by infrastructural limitations, ethical uncertainty, and inequities in access (Mbangeleli and Funda, 2024; Funda and Mbangeleli, 2024). Research shows that AI tools have the potential to improve student engagement, personalization, and administrative efficiency, yet their integration requires ethical frameworks and national policies that address data governance, transparency, and fairness (Afolabi, 2024; Opesemowo and Adekomaya, 2024).

Swahili, though one of Africa's most widely spoken languages, remains underrepresented in natural language processing (NLP) due to limited annotated datasets and digitized academic resources (Shikali and Mokhosi, 2020; Wanjawa and Muchemi, 2020; Mathayo and Kondoro, 2024). These limitations continue to affect the performance of AI models in tasks such as translation, summarization, question answering, and academic content generation (Wanjawa et al., 2022). Recent research has explored various strategies to overcome these challenges, including retrieval-augmented generation(RAG), hybrid summarization frameworks, and multilingual pretraining adapted to African languages (Ndimbo et al., 2025; Alghamdi et al., 2024). Efforts to address Swahili's morphological complexity, particularly in verb forms have also contributed valuable linguistic resources for improving tokenization and syntactic modeling (Mathayo and Kondoro, 2024). While these developments offer promising directions, most AI tools remain poorly aligned with Swahili's academic writing norms, highlighting the need for more targeted adaptation and fine-tuning for educational use cases (Mwansoko, 2003).

At a continental level, scholars are calling for the development of linguistically inclusive AI models. Kshetri (2024) and Shahid et al. (2025) argue that low-resource language users remain disadvantaged due to colonial data gaps and systemically biased LLM training pipelines. Raychawdhary et al.

(2024) demonstrates how language-adaptive pretraining improves NLP outcomes across African languages, including Swahili, but stresses the need for broader investment in multilingual AI resources. These studies reinforce the urgent need to adapt generative AI to the context and complexity of languages like Swahili.

Ethical concerns also dominate the discourse on AI in African education. Scholars emphasize the importance of embedding AI ethics education in university curricula and creating institution-specific policy frameworks that guide responsible AI use (Holmes et al., 2021; Ahmed et al., 2025; Ayandibu, 2024). In Nigeria and Kenya, for instance, the absence of national AI regulation has raised alarms about data privacy, algorithmic bias, and transparency in automated decision-making (Afolabi, 2024; Wang'ang'a, 2024). These issues are especially critical in regions where students face high digital vulnerability due to weak infrastructure and limited AI literacy (Chisom et al., 2024; Maina and Kuria, 2024).

While prior research has investigated AI adoption in African education and the development of NLP for low-resource languages, few studies have directly focused on Swahili academic writing support. Much of the current literature concentrates on machine translation, sentiment analysis, or chatbot development, with little attention given to academic genre conventions, citation generation, or discipline-specific writing (Murindanyi et al., 2023; Raychawdhary et al., 2024). Our study fills this gap by examining how Swahili-speaking university students use AI writing assistants in academic settings, what barriers they face, and how AI systems can be redesigned to align with linguistic, cultural, and infrastructural realities in Tanzania.

This work contributes to ongoing efforts to make AI more inclusive, particularly in underrepresented language contexts. By grounding our analysis in the lived experiences of Tanzanian university students, we offer new insights into AI accessibility, trust, and ethical concerns, and we propose practical strategies for integrating Swahili into AI-powered academic tools. Our findings support broader calls for African-led AI development that prioritizes language equity, student-centered design, and sustainable AI literacy programs in higher education.

3 Methodology

3.1 Survey Design and Structure

This study employed a structured online survey to investigate the adoption and use of AI writing assistants among university students in Tanzania. The survey was designed based on the *Unified Theory of Acceptance and Use of Technology 3 (UTAUT3)* framework, incorporating best practices from prior studies on AI in education (Rahmi et al., 2024; Shibani and Shum, 2024). The questionnaire was structured into four key sections:

1. **Demographics**: Collected participants' university affiliation, year of study, academic discipline, and gender.

2. **AI Usage and Adoption**: Examined AI tool usage frequency, primary applications (e.g., writing assistance, research, coding), and access barriers.

3. **Technology Adoption Constructs (UTAUT3)**: Measured factors such as *performance expectancy, effort expectancy, social influence, facilitating conditions, price value, hedonic motivation, and habit.*

4. **Trust and Ethical Considerations**: Investigated students' concerns about trust, plagiarism, privacy, and AI-generated content reliability (Lee, 2024; Voss et al., 2023).

To ensure a comprehensive understanding, the survey incorporated various question types, some of which are outlined in Table 1.

The full survey instrument is provided in the Appendix for transparency and reproducibility.

3.2 Participant Recruitment and Sampling

A convenience sampling approach was used to recruit participants through *WhatsApp Messenger groups* following a "do it and refer a friend" strategy. The survey was specifically limited to university and college students in Tanzania. No restrictions were placed on university type, but given the online distribution method, participation was likely skewed towards students with digital access.

The survey was conducted over four weeks, from January 10 to February 4, 2025, receiving 1,005 valid responses from students across various academic disciplines. Table 2 summarizes participant demographics.

Survey Section	Sample Question
Demographics	- What is your academic discipline? - What year of study are you in?
AI Usage	- How frequently do you use AI tools like ChatGPT for academic purposes? (Daily, Weekly, Monthly, Rarely, Never) - What are your primary use cases for AI tools? (Writing assistance, Research, Coding, etc.)
Technology Adoption	- AI tools help me complete tasks faster and more efficiently.
Challenges	- Infrastructure limitations prevent me from fully utilizing AI tools.
Trust & Ethics	- I trust AI tools like ChatGPT to provide accurate and unbiased information. - What is the biggest challenge you face when using AI tools?

Table 1: Sample survey questions used in the study, categorized by survey section and question type.

Category	Percentage (%)
Gender	
Male	35.9
Female	63.5
Prefer not to say	0.6
Year of Study	
Professional Courses	1.94
Diploma	4.79
Undergraduate	86.14
Postgraduate	7.14
How long have you been using AI Services?	
Less than year	3.08
1 year	6.37
2 years	25.87
3 years	41.79
4 years	17.91
5 years and above	4.78
Never	0.20

Table 2: Participant demographics across gender, year of study, and university type.

3.3 Enhancing Reproducibility

To ensure transparency and allow for replication, several methodological details are provided. The survey was conducted online via Google Forms and distributed primarily through WhatsApp Messenger groups. A snowball sampling approach was employed, wherein participants were encouraged to share the survey with their peers, facilitating broader participation. Data collection took place over a period of four weeks, from January 10 to February 4, 2025.

In terms of ethical considerations, all participants provided informed consent before taking part in the study. The survey introduction clearly explained how their data would be used, emphasizing that participation was voluntary and that respondents could opt in or out freely. To protect confidentiality, no personally identifiable information was collected, ensuring full anonymity. Additionally, all responses were securely stored on an encrypted cloud platform with access restricted to the research team, safeguarding data integrity. By detailing these measures, the study upholds transparency, replicability, and ethical integrity in AI adoption research.

4 Results and Discussion

4.1 Supporting Learning Processes and Academic Outcomes

Our findings indicate that **85%** of surveyed students use AI writing assistants for academic tasks, with **32.2%** using them daily and **36.4%** on a weekly basis. The most common applications include writing assistance, research support, coding help, and content summarization. Students frequently rely on AI tools for brainstorming and structuring essays, refining their writing style, and improving coherence in their academic work. Engineering and computer science students reported using AI for debugging, code generation, and understanding programming concepts. Additionally, AI tools were widely used for summarizing complex research papers, simplifying academic language, and assisting students in exam preparation. These patterns are visually illustrated in Figure 1, which shows a clear majority of students using AI tools regularly.

Despite these advantages, a significant portion

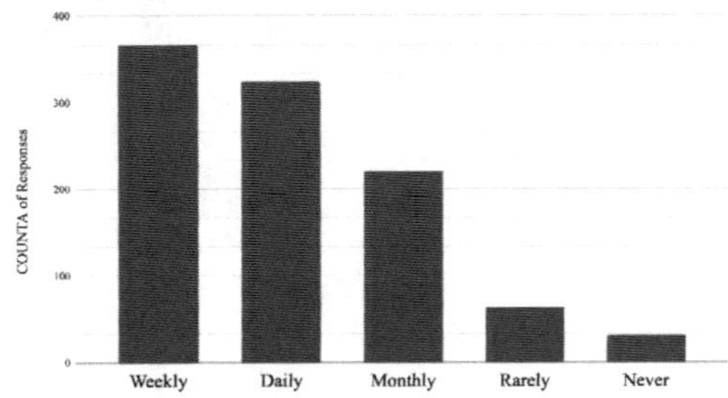

Figure 1: Frequency of AI Tool Usage for Academic Purposes among Tanzanian University Students.

of students expressed concerns about the depth and accuracy of AI-generated content. One student commented,

> "Sometime am not getting the right answer."

Another added,

> "They are not detailed when searching for relevant topics... you need to pay expensively to access additional features."

These quotes reflect students' frustration with the limitations of free or general-purpose AI tools, especially regarding their reliability in producing accurate and context-rich academic responses. Such concerns align with a growing body of literature highlighting the issue of hallucinations in large language models (LLMs), where AI-generated outputs may appear fluent and coherent yet contain factual errors or misleading information (Guerreiro et al., 2023; Perkovic et al., 2024; McIntosh et al., 2024). This issue is particularly problematic in academic contexts, where precision and evidence-based writing are essential.

A smaller but notable group raised concerns around over-reliance and ethics. One student remarked,

> "It reduces my critical thinking skills because I rely on AI to structure my essays instead of thinking through them myself."

Another simply noted,

> "Ethically, AI shouldn't be trusted full."

These quotes reflect broader concerns about cognitive offloading and diminished critical thinking when students rely heavily on AI (Fan et al., 2022; Nguyen et al., 2024). Scholars emphasize that the opacity of AI systems complicates accountability and autonomy, especially when learners lack insight into how outputs are generated (Osasona et al., 2024; Ashok et al., 2022). Broader ethical risks such as bias, privacy, and inequality are especially pronounced in education, where students may uncritically trust AI-generated content (Huang et al., 2023). These concerns underscore the need for clear institutional guidelines and AI literacy to ensure responsible and informed use.

To address these challenges, universities should introduce AI literacy programs that promote responsible use and encourage verification of AI outputs. Developers, on the other hand, must enhance transparency by enabling citation generation and explanation features in AI tools.

4.2 Developing AI Writing Assistants for Underrepresented Languages and Writing Tasks

A key finding from the survey is that **68.8%** of students expressed a preference for Swahili integration in AI tools, with **31.7%** strongly agreeing and **37.1%** agreeing. This preference is clearly depicted in Figure 2, which shows the distribution of student responses across the Likert scale.

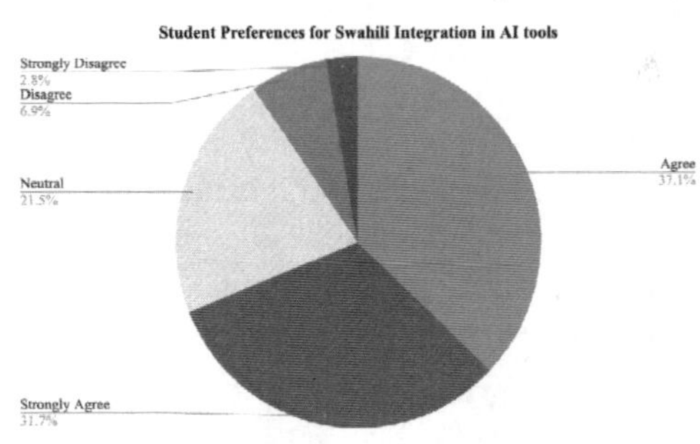

Figure 2: Student Preferences for Swahili Integration in AI Tools. Based on Likert scale survey responses.

Many students cited difficulties with AI-generated content that does not align with Tanzanian academic and cultural expectations. One respondent noted,

> "AI-generated responses often lack local context and do not fit Tanzanian academic writing conventions."

Another shared,

> "Most AI-generated information is too Eurocentric, making it hard to use for our coursework, which requires African and Tanzanian perspectives."

Student concerns about AI-generated content lacking Tanzanian relevance reflect broader research showing that most AI systems embed Western cultural norms, often misaligning with local academic expectations (Prabhakaran et al., 2022; Tao et al., 2023). This is especially limiting in disciplines reliant on contextualized writing. Users in collectivist societies, like Tanzania, often prefer AI that aligns with communal values, yet current tools rarely meet this need (Barnes et al., 2024). Despite the strong overall preference for Swahili integration, 21.5% of students remained neutral, while 9.7% expressed no desire for its inclusion.

To improve Swahili representation in AI, developers should collaborate with Tanzanian universities to create high-quality Swahili datasets and train AI systems on localized academic corpora. Equally important, greater support should be directed toward community-led initiatives such as Masakhane and AfricaNLP, which play a crucial role in advancing African language technologies through grassroots research, open collaboration, and regional expertise (Orife et al., 2020).

4.3 Accessibility and Inclusion Challenges in AI Adoption

Accessibility remains a major barrier to AI adoption among Tanzanian university students, particularly those from underprivileged or rural backgrounds. Many reported struggling with the high cost of subscriptions, poor internet connectivity, and a lack of personal digital devices. One respondent stated,

> "Poor network accessibility and data costs make it hard to use AI tools effectively."

Another shared,

> "I struggle to access AI tools because of high subscription fees and unstable internet."

Others called for more institutional support, with one participant suggesting,

> "Increase awareness and friendly subscriptions."

These challenges are visualized in Figure 3, which categorizes the most common barriers raised in open-ended survey responses.

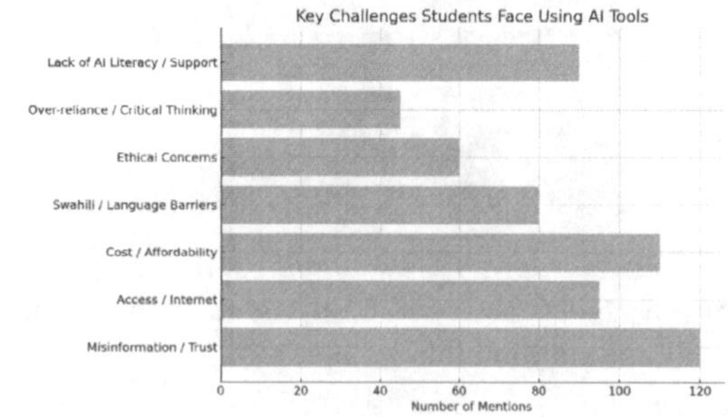

Figure 3: Key Challenges Students Face When Using AI Tools, based on qualitative responses.

In addition to affordability and infrastructure limitations, students highlighted gaps in institutional support. Fewer than 25% reported receiving formal AI training or encouragement from lecturers to engage with AI tools. Students with disabilities also expressed concerns about the lack of accessibility features, such as screen readers and voice input, which hinder equal participation.

Figure 4 presents a word cloud capturing the most frequently mentioned themes in student feedback, further emphasizing recurring concerns around cost, internet access, and inclusivity.

Figure 4: Word Cloud of Student Responses on AI Challenges and Improvements. Larger words indicate more frequent mentions.

These findings echo broader concerns in the literature about digital divides in low-resource settings, where infrastructural and economic barriers limit access to educational technologies (Kivaisi et al., 2023; Xu, 2024). To address these disparities, we recommend the development of lightweight, offline-compatible AI models, subsidized access through universities, and inclusive AI literacy programs that support students across all backgrounds and abilities.

5 Conclusion

This study provides a comprehensive examination of the adoption, challenges, and opportunities associated with AI writing assistants in Tanzanian universities. The findings reveal high levels of student engagement with AI tools particularly for academic writing, research, and coding but also surface critical barriers that hinder equitable and effective use. These include limited support for Swahili and other low-resource languages, infrastructure and cost-related accessibility issues, and ethical concerns related to over-reliance, misinformation, and academic integrity. Three core insights emerge from this research. First, linguistic gaps persist: although a majority of students prefer AI tools that support Swahili, most current systems lack adequate localization for Tanzanian academic contexts. Second, accessibility remains a challenge: unstable internet access, high subscription costs, and the digital divide disproportionately affect students in rural or low-income settings. Third, institutional support is inconsistent: students lack structured AI literacy programs, and few universities have established clear guidelines on ethical AI use or integration into curricula.

To address these gaps, we recommend several targeted interventions. Policymakers and universities should establish national and institutional frameworks for AI ethics and digital inclusion. This includes investing in localized Swahili-language AI datasets, promoting open-source AI development, and ensuring affordable or subsidized access to AI tools for students. Universities should embed AI literacy training into academic programs, encouraging responsible and critical use of AI writing assistants. AI developers, in turn, must create lightweight, offline-compatible models that are inclusive of low-bandwidth users and students with disabilities. Broadly, this study underscores the need for AI technologies that are not only accessible, but also contextually and culturally relevant. By bridging linguistic and technological divides, AI writing assistants can serve as inclusive tools that support learning across diverse educational contexts. For regions like Tanzania and the broader Global South this research contributes to growing calls for AI systems that promote ethical innovation, educational equity, and digital justice in low-resource settings.

Limitations

While this study offers valuable insights into the adoption and challenges of AI writing assistants in Tanzanian universities, it is not without limitations. The use of convenience and snowball sampling via WhatsApp may have introduced selection bias, favoring digitally connected and AI-aware students while underrepresenting those from rural areas or with limited internet access. The data is self-reported, which may be affected by recall and social desirability bias, and the absence of interviewer support could have led to varied interpretations of survey items. Although the survey included open-ended questions, the qualitative data was limited in depth and could be enriched by follow-up interviews or focus groups to capture more nuanced perspectives, particularly from students with disabilities or those using Swahili in academic contexts. Additionally, the study is geographically limited to Tanzanian universities and does not account for educator or institutional viewpoints, which are vital to understanding broader AI policy and integration. Finally, while ChatGPT and similar tools were referenced, the study did not conduct a comparative analysis of different AI platforms or evaluate their technical accuracy, especially in low-resource language settings. These limitations suggest opportunities for deeper, more inclusive future research.

References

Adewale Afolabi. 2024. Ethical issues in artificial intelligence adoption in african higher education institutions in nigeria. *African Journal of Information and Knowledge Management*.

Antwi-Boampong Ahmed, David King Boison, K. K. Hiran, Manish Dadhich, and Ebenezer Malcalm. 2025. Half a decade of artificial intelligence in education in africa: Trends, opportunities, challenges and future directions. *Journal of Engineering Education Transformations*.

Jawaher Alghamdi, Yuqing Lin, and Suhuai Luo. 2024. Fake news detection in low-resource languages: A novel hybrid summarization approach. *Knowl. Based Syst.*, 296:111884.

M. Ashok, Rohit Madan, Anton Joha, and U. Sivarajah. 2022. Ethical framework for artificial intelligence and digital technologies. *Int. J. Inf. Manag.*, 62:102433.

Elizabeth Oluwakemi Ayandibu. 2024. Examining the integration of tiktok-based learning in secondary business studies education: A south african perspective on digital teaching innovation. *International Journal of Innovative Technologies in Economy*.

Aaron J. Barnes, Yuanyuan Zhang, and Ana Valenzuela. 2024. Ai and culture: Culturally dependent responses to ai systems. *Current opinion in psychology*, 58:101838.

Elizabeth Carroll. 2018. Linguistic diversity as resource: English language learners in a university writing center.

Onyebuchi Nneamaka Chisom, Chika Chioma Unachukwu, and Blessing Osawaru. 2024. Review of ai in education: Transforming learning environments in africa. *International Journal of Applied Research in Social Sciences*, 5(10).

Mingming Fan, Xianyou Yang, Tsz Tung Yu, Vera Q. Liao, and Jian Zhao. 2022. Human-ai collaboration for ux evaluation: Effects of explanation and synchronization. *Proceedings of the ACM on Human-Computer Interaction*, 6:1 – 32.

Vusumzi Funda and Noluthando Mbangeleli. 2024. Artificial intelligence (ai) as a tool to address academic challenges in south african higher education. *International Journal of Learning, Teaching and Educational Research*.

Nuno M. Guerreiro, Duarte M. Alves, Jonas Waldendorf, B. Haddow, Alexandra Birch, Pierre Colombo, and André Martins. 2023. Hallucinations in large multilingual translation models. *Transactions of the Association for Computational Linguistics*, 11:1500–1517.

Wayne Holmes, K. Porayska-Pomsta, Kenneth Holstein, Emma Sutherland, Toby Baker, S. B. Shum, O. Santos, Mercedes T. Rodrigo, M. Cukurova, I. Bittencourt, and K. Koedinger. 2021. Ethics of ai in education: Towards a community-wide framework. *International Journal of Artificial Intelligence in Education*, 32:504 – 526.

Changwu Huang, Zeqi Zhang, Bifei Mao, and X. Yao. 2023. An overview of artificial intelligence ethics. *IEEE Transactions on Artificial Intelligence*, 4:799–819.

Alexander R. Kivaisi, Qingjie Zhao, and Jimmy T. Mbelwa. 2023. Swahili speech dataset development and improved pre-training method for spoken digit recognition. *ACM Transactions on Asian and Low-Resource Language Information Processing*, 22:1 – 24.

N. Kshetri. 2024. Linguistic challenges in generative artificial intelligence: Implications for low-resource languages in the developing world. *Journal of Global Information Technology Management*, 27:95 – 99.

Sue-Jin Lee. 2024. Analyzing the use of ai writing assistants in generating texts with standard american english conventions: A case study of chatgpt and bard. *The CATESOL Journal*.

T. J. Maginga, S. J. Kutuku, H. M. Hamza, G. G. Mulokozi, and J. Nsenga. 2024. Mkulimagpt: Equitable ai use via a swahili chatbot for maize farming system in tanzania. *African Journal of Agriculture and Food Science*.

Anthony M. Maina and Jane Kuria. 2024. Building an ai future: Research and policy directions for africa's higher education. In *2024 IST-Africa Conference (IST-Africa)*, pages 01–09.

Cesilia Mambile and Augustino Mwogosi. 2025. Transforming higher education in tanzania: unleashing the true potential of ai as a transformative learning tool. *Technological Sustainability*, 4(1):51–76.

Irene Masiringi Mathayo and Alfred Malengo Kondoro. 2024. Unveiling swahili verb conjugations: A comprehensive dataset for low-resource nlp. In *Proceedings of the 2024 8th International Conference on Natural Language Processing and Information Retrieval (NLPIR 2024)*, page 8.

Noluthando Mbangeleli and Vusi Funda. 2024. Mapping the evidence around the use of ai-powered tools in south african universities: A systematic review. *International Conference on Education Research*.

Timothy R. McIntosh, Tong Liu, Teo Susnjak, Paul Watters, Alex Ng, and Malka N. Halgamuge. 2024. A culturally sensitive test to evaluate nuanced gpt hallucination. *IEEE Transactions on Artificial Intelligence*, 5:2739–2751.

Anass Moussa and Hassan Belhiah. 2024. Beyond syntax: Exploring moroccan undergraduate with ai-assisted writing. *Arab World English Journal*.

Sudi Murindanyi, Brian Afedra Yiiki, Andrew Katumba, and J. Nakatumba-Nabende. 2023. Explainable machine learning models for swahili news classification. *Proceedings of the 2023 7th International Conference on Natural Language Processing and Information Retrieval*.

H. Mwansoko. 2003. Swahili in academic writing. *Nordic Journal of African Studies*, 12:265–276.

Edmund V. Ndimbo, Qinxuan Luo, Gimo C. Fernando, Xu Yang, and Bang Wang. 2025. Leveraging retrieval-augmented generation for swahili language conversation systems. *Applied Sciences*.

U. Negeri, Maulana Malik, Ibrahim Malang, S. R. Yazid, and Dzulfikri Dzulfikri. 2024. Chatgpt, smart writing assistant chatbot for students: An analysis of its drawbacks. *Abjadia : International Journal of Education*.

Andy Nguyen, Yvonne Hong, Belle Dang, and Xiaoshan Huang. 2024. Human-ai collaboration patterns in ai-assisted academic writing. *Studies in Higher Education*, 49:847 – 864.

O. Opesemowo and Victoria Adekomaya. 2024. Harnessing artificial intelligence for advancing sustainable development goals in south africa's higher education system: A qualitative study. *International Journal of Learning, Teaching and Educational Research.*

Iroro Orife, Julia Kreutzer, Blessing K. Sibanda, Daniel Whitenack, Kathleen Siminyu, L. Martinus, Jamiil Toure Ali, Jade Z. Abbott, Vukosi Marivate, Salomon Kabongo KABENAMUALU, Musie Meressa, Espoir Murhabazi, Orevaoghene Ahia, Elan Van Biljon, A. Ramkilowan, Adewale Akinfaderin, A. Oktem, Wole Akin, Ghollah Kioko, and 6 others. 2020. Masakhane - machine translation for africa. *ArXiv*, abs/2003.11529.

Femi Osasona, Olukunle Oladipupo Amoo, Akoh Atadoga, Temitayo Oluwaseun Abrahams, Oluwatoyin Ajoke Farayola, and Benjamin Samson Ayinla. 2024. Reviewing the ethical implications of ai in decision making processes. *International Journal of Management Entrepreneurship Research.*

Gabrijela Perkovic, Antun Drobnjak, and Ivica Boticki. 2024. Hallucinations in llms: Understanding and addressing challenges. *2024 47th MIPRO ICT and Electronics Convention (MIPRO)*, pages 2084–2088.

Vinodkumar Prabhakaran, Rida Qadri, and Ben Hutchinson. 2022. Cultural incongruencies in artificial intelligence. *ArXiv*, abs/2211.13069.

Shamola Pramjeeth and Priya Ramgovind. 2024. Generative artificial intelligence (ai) tools in higher education: A moral compass for the future? *African Journal of Inter/Multidisciplinary Studies.*

Regina Rahmi, Zahria Amalina, Andriansyah Andriansyah, and Adrian Rodgers. 2024. Does it really help? exploring the impact of al-generated writing assistant on the students' english writing. *Studies in English Language and Education.*

Nilanjana Raychawdhary, Amit Das, Sutanu Bhattacharya, Gerry V. Dozier, and Cheryl D. Seals. 2024. Optimizing multilingual sentiment analysis in low-resource languages with adaptive pretraining and strategic language selection. *2024 IEEE 3rd International Conference on Computing and Machine Intelligence (ICMI)*, pages 1–5.

Soham Sabharwal and Rohan Sahni. 2024. Tackling the problem of multilingualism in voice assistants. *International Journal of Electrical, Electronics and Computers.*

Farhana Shahid, Mona Elswah, and Aditya Vashistha. 2025. Think outside the data: Colonial biases and systemic issues in automated moderation pipelines for low-resource languages.

A. Shibani and S. B. Shum. 2024. Ai-assisted writing in education: Ecosystem risks and mitigations. *ArXiv*, abs/2404.10281.

Casper S. Shikali and Refuoe Mokhosi. 2020. Enhancing african low-resource languages: Swahili data for language modelling. *Data in Brief*, 31.

Cuiping Song and Yanping Song. 2023. Enhancing academic writing skills and motivation: assessing the efficacy of chatgpt in ai-assisted language learning for efl students. *Frontiers in Psychology*, 14.

Eva Syarifah and Afief Fakhruddin. 2024. Exploring students' experience in using ai to assist their writing. *Journal of English Language Learning*, 8:558–564.

Yan Tao, Olga Viberg, Ryan S. Baker, and René F. Kizilcec. 2023. Cultural bias and cultural alignment of large language models. *PNAS Nexus*, 3.

E. Tibategeza and Theodorus du Plessis. 2012. Language-in-education policy development in tanzania: An overview. *Language Matters*, 43:184 – 201.

Faye-Marie Vassel, Evan Shieh, Cassidy R. Sugimoto, and T. Monroe-White. 2024. The psychosocial impacts of generative ai harms. pages 440–447.

Erik Voss, Sara T. Cushing, G. Ockey, and Xun Yan. 2023. The use of assistive technologies including generative ai by test takers in language assessment: A debate of theory and practice. *Language Assessment Quarterly*, 20:520 – 532.

A. W. Wang'ang'a. 2024. Consequences of artificial intelligence on teaching and learning in higher education in kenya: Literature review. *East African Journal of Education Studies.*

B. Wanjawa and Lawrence Muchemi. 2020. Using semantic networks for question answering - case of low-resource languages such as swahili. pages 278–285.

Barack Wanjawa, Lilian Wanzare, Florence Indede, Owen McOnyango, Lawrence Muchemi, and Edward Ombui. 2022. Kenswquad – a question answering dataset for swahili low resource language.

Utami Widiati, Diyenti Rusdin, Inda Indrawati, Marzuki, and N. Govender. 2023. The impact of ai writing tools on the content and organization of students' writing: Efl teachers' perspective. *Cogent Education*, 10.

Qian Xu. 2024. The impact of new media technology applications on educational equity in rural areas. *Education Journal.*

Eunjyu Yu and Suny Canton. 2023. Intelligent enough? artificial intelligence for online learners. *The Journal of Educators Online.*

Xin Zhao. 2022. Leveraging artificial intelligence (ai) technology for english writing: Introducing wordtune as a digital writing assistant for efl writers. *RELC Journal*, 54:890 – 894.

Appendix A: Survey Instrument

The full student survey used in this study is available at the following link: https://forms.gle/JEfp3MbH42Uwq78d8

This includes all demographic, Likert scale, multiple-choice, and open-ended questions used to assess AI writing assistant usage, accessibility, and attitudes.

From Crafting Text to Crafting Thought: Grounding Intelligent Writing Support to Writing Center Pedagogy

Yijun Liu and Tal August
Siebel School of Computing and Data Science
University of Illinois Urbana-Champaign
{yijun6, taugust}@illinois.edu

Abstract

Intelligent writing support tools have evolved from solving surface-level issues to collaborating and creating language with writers. Along with these new capabilities come concerns that generated fluent text can impact writers' processes in unintended ways, especially for students. In this workshop paper, we look to a similar transition that writing centers experienced over the last century, which shifted focus from fixing surface-level issues to maintaining student writer voices. We interviewed 10 current writing tutors and grounded their described practices with ideas proposed in writing center literature. We employed these strategies in developing an intelligent writing tool prototype. We describe the design of our tool and discuss potential evaluations along with how to foster deeper relationships between writers and writing centers using intelligent writing tools.

1 Introduction

With the emergence of large language models (LLMs) and the advanced text processing capabilities they entail, writing tools have undergone a fundamental transformation from fixing surface-level issues to creating spaces for collaboration and co-creation between writers and AI agents. Commercial systems and research prototypes alike have expanded beyond suggesting grammar, spelling, and sentence structure revisions (Ding and Zou, 2024) to helping writers reflect on the logical coherence and flow of their writing (Dang et al., 2022), overcome writer's block (Tica and Krsmanović, 2024), gain new perspectives and ideas (Gero et al., 2022; Gero and Chilton, 2019), and develop deeper awareness of potential reader audiences (Benharrak et al., 2024). This transformation has fostered surging interest in both Human-Computer Interaction (HCI) and Natural Language Processing (NLP) communities to develop systems and agents that can aid writers throughout their diverse writing practices.

Yet, it is not clear how writing tools will impact these writing practices, for better or worse. This concern is especially vital for student writers, who are still developing their own writing processes (Andre and Schneider, 2004; Moore, 2016). Writing tools hold the promise of supporting student learning, but the fluent text generated by many tools might dilute students' perception of ownership (Islam and Greenwood, 2024) or open up risks of plagiarism (King and ChatGPT, 2023).

The transition in writing tools today—and the concerns this transition raises—echoes the evolution of university writing centers over the last century. Around 80 years ago, writing centers, then referred to as writing "labs" or "clinics," began emerging at universities across the United States, aimed at addressing student writing problems (Carino, 1995, 1996). Much like how many writers today use automated writing assistants to finalize their writing, these centers functioned as fix-up shops, "cleaning up" students' papers individually before submission (Carino, 1995; North, 1984). 40 years later the purpose of writing centers began to shift. Writing centers became more writer-centered rather than curriculum-centered, process-oriented rather than product-oriented, and collaborative rather than instructional (Carino, 1995; North, 1984). In response to growing concerns of student ownership and plagiarism amid these changes, writing centers developed strategies that realized the vision of collaborative writing spaces while centering the student within the writing process (Brooks, 1991; Ryan and Zimmerelli, 2012; Thompson and Mackiewicz, 2011). Writing centers have since become a widespread and successful resource across institutions worldwide (Archer, 2010; Tan, 2011), demonstrating the value of collaborative support in students' writing (Boquet and Lerner, 2008).

In this workshop paper, we explore the parallels between writing centers and intelligent writing

Proceedings of the Fourth Workshop on Intelligent and Interactive Writing Assistants (In2Writing 2025), pages 47–61
May 4, 2025

tools to rethink the roles of writing support tools in the age of LLMs. We ask the question, **how can intelligent writing support tools facilitate writer-centered, process-oriented, and collaborative writing sessions?** To answer this question, we first conducted an interview study with 10 current writing tutors at 3 US-based university writing centers to explore their strategies during writing sessions and their experiences with AI in writing. This formative study grounded the high-level ideas proposed in writing center literature (North, 1984; Highline Writing Center, 2024; Thompson and Mackiewicz, 2011) to concrete practices. We synthesized these practices into design guidelines focused on creating writer-centered, process-oriented, and collaborative writing sessions.

We illustrate how writing center strategies can guide the development of writing support tools by developing an LLM-based prototype writing tool, *Writor*, based on our design guidelines. *Writor* supports two writing stages based on the stages described to us by the writing tutors (§3) and prior writing center literature (§2): goal setting (§5.2) and editing (§5.3). In the goal setting stage, *Writor* prompts the writer to reflect on the assignment and potential readers, synthesizing a set of goals with writer input. Using these goals, *Writor* provides feedback and suggestions to writers grounded to a submitted draft in the editing stage. Writers can follow up on feedback or request additional feedback by highlighting sections of their text.

Crucially, *Writor* is designed to never give text verbatim to a writer. Instead, *Writor* employs feedback strategies tutors highlighted in our interviews, such as asking questions, providing writing suggestions that are topically distinct from the current writing, or pointing to sections of a writers' own text that can serve as guides for revision. We end by discussing potential evaluations of *Writor* and ways to foster relationships between writers, writing centers, and intelligent writing tools.

2 Related Work

2.1 Writing with AI

AI-powered writing tools now span a spectrum of feedback provision, from surface-level grammar and spelling corrections such as Grammarly[1] to broader adjustments to structure (Weber et al., 2024; Meyer et al., 2024; Han et al., 2024; Yang et al., 2024), language (Wambsganss et al., 2022; Meyer et al., 2024; Han et al., 2024), and adherence to writing requirements (Dai et al., 2023; Han et al., 2024). These tools have shifted from simple rule-based systems (Ding and Zou, 2024; Ware, 2011) to sophisticated AI-driven assistants that analyze and generate writing feedback at multiple levels.

To support writers, AI tools employ a range of feedback techniques. Some use Socratic questioning to prompt deeper reflection and critical thinking (Kim and Tan, 2023; Arnold et al., 2021), while others provide continuous summaries to help writers reflect through their writing processes (Dang et al., 2022). Some AI writing assistants, such as those explored by Kreminski and Martens (2022), attempt to align feedback with a writer's values and intentions, ensuring that suggestions are contextually relevant. Gero et al. (2023) also points out having conversational exchanges with computers as a form of receiving feedback. Additionally, many AI systems take a generative approach for feedback, offering text suggestions or rewriting sections for the writer (Yang et al., 2024; Ding and Zou, 2024).

In addition to feedback-oriented tools, many writing assistants offer more direct intervention. Systems like CoAuthor (Lee et al., 2022) and Wordcraft (Yuan et al., 2022) actively participate in text creation. The widespread usages of general-purpose LLMs has further accelerated this trend, as users can employ these models to draft texts such as emails and essays (King and ChatGPT, 2023). This direct generation approach raises important questions about authorship (Islam and Greenwood, 2024) and what it means to develop authentic writing skills in an AI-augmented environment (Tseng and Warschauer, 2023).

Considering the ethical concerns surrounding generative texts and need for a structured approach to effective writing feedback, we draw on existing writing and writing pedagogy theories to inform AI writing support. These pedagogical frameworks highlight writer agency, process over product, and non-directive feedback (Ryan and Zimmerelli, 2012; Duke Writing Center, 2024; Highline Writing Center, 2024; North, 1984), offering a principled alternative to fully generative approaches.

To situate our work in the broader landscape of writing assistant design, we build on the framework proposed by Lee et al. (2024), which maps five key aspects of writing assistants: task, user, technology, interaction, and ecosystem. Our work contributes

[1] www.grammarly.com

most directly to the user, interaction, and ecosystem aspects, focusing on how writing assistants can embody principles from writing center pedagogy to better support writers' learning and development.

2.2 Writing and Writing Center Pedagogy

Current writing center pedagogy has been largely influenced by North (1984)'s seminal essay "The Idea of a Writing Center" in 1984. Since then, these ideas have evolved into more specific strategies. This section synthesizes writing center pedagogy into three distinct, interconnected themes of writing support: 1) writer-centered, 2) process-oriented, and 3) collaborative.

The *writer-centered approach* tailors support to "the writers it serves" rather than to fixed curricula (North, 1984). To foster a writer-centered environment, writing center literature has developed a set of individualized scaffolding techniques. One key type of scaffolding is motivational scaffolding, which aims to cultivate students' interests in writing tasks and encourage their persistent engagement with writing processes (Ryan and Zimmerelli, 2012; Mackiewicz and Thompson, 2013; Cromley and Azevedo, 2005; David Wood, 1976). Some motivational scaffolding practices include offering genuine praise for specific accomplishments, expressing encouragement that builds confidence, and demonstrating sympathy and empathy regarding the difficulties inherent in complex writing tasks (Mackiewicz and Thompson, 2013). Other scaffolding techniques include setting agendas with writers oriented around their goals (Ryan and Zimmerelli, 2012), negotiating priorities for the sessions (Ryan and Zimmerelli, 2012), and acknowledging writers' cultural and linguistic backgrounds to adjust tutoring styles (Kilborn, 1994).

A *process-oriented approach* to writing instruction emphasizes developing writers' skills over writers' texts (North, 1984). One influential framework within this approach is minimalist tutoring. Initially focused on promoting student ownership of their work (Braun and Clarke, 2006), minimalist tutoring later evolved into a widely accepted strategy for fostering student learning by minimizing direct intervention (Ryan and Zimmerelli, 2012). Instead of providing students with explicit corrections, minimalist tutoring encourages them to engage actively in the writing process (Brooks, 1991). In minimalist, non-directive tutoring, tutors facilitate discussion, prompting students to articulate their thoughts, evaluate their arguments, and take control of revisions (Ryan and Zimmerelli, 2012; Brooks, 1991; Clark, 2001). Ultimately, the goal of minimalist tutoring is to cultivate independent writers who can critically assess and refine their work (Ryan and Zimmerelli, 2012).

Writing center literature further reinforces this process-oriented philosophy through several scaffolding techniques to give feedback that encourages students to engage with their writing and build up their writing skills (Ryan and Zimmerelli, 2012). Key scaffolding strategies include reacting as a reader, where tutors provide feedback from the perspective of an imagined reader; prompting for clarification, where tutors ask open-ended questions to encourage students to expand on their ideas; and metacommentary, where tutors explain the reasoning behind feedback to help students internalize the revision process (Ryan and Zimmerelli, 2012).

For providing feedback, writing centers employ a Higher Order and Lower Order Concerns framework (HOCs and LOCs, respectively). The framework prioritizes writing revisions by addressing HOCs—global issues like argumentation, organization, and clarity—before LOCs such as grammar and punctuation (Purdue Online Writing Lab (OWL), 2024; Duke Writing Center, 2024; Highline Writing Center, 2024). This framework further encourages tutors to touch on the high-level issues to foster learning and the writing process.

A *collaborative approach* in writing centers emphasizes partnership between tutors and writers rather than a hierarchical instructional model (North, 1984). Instead of tutors simply directing students, both parties engage in dialogue. Writing center literature shows that collaborative approaches encourage critical thinking (Bruffee, 1984) and deeper engagement with writing (Manning et al., 2012; Thompson, 2009). Through discussion, tutors provoke thought in a social context, encouraging active learning (Bruffee, 1984).

Moreover, writing itself is often viewed as a re-externalized conversation, meaning that the writing process mirrors the way ideas are developed and refined through dialogue (Bruffee, 1984; McAndrew and Reigstad, 2001). By engaging in dialogic interactions about their writing, students can improve their ability to articulate ideas clearly, refine their arguments, and thereby develop stronger writing skills overall (Ryan and Zimmerelli, 2012).

3 Interview Study

Writing center principles introduce a framework to help focus the development of intelligent writing tools. To ground the writing center principles introduced in §2 into practical guidelines, we examined how writing tutors implement them in real tutoring sessions through semi-structured interviews.

The study was guided by two research questions:

1. What strategies do writing tutors use to support students, and how are these strategies implemented during tutoring sessions?

2. What are tutors' perspectives on how AI could support or transform writing center practices?

This study was approved by the relevant Institutional Review Board. The interview schedule is included in the Appendix A.

3.1 Procedure

We recruited 10 writing center tutors (6 graduate, 4 undergraduate) from three universities (2 private, 1 public) located in the United States [2]. Recruitment was done through university email lists, fliers, and participant referrals. Tutoring experience ranged from 3 months to 5 years (mean=1.95 years, SD=1.54 years). All interviews were conducted via Zoom in English. Each interview lasted approximately one hour, and each participant was compensated with a $20 Amazon gift card. Each interview was audio-recorded, transcribed, and anonymized.

To identify themes and strategies tutors used to support student writing processes, we conducted a reflexive thematic analysis on the transcribed interviews following (Braun and Clarke, 2006). One author familiarized themselves with the interview data and made initial notes on tutoring strategies and themes. This author created an initial set of codes for individual strategies (e.g., "reading aloud") and iterated on these codes through discussions with another author. Iteration happened weekly during in-person discussions over the course of a month and included the second author and first author recoding the same interview transcript and meeting to resolve differences in codes. Following iteration, the authors reviewed the strategies and transcripts collectively to assess supporting evidence for each strategy. After refining the strategies, the first author revisited the data and checked for consistency between strategies and observations from the study. Below we describe the strategies surfaced by our interviews, organized around the writing center literature's characterization of writing support as *writer-centered*, *process-oriented*, and *collaborative*.

3.2 Writing Support is *Writer-Centered*

Empathy and Building Confidence. *"How do you feel?"* Six out of ten tutors mentioned this specific phrase during their interviews as they described what they would typically say to students. Empathy and confidence building emerged as an important writer-centered approach, often mentioned as a means of *motivational scaffolding* in writing center literature (Ryan and Zimmerelli, 2012; Mackiewicz and Thompson, 2013). For example, P5 mentioned listening to and reassuring students when they feel frustrated with reviewer comments or their relationship with advisors, while P7 deliberately tried to build emotional rapport to help students feel more comfortable during sessions.

This foundation of empathy naturally fed into confidence-building, where tutors used encouraging language and praise to help students recognize their own progresses. Five tutors used encouraging language and verbal compliments to affirm students' writing abilities. For example, P2 emphasized the importance of helping students recognize their own progress, creating an environment where student can believe that, *"Yes, [student] can be a writer;"* P5 described boosting students' confidence by reassuring them that their writing was already strong, particularly for those experiencing imposter syndrome or writing in a non-native language.

Preserving Students' Voices. Another crucial aspect of the writer-centered approach was preserving students' voices in writing. Six tutors emphasized the importance of maintaining students' original meaning and personal characteristics in their writing. As P2 noted, they prefer to *"keep them[students' writings] as a kind of personal characteristic."* P8 highlighted their training to ensure *"it's the students' ideas that we're working with"* rather than imposing their own thoughts. P3 also employed a strict rule in giving students no more than four continuous words to ensure this, because *"sometimes I say a sentence, and they[students] go: 'Oh, that's what I like.'"* This focus on preserving student voices and maintaining ownership aligns with many centers' minimalist, non-directive

[2] According to participants, their writing centers were typically fully booked.

tutoring (Thompson and Mackiewicz, 2011).

Centering the Writer with AI. Five tutors brought up issues related to plagiarism raised by supervisors or students when discussing AI in tutoring contexts. Tutors argued that any AI writing support should prioritize student voices by adopting non-directive, minimalist feedback.

3.3 Writing Support is *Process-Oriented*

Using Examples and Analogies. Process-oriented writing support strategies emerged as a significant theme in our study. We identified three key strategies, with each being independently mentioned by eight tutors during our interviews. First, tutors emphasized the use of examples and analogies to facilitate student learning and comprehension. They provided a wide range of examples, from providing sentence structure options to sharing personal experiences for understanding writing contexts. They also used analogies to clarify complex concepts. For instance, P3 described using a simple topic–such as apples–to illustrate how to structure an introduction: *"If I was writing a paper on apples, I would start with a broader history of apples and how they fit into my thesis, and then gradually lead into the thesis itself."*

Providing Reader-Perspective. Second, eight tutors delivered feedback from a reader's perspective rather than a purely instructional standpoint. Instead of providing directive feedback as tutors, they shared their reactions and understanding of the text as readers, helping students recognize how their writing affects their audience. For example, P9 provided their perspective as a reader and asked clarifying questions accordingly by asking questions like, *"I also noticed [something] as I was reading...maybe you could expand here?"*

Understanding Prompts. Third, tutors ensured students thoroughly understood assignment prompts to maintain alignment with instructor expectations. Specifically, this involved having students explain prompts in their own words and collaboratively reading instructions to establish shared understanding. For instance, P6 emphasized checking for misalignment, noting that if students explained the instructions differently from how they initially interpreted them, they would *"literally point to parts of the instructions and say, 'When your instructor says to add more ethos to your paper, what does ethos mean?'"*

Orienting Process in AI. Organization and planning was the most highly regarded capability of AI tools among tutors. Tutors shared their experiences using AI for organization, flow, generating ideas, and outlining. Three tutors reported using AI for these purposes in their own writing, while one tutor had experience using AI for writing tutoring. In total, six tutors perceived that AI could be effectively employed in writing tutoring for process-oriented tasks, making it the most highly perceived capability of AI.

3.4 Writing Support is *Collaborative*

Tutoring is Conversational. *"Sometimes they show the writing... I say, close your laptop for a second, and I close my laptop, too, and I say, like, talk to me,"* P6 said. Six tutors highlighted how conversation forms the foundation of collaborative writing support. Tutors actively created opportunities for dialogue rather than delivering one-way instruction. Some tutors, like P6 and P8, intentionally asked students to close their laptops to facilitate conversation, shifting focus from the written text to the verbal expression of ideas. Tutors also engaged in back-and-forth discussions instead of direct instruction about writing strategies and clarity, as noted by P4 and P9. Additionally, P7 emphasized that conversation is central to their tutoring philosophy, using dialogue as a primary tool for helping students develop their ideas.

Understanding Expectations. Rather than prescribing solutions, five tutors described a collaborative process of understanding writers' expectations. Tutors usually dedicated initial session time to mutual exploration of achievable goals for the session that are *"the most helpful to [the writer]"*, as P7 noted. This approach positioned writers as active participants rather than passive recipients of instruction, creating a shared understanding that guided their collaborative work rather than imposing a tutor-directed agenda. *"[The way] we're trained isn't necessarily like we're gonna go through and tell you everything,"* P9 emphasized.

Collaborative in AI System. While tutors did not specifically mention AI's capabilities in fostering a similar collaborative writing space, five tutors highlighted that they found AI tools often hard to comprehend writings. Unlike human tutors who facilitated back-and-forth conversations, AI systems seemed only capable of engaging in vague discussion. As P6 noted, *"ChatGPT sounds like the classmate who didn't do the reading, but still has to participate in class."*

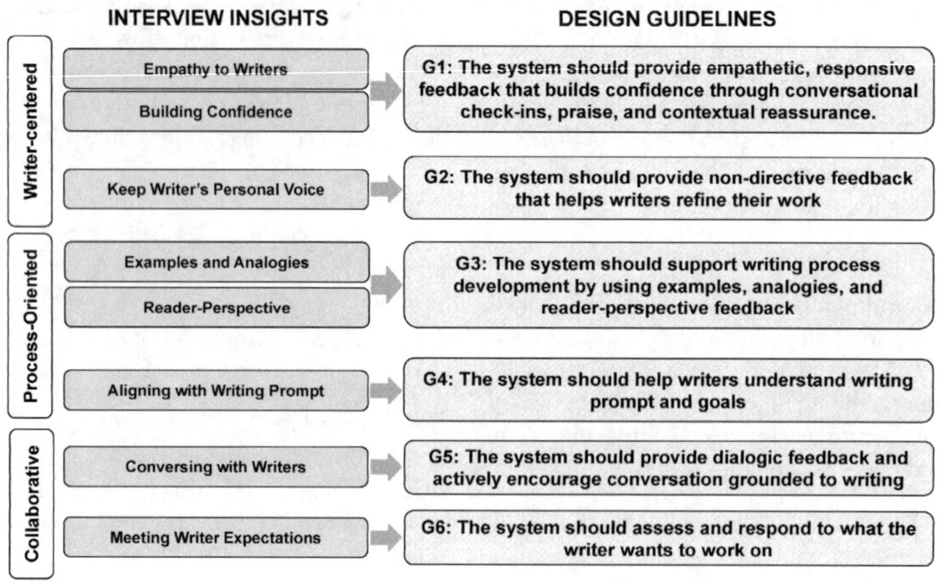

Figure 1: Interview insights and design principles categorized by writer-centered, process-oriented, and collaborative. Based on insights from formative interviews with writing tutors, we identified six core design principles.

3.5 Limitation

One limitation of this interview study is to only interview writing center tutors. We chose to interview tutors because they are trained practitioners who intentionally apply writing center principles in practice. Their perspective offers insights into the rationale behind specific strategies–how and why they implement them. Since our goal was to translate these principles into actionable AI design guidelines, understanding the intentional practices of tutors was critical. However, we acknowledge that students' perspectives are also crucial for understanding how these strategies are received and experienced. Future work should incorporate student voices to gain a more comprehensive view of effective writing support.

4 Design Goals

We translate tutoring practices from our interviews into actionable design goals for intelligent writing support systems, as shown in Fig.1. We unified guidelines around how we perceived these strategies interacting based on interviews with tutors and writing center literature. "Empathy to Writers" and "Building Confidence" were merged into G1, as both contribute to motivational scaffolding. "Examples and Analogies" and "Reader-Perspective" were combined into G3, as both are instructional strategies tutors used in sessions to support process-oriented learning.

5 System Design

We illustrate how our design guidelines can inform the design of intelligent writing tools by developing *Writor*, an intelligent writing tool that aims to provide process-oriented, writer-centered, and collaborative writing support.

5.1 System Architecture & Workflow

Writor utilizes a client-server architecture with a Flask-based backend and a JavaScript frontend. The system operates in two key stages: (1) a preparation and goal-setting stage, where writers input context, upload texts, and define their writing objectives, and (2) an editing stage, where they receive and engage with AI-generated feedback. The backend integrates prompting to OpenAI's GPT-4o for writing analysis and Firebase Firestore to store session data and interaction history. All prompts for *Writor* are included in Appendix B.

5.2 Preparation & Goal Setting

Writor begins with a preparation and goal setting stage designed to help writers define their writing objectives. *Writor* prompts the writer to input their writing task details and specify areas they want to improve. Based on the writer's input, *Writor* generates a list of five suggested goals. One of these generated goals focuses on the potential readers and their expectations, encouraging writers to consider their audience from the beginning. Writers can then select which of the generated goals to use and write in their own additional goals. By encouraging writers to discuss their goals for the writing session, their current assignment, and potential readers, *Writor* aims to address **G4** (Design Guideline 4) and **G6**. A writer's selected goals—along with the writing task details and a working draft of the text itself—are then sent to the backend for analysis. The prompts used for synthesizing goals are illustrated in Fig.3 in Appendix B.

5.3 Editing Stage

Following goal-setting, *Writor* enables writers to directly edit their text guided by feedback from the system. *Writor* automatically fills the writer's working draft (uploaded in the goal-setting stage, §5.2) to a text editor (Fig.2). Feedback based on the writers' selected goals are overlayed on the text as highlighted sentences (Fig.2c) with corresponding cards in the right sidebar (Fig.2e). If writers wish to remind themselves of their submitted goals, they can do so by expanding the goal panel in the upper left corner of the interface (Fig.2a). Below we describe the individual interface elements that support the editing stage.

5.3.1 Text Editor

The text editor on the left panel serves as the core space for writing and revising. It provides basic text formatting tools including bold, italic, and underline. The two key features in the editors are:

- **Interactive Highlighting (Fig.2c)**: Each suggestion or comment generated by *Writor* is linked directly to spans of the writer's text. These spans are shown as highlights within the text editor, color-coded to either praise or feedback (described in more detail in §5.3.2). When clicked, a highlighted span will scroll the associated feedback card into view. If the feedback card is clicked on the right sidebar, the associated highlight will be emphasized with greater highlight saturation.

- **Highlight & Get Feedback Button (Fig.2b)**: While *Writor* generates initial feedback when a writer begins the editing stage, the text interface also allows writer-initiated feedback. A writer can highlight any sentence within the text editor and request feedback from *Writor* via an open-ended prompt. This function gives writers the flexibility to initiate feedback at any place in the text, addressing **G6**.

5.3.2 Feedback Sidebar

The primary interaction *Writor* provides is through a feedback sidebar (Fig.2e). The feedback sidebar presents praise for specific strengths within the document **(G1)** and areas for improvement. For each area of improvement, the generated feedback includes one or more non-directive strategy: asking questions **(G5)**, providing examples and analogies, or offering a reader perspective **(G3)**.

All pre-populated cards (for both praise and areas for improvement) are arranged in the order they appear in the text. Each card includes a header summarizing the feedback followed by generated feedback. Different background colors distinguish praise, problem areas, and self-highlighted cards, with praise cards featuring icons for additional emphasis. Background colors are coordinated with highlighted spans in the text editor.

Each card allows a writer to ask follow-up questions or engage in open-ended discussions **(G5)**, grounded to specific feedback. A *Find Example* button below the chat bar enables an additional strategy: finding examples within the writer's own text that might be a first step to addressing the current issue **(G3 & G5)**. When writers request examples via the Find Examples button, the system searches the document for successful implementations within the writer's own text addressing the identified critique. If no examples can be found, *Writor* provides analogies or examples on a different topic (e.g., P3's use of a basic topic like apples to illustrate a suggested revision).

All prompts for feedback include the writing task details, the writer's selected goals, and the writing itself (Appendix B). We limit initial feedback to five items and three praises in order to not overwhelm writers with long lists of generated feedback. The prompting strategy for areas of improvement follows the following pipeline and is shown in Appendix B, Fig.8:

1. HOC Identification: Identifies high-order concerns based on the writer's selected goals **(G6)**; if no HOCs are selected, infers HOCs automatically based on goals.

2. Sentence-Level Analysis: Maps identified HOCs to specific sentences, focusing on the most significant issues (limited to top 5).

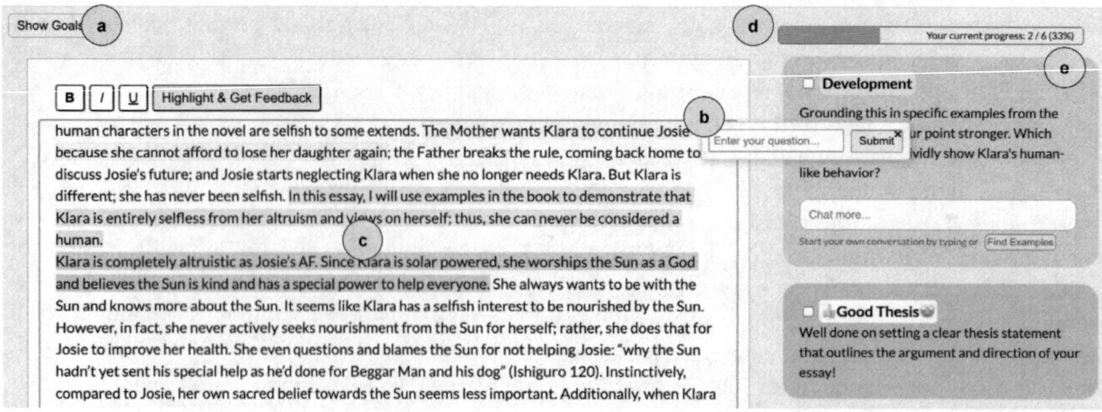

Figure 2: Edit Interface of *Writor*: (a) Expandable button for viewing selected writing goals; (b) Highlight & Get Feedback for user-initiated analysis; (c) Interactive highlighting that connects feedback to specific text; (d) Progress bar for tracking addressed feedback items; (e) Problem area feedback and praise cards.

3. Feedback Type Selection: Determines the most appropriate feedback approach (e.g., reader-perspective feedback) for each identified sentence.

4. Final Feedback Creation: Generates concise (under 600 characters) feedback using the feedback type paired with open-ended questions to promote writer engagement.

Writor is still a prototype, and we are currently planning additional refinements to the system. Among these refinements are import and export functionalities so writers can easily include *Writor* in their existing workflows. Text will be exported as plain text, while all *Writor* comments will be exported as an additional JSON with mapping to the original text. We also plan to further evaluate *Writor*'s generated output to ensure that suggestions are indeed specific to highlighted spans, suggestions consistently follow the feedback strategies we employ, and that the current prompts are robust to repeated requests for usable text.

6 Discussion & Future Work

In this workshop paper, we look to writing centers as one vision of writing technology that appropriately supports diverse student writing tasks. Our interviews with writing tutors (§3) and resulting design guidelines (Fig.1) illustrate ways that writing tools can support students in developing their writing by centering the student in a collaborative, dialogic process. Growing concerns about academic integrity (King and ChatGPT, 2023) and over-reliance on text generation (Zhou and Sterman, 2024) present an opportunity to re-imagine intelligent writing tools from content generators to process facilitators. Our prototype writing tool, *Writor*, illustrates one approach to this new paradigm, encouraging writers to engage with and refine their own writing rather than relying on AI-generated revisions. Below we discuss potential evaluations of *Writor* and further refinements that we are excited to pursue.

Proposed Evaluations We plan to evaluate *Writor* in a controlled experimental study comparing *Writor* with a chat interface. The study will be a counterbalanced within-subjects experiment comparing *Writor*'s writing feedback with a basic chat canvas interface. The basic chat interface will replicate open-ended chat interactions with a text editor (e.g., a chat sidebar with document and highlighted context). Participants will come in with two pieces of writing, one focused on argumentation (e.g., an argumentative essay) and one on professional communication (e.g., a cover letter). We selected argumentative essays and cover letters because these were the two most frequently mentioned and distinctly different genres discussed by tutors in our interviews. Each participant will use either the chat interface or *Writor* to revise each of their documents for 20-30 minutes. Following each revision, participants will complete a brief questionnaire about their experience with the tool and their overall perception of their final document and revision process. After using both tools, we will conduct semi-structured interviews to gather feedback about participants' interaction with both feedback approaches. We will compare editing behavior, qualitative feedback on the writing experience, and final documents across the conditions. We also are brainstorming a more free-form deployment where students can use *Writor* in a classroom assignment and provide lightweight, in-situ signals on *Writor*'s feedback (e.g., thumbs-up) over the course of the writing assignment (e.g., 2-3 weeks).

We also plan to evaluate the model's suggestions in isolation with writing center tutors. In this study, tutors will rate AI-generated critiques and praises on argumentative essays and cover letters via surveys. Each writing sample will be paired with five critiques and five praises generated by the model. Tutors will rate each feedback item on dimensions such as accuracy, specificity, actionability, tone, overall quality, and adoption willingness. This evaluation complements the interactive user study by assessing how writing experts perceive the standalone quality of the model's feedback.

Fostering connections to writing centers One risk of *Writor*'s (or similar tools') success is the diversion of interest from writing centers themselves. Writing centers provide more than non-directive, process-oriented feedback: they create social scaffolding for students and provide a first step for students accessing additional resources (Mackiewicz and Thompson, 2018; Thompson and Mackiewicz, 2011; North, 1984). Automated tools can bring significant benefits of scale, access, and personalization, but writing centers provide benefits inherent to the social context of interacting with other humans. Instead of seeing *Writor* as a threat to writing centers, we seek to provide a first step for students seeking support in their writing that works synergistically with writing centers. One way we are considering approaching this connection is by providing writing center tutors from our formative study with *Writor* and gathering their feedback on (1) how effective they perceive *Writor*'s support to be and (2) how they could see *Writor* integrating as a first (or later) step in their process working with students. Following our conversations with writing tutors, we are considering offering participants in our evaluation with the option of seeking writing support from local writing centers (with their permission) after interacting with *Writor*.

References

Jo-Anne Andre and Barbara Schneider. 2004. The Transition from Academic to Workplace Writing: Students Talk about their Experiences. *Discourse and Writing/Rédactologie*, 20(1):39–59. Number: 1.

Arlene Archer. 2010. Challenges and potentials for writing centres in south african tertiary institutions. *South African Journal of Higher Education*, 24:495–510.

Kenneth C. Arnold, April M. Volzer, and Noah G. Madrid. 2021. Generative models can help writers without writing for them. In *Proceedings of the ACM IUI 2021 Workshops*, pages 1–6. CEUR Workshop Proceedings.

Karim Benharrak, Tim Zindulka, Florian Lehmann, Hendrik Heuer, and Daniel Buschek. 2024. Writer-defined ai personas for on-demand feedback generation. In *Proceedings of the 2024 CHI Conference on Human Factors in Computing Systems*, CHI '24, New York, NY, USA. Association for Computing Machinery.

Elizabeth H. Boquet and Neal Lerner. 2008. After "the idea of a writing center". *College English*, 71(2):170–189.

Virginia Braun and Victoria Clarke. 2006. Using thematic analysis in psychology. *Qualitative research in psychology*, 3(2):77–101.

Jeff Brooks. 1991. Minimalist tutoring: Making the student do all the work. *Writing Lab Newsletter*, 15(6):1–4.

Kenneth A. Bruffee. 1984. Peer tutoring and the 'conversation of mankind'. In Gary A. Olson, editor, *Writing Centers: Theory and Administration*, page 12. National Council of Teachers of English (NCTE), Urbana, IL.

Peter Carino. 1995. Early writing centers: Toward a history. *The Writing Center Journal*, 15(2):103–115.

Peter Carino. 1996. Open admissions and the construction of writing center history: A tale of three models. *The Writing Center Journal*, 17(1):30–48.

Irene Clark. 2001. Perspectives on the directive/non-directive continuum in the writing center. *The Writing Center Journal*, 22(1):33–58.

Jennifer G. Cromley and Roger Azevedo. 2005. What do reading tutors do? a naturalistic study of more or less experienced tutors in reading. *Discourse Processes*, 40:83–113.

Wei Dai, Jionghao Lin, Flora Jin, Tongguang Li, Yi-Shan Tsai, Dragan Gasevic, and Guanliang Chen. 2023. Can large language models provide feedback to students? a case study on chatgpt. Preprint.

Hai Dang, Karim Benharrak, Florian Lehmann, and Daniel Buschek. 2022. Beyond text generation: Supporting writers with continuous automatic text summaries. In *Proceedings of the 35th Annual ACM Symposium on User Interface Software and Technology*, UIST '22, New York, NY, USA. Association for Computing Machinery.

Gail Ross David Wood, Jerome S. Bruner. 1976. The role of tutoring in problem solving. *Journal of Child Psychology and Child Psychiatry*, 17:89–100.

Lanping Ding and Di Zou. 2024. Automated writing evaluation systems: A systematic review of grammarly, pigai, and criterion with a perspective on future directions in the age of generative artificial intelligence. *Education and Information Technologies*, 29:14151–14203.

Duke Writing Center. 2024. *Revision Strategies: HOCs and LOCs*. Retrieved from shortened-hoc-v-loc-handout-1.original.pdf.

Katy Ilonka Gero and Lydia B. Chilton. 2019. Metaphoria: An algorithmic companion for metaphor creation. In *Proceedings of the 2019 CHI Conference on Human Factors in Computing Systems*, CHI '19, page 1–12, New York, NY, USA. Association for Computing Machinery.

Katy Ilonka Gero, Vivian Liu, and Lydia Chilton. 2022. Sparks: Inspiration for science writing using language models. In *Proceedings of the 2022 ACM Designing Interactive Systems Conference*, DIS '22, page 1002–1019, New York, NY, USA. Association for Computing Machinery.

Katy Ilonka Gero, Tao Long, and Lydia B Chilton. 2023. Social dynamics of ai support in creative writing. In *Proceedings of the 2023 CHI Conference on Human Factors in Computing Systems*, CHI '23, New York, NY, USA. Association for Computing Machinery.

Jieun Han, Haneul Yoo, Junho Myung, Minsun Kim, Hyunseung Lim, Yoonsu Kim, Tak Yeon Lee, Hwajung Hong, Juho Kim, So-Yeon Ahn, and Alice Oh. 2024. Llm-as-a-tutor in efl writing education: Focusing on evaluation of student-llm interaction. *Preprint*, arXiv:2310.05191.

Highline Writing Center. 2024. Basic theories of tutoring: Hocs and locs. Accessed: 2024-09-17.

Gazi Islam and Michelle Greenwood. 2024. Generative artificial intelligence as hypercommons: Ethics of authorship and ownership. *Journal of Business Ethics*, 192(4):659–663.

Judith Kilborn. 1994. Cultural diversity in the writing center: Defining ourselves and our challenges. *The Writing Lab Newsletter*, 19(1):7–10.

Tae Wook Kim and Quan Tan. 2023. Repurposing text-generating ai into a thought-provoking writing tutor. *Preprint*, arXiv:2304.10543.

Michael R. King and ChatGPT. 2023. A conversation on artificial intelligence, chatbots, and plagiarism in higher education. *Cellular and Molecular Bioengineering*, 16:1–2.

Max Kreminski and Chris Martens. 2022. Unmet creativity support needs in computationally supported creative writing. In *Proceedings of the First Workshop on Intelligent and Interactive Writing Assistants (In2Writing 2022)*, pages 74–82, Dublin, Ireland. Association for Computational Linguistics.

Mina Lee, Katy Ilonka Gero, John Joon Young Chung, Simon Buckingham Shum, Vipul Raheja, Hua Shen, Subhashini Venugopalan, Thiemo Wambsganss, David Zhou, Emad A. Alghamdi, Tal August, Avinash Bhat, Madiha Zahrah Choksi, Senjuti Dutta, Jin L.C. Guo, Md Naimul Hoque, Yewon Kim, Simon Knight, Seyed Parsa Neshaei, Antonette Shibani, Disha Shrivastava, Lila Shroff, Agnia Sergeyuk, Jessi Stark, Sarah Sterman, Sitong Wang, Antoine Bosselut, Daniel Buschek, Joseph Chee Chang, Sherol Chen, Max Kreminski, Joonsuk Park, Roy Pea, Eugenia Ha Rim Rho, Zejiang Shen, and Pao Siangliulue. 2024. A design space for intelligent and interactive writing assistants. In *Proceedings of the CHI Conference on Human Factors in Computing Systems*, CHI '24, New York, NY, USA. Association for Computing Machinery.

Mina Lee, Percy Liang, and Qian Yang. 2022. Coauthor: Designing a human-ai collaborative writing dataset for exploring language model capabilities. In *Proceedings of the 2022 CHI Conference on Human Factors in Computing Systems*, CHI '22, New York, NY, USA. Association for Computing Machinery.

Jo Mackiewicz and Isabelle Thompson. 2013. Motivational scaffolding, politeness, and writing center tutoring. *The Writing Center Journal*, 33(1):38–73.

Jo Mackiewicz and Isabelle Thompson. 2018. *Talk about writing: The tutoring strategies of experienced writing center tutors*. Routledge.

Kellye Manning, Courtney Goff, and Amanda McCain. 2012. *A Synthesis of Qualitative Studies of Writing Center Tutoring, 1983-2006*. Peter Lang Inc., International Academic Publishers.

Donald A. McAndrew and Thomas J. Reigstad. 2001. *Tutoring Writing: A Practical Guide for Conferences*. Boynton-Cook.

Jennifer Meyer, Thorben Jansen, Ronja Schiller, Lucas W. Liebenow, Marlene Steinbach, Andrea Horbach, and Johanna Fleckenstein. 2024. Using llms to bring evidence-based feedback into the classroom: Ai-generated feedback increases secondary students' text revision, motivation, and positive emotions. *Computers and Education: Artificial Intelligence*, 6:100199.

Kaleigh Moore. 2016. Study: Poor writing skills are costing businesses billions.

Stephen M. North. 1984. The idea of a writing center. *College English*, 46(5):433–446.

Purdue Online Writing Lab (OWL). 2024. Higher order concerns (hocs) and lower order concerns (locs). Accessed: 2024-09-17.

Leigh Ryan and Lisa Zimmerelli. 2012. *The Oxford Guide for Writing Tutors: Practice and Research*. Oxford University Press, New York.

Bee-Hoon Tan. 2011. Innovating writing centers and online writing labs outside north america. *Asian EFL Journal*, 13(2):391–417.

Isabelle Thompson. 2009. Scaffolding in the writing center: A microanalysis of an experienced tutor's verbal and nonverbal tutoring strategies. *Written Communication*, 26(4):417–453.

Isabelle Thompson and Jo Mackiewicz. 2011. *The Synthesis of Qualitative Studies of Writing Center Tutoring, 1983-2006*. Peter Lang Inc., International Academic Publishers, New York.

Lena Tica and Ivana Krsmanović. 2024. Overcoming the writer's block? exploring students' motivation and perspectives on using chatgpt as a writing assistance tool in esp. *ELOPE: English Language Overseas Perspectives and Enquiries*, 21(1):129–149.

Waverly Tseng and Mark Warschauer. 2023. Ai-writing tools in education: if you can't beat them, join them. *Journal of China Computer-Assisted Language Learning*, 3(2):258–262.

Thiemo Wambsganss, Matthias Soellner, Kenneth R Koedinger, and Jan Marco Leimeister. 2022. Adaptive empathy learning support in peer review scenarios. In *Proceedings of the 2022 CHI Conference on Human Factors in Computing Systems*, CHI '22, New York, NY, USA. Association for Computing Machinery.

Paige Ware. 2011. Computer-generated feedback on student writing. *TESOL Quarterly*, 45(4):769–774.

Florian Weber, Thiemo Wambsganss, Seyed Parsa Neshaei, and Matthias Soellner. 2024. Legalwriter: An intelligent writing support system for structured and persuasive legal case writing for novice law students. In *Proceedings of the 2024 CHI Conference on Human Factors in Computing Systems*, CHI '24, New York, NY, USA. Association for Computing Machinery.

Kexin Bella Yang, Sungjin Nam, Yuchi Huang, and Scott Wood. 2024. Rhetor: Providing llm-based feedback for students' argumentative essays. In *Technology Enhanced Learning for Inclusive and Equitable Quality Education*, pages 201–205, Cham. Springer Nature Switzerland.

Ann Yuan, Andy Coenen, Emily Reif, and Daphne Ippolito. 2022. Wordcraft: Story writing with large language models. In *Proceedings of the 27th International Conference on Intelligent User Interfaces*, IUI '22, page 841–852, New York, NY, USA. Association for Computing Machinery.

David Zhou and Sarah Sterman. 2024. Ai.llude: Investigating rewriting ai-generated text to support creative expression. In *Proceedings of the 16th Conference on Creativity & Cognition*, C&C '24, page 241–254, New York, NY, USA. Association for Computing Machinery.

A Interview Questions

Opening (5-8 min)

- Welcome and introduction.
- Brief overview of the research project and purpose of the interview.
- Present the consent form; assure confidentiality and explain that the interview will be recorded for research purposes; give time for the participants to ask questions about the consent form.
- Obtain consent.

Body (50 min)

Tutor Background (5 min)

- Can you tell me about your experience as a writing tutor?
- How long? Where? Which grade level?
- What kinds of articles and students do you mostly work with? At what stages of writing?

Tutoring Approaches and Strategies (15 min)

- **[Grounded to a scenario the tutor described earlier]** We want to focus on the editing stage, where students come in and present a draft. What kinds of strategies do you usually use?
- Can you give examples of non-directive tutoring strategies, such as scaffolding, that you use for advising on a draft? How effective do you find these? Do you think students find these approaches useful?
- How do you balance offering guidance while ensuring that students retain ownership of their writing?
- What kinds of questions or prompts do you find most effective for helping students think critically about their writing?
- If you find out that a student might be using a language model to write their script, what guidance do you think is most necessary to give them?

AI & Writing (24 min)

- Do you use AI during your sessions? If so, how?
- How do you feel about students' writing after ChatGPT and other large language models gained tremendous popularity? What are your opinions on these tools from a writing tutor's perspective?
- How might an AI writing support tool complement the work done in writing centers? Are you using any AI tools right now during your sessions?
- How could AI augment or help before, during, or after tutoring sessions with you?
- What opportunities do you see for expanding access to writing support through AI?
- How could an AI tool potentially address common issues you encounter in tutoring sessions?

Closing (6 min)

- Is there anything else you'd like to share about your experience as a tutor or your thoughts on integrating writing center strategies into AI systems?
- Do you have any concerns or suggestions for the direction of this research project?
- Based on your experience, what advice would you give to developers creating an AI writing support tool?

Conclusion (2 min)

- Thank the tutor for their time and insights.
- Explain the next steps in the research process, restating how the interview data will be used.

B Prompts

Prompt for Generating Goals

Here is the writing prompt and potential requirements: '{writing_prompt}' Please analyze what the expected goals are for the writing to fit the prompt and any grading rubrics or requirements. The user also has their expectations for the editing service, which are: {edit_expectations}. Given the information about the writing prompt and areas that users want to work on, provide the top 4 goals that the user should aim for in their writing. Goal 5 should be a goal aimed at satisfying any potential readers' expectations for the writing. The writing type and potential readers are described here: {reader}. Be specific in your goals, refrain from broad goals. Return ONLY a JSON object with the following structure:

```
{
  "goals": [
    "Goal 1",
    "Goal 2",
    "Goal 3",
    "Goal 4",
    "Goal 5"
  ]
}
```

Replace the placeholder goals with the actual goals. Do not include any extra text.

Figure 3: Prompt for Generating Goals

Prompt for Praise Feedback Generation

Please identify the sentences that the writer did well and provide encouraging feedback for them. Here is the complete writing:{text}. The category should always include a praise word like "Good Thesis", "Excellent Analysis".
Return your response in JSON form only for the top 3 most significant sentences, keep the feedback under 300 characters, be concise yet constructive.

```
{
    "Encouragement": [
        {
            "Sentence": "To conclude, Klara can never be considered a human because she never
                        acknowledges herself.",
            "Feedback": "Great job on referring back to the thesis for conclusion!",
            "Category": "Great Conclusion"
        }
    ]
}
```

Figure 4: Prompt for Praise Feedback Generation

Context Prompt for Chats

Here is the entire writing for context: {text}. We are now conversing about the specific sentence needing clarification or feedback, which is: {sentence}. You have previously provided feedback on the sentence, which is {sentence_feedback}. The conversation so far is: {conversation}
Please try to answer the question and give feedback according to the context.
Follow these guildelines: Do not directly provide the answer, but guide the writer toward the answer. Do not give any text to copy and paste directly into the writing.Instead, provide examples or feedback to help the writer understand how to improve their writing.
If the user insists on a direct answer, respond with: "I can't provide a direct answer."
Keep your response under 400 characters.

Figure 5: Context Prompt for Chats

Prompt for Self-Highlighted Feedback

User has a question about the selected sentence in the writing: {sentence} The question is: {question}. Please provide a short, concise, emphatic, and encouraging feedback answering the user's question and specific to the sentence. Here is the complete writing:{text} Keep in mind these are the user's goals for the writing: {writer_goals_selected}. Keep the feedback under 400 characters, be concise yet constructive. Return your response in JSON form, **never** give users anything to copy and paste directly into their essay.

```
{
    "Feedback": "This is my empathic feedback."
}
```

Figure 6: Prompt for Self-Highlighted Feedback

Prompt for Finding Examples

We have identified a problem with the following sentence in the essay: {sentence} The problem is: {problem} Now, here's the full essay for context: {essay}
Can you find examples from the essay where the writer has done well in addressing this kind of problem? If so, please provide that example. If not, please provide an analogy or example from a different context that could help the writer understand how to address this problem.
Follow these guidelines: Provide **only one example**; Use second-person pronouns like "you". Limit your response to 600 characters. Do **not** provide any text that can be directly copied and pasted into the essay.

```
{
    "Feedback": "This is my empathic feedback with user's examplary quotes."
}
```

Figure 7: Prompt for Finding Examples

Prompt for Problem Area Feedback Generation

Step 1: HOC Identification
Given the following writing, writing details, and writer's goals, identify up to 4 major high-order concerns (HOCs) that need urgent revision. Ensure these concerns align with the assignment goals or highlight major flaws not mentioned in the goals. High-order concerns include: Thesis/Argument: Whether the main argument is clear and well-structured; Organization: The logical flow and structure of ideas; Development: Whether evidence, examples, and reasoning support arguments.; Audience and Purpose: How well the writing communicates its purpose to the intended audience. Writing Details: {writing_detail} Writer's Goals: {writer_goals_selected} Writing: {text} Return response in JSON format:

```
{"HOCs": [
    {"Issue": "Thesis", "Reason": "The thesis is vague and lacks specificity."},
]}
```

Step 2: Sentence-Level Issue Identification
The writing focuses on the following issues: {hoc_results}. Identify the problematic sentences related to these issues. If a new sentence is needed, highlight the previous sentence where the new sentence should be inserted. Writing: {text}Return response in JSON format (top 5 most significant issues only):

```
{"Sentences": [
    {
        "Sentence": "The central idea for the essay is on apple.",
        "HOC": "Thesis",
        "Reason": "The thesis is unclear and lacks specificity."
    }
]}
```

Step 3: Feedback Type Selection
There are two types of feedback: Reader-Perspective Feedback: Describes how the sentence is perceived by the reader; Example/Analogy Feedback:Provides examples or analogies to clarify improvements. List of problematic sentences with reasons: {sentence_results} Writing: {text} Determine the most appropriate feedback type and return in JSON format:

```
{"Feedback_type": [
    {
        "Sentence": "The central idea for the essay is on apple.",
        "HOC": "Thesis",
        "Reason": "The thesis is unclear and lacks specificity.",
        "FeedbackType": "Example/Analogy"
    }
]}
```

Step 4: Final Feedback Creation
Provide feedback for the identified issues with an empathic and encouraging tone. Use the selected feedback type. Feedback Type List: {type_results} Writing Details: {writing_detail} Writer's Goals: {writer_goals_selected} Writing: {text}. Guidelines: 1) Keep feedback under 600 characters 2) End each feedback item with an open-ended question to promote engagement. 3) Do **not** provide text for users to copy and paste into their writing.

```
{"Feedback": [
    {
        "Sentence": "The central idea for the essay is on apple.",
        "HOC": "Thesis",
        "Reason": "The thesis is unclear and lacks specificity.",
        "FeedbackType": "Example/Analogy",
        "Feedback": "A good thesis on pear is:[thesis]. Can you think about using similar strategy?"
    }
]}
```

Figure 8: Prompt for Problem Area Feedback Generation

Interaction-Required Suggestions for Control, Ownership, and Awareness in Human-AI Co-Writing

Kenneth C. Arnold
Calvin University
kcarnold@alum.mit.edu

Jiho Kim
Calvin University
jihokim8@acm.org

Abstract

This paper explores interaction designs for generative AI interfaces that necessitate human involvement throughout the generation process. We argue that such interfaces can promote cognitive engagement, agency, and thoughtful decision-making. Through a case study in text revision, we present and analyze two interaction techniques: (1) using a predictive-text interaction to type the assistant's response to a revision request, and (2) highlighting potential edit opportunities in a document. Our implementations demonstrate how these approaches reveal the landscape of writing possibilities and enable fine-grained control. We discuss implications for human-AI writing partnerships and future interaction design directions.

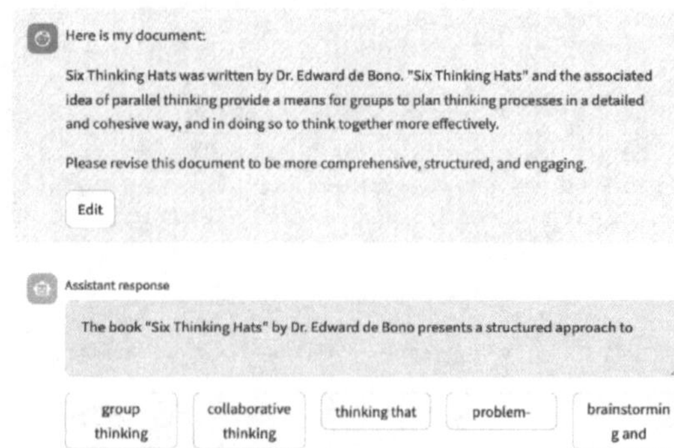

Figure 1: Predictive text interaction repurposed to type the assistant's response

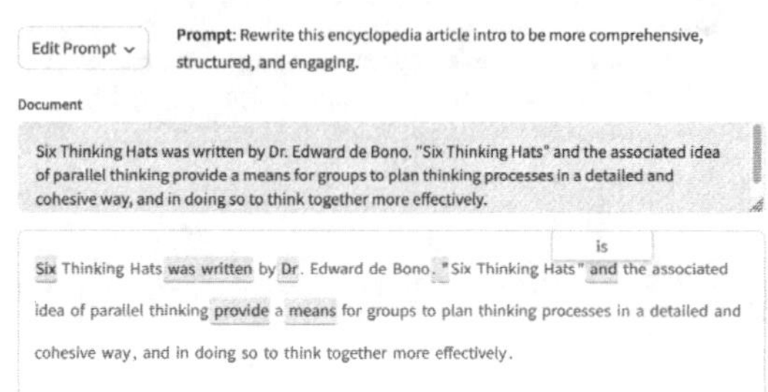

Figure 2: Highlighting opportunities for divergent choices

1 Introduction

Current chatbot interfaces for large language models like ChatGPT, Claude, and Gemini limit interaction to a turn-taking conversation, even though the underlying models could support more versatile interactions, especially for writing tasks.

In this paper, we begin to explore the design space of interactions that people can have with model outputs, focusing on the potential opportunities presented by interactions where human initiative is *required* for completing a task. Although these interactions are, by construction, less efficient at producing plausible outputs, we aim to explore the potential benefits they might offer in control, ownership, visibility of the solution space, and feedback for model tuning.

We present two interaction techniques for revision in writing: predictive-text and opportunity highlighting. The first technique adapts the familiar predictive-text interaction (top-k suggestions or free typing) found on mobile devices to allow people to type the *assistant's response* word by word. The second technique visualizes alternative (and sometimes divergent) choices for revising text according to a writer-specified goal.

2 Design Principles

AI support for writing has evolved primarily along two interaction paradigms: conversational exchanges with an assistant (as in modern chatbots) and editorial feedback systems (like inline markup in Grammarly or reflection tools like Impressona (Benharrak et al., 2024) and Textfocals (Kim et al., 2024). While these paradigms have proven useful, they both place the AI in a position of either generating content or evaluating it, with humans primarily reacting to AI output.

Proceedings of the Fourth Workshop on Intelligent and Interactive Writing Assistants (In2Writing 2025), pages 62–68
May 4, 2025 ©2025 Association for Computational Linguistics

We propose interaction-required approaches that fundamentally shift this dynamic by necessitating ongoing human involvement throughout the generation process. Our approach is guided by three design principles that emphasize cognitive partnership between humans and AI systems:

Prioritize cognitive engagement over efficiency Although AI assistance can speed task completion, using it without cognitive engagement can lead to overconfidence (Fernandes et al., 2025), errors (Dakhel et al., 2023), and skill stagnation (Gajos and Mamykina, 2022). Interactions can instead be designed to encourage writers' thoughtful participation rather than optimizing solely for speed or ease. This principle addresses how AI systems can support authentic self-expression, ownership, and accountability in writing, which many writers desire (Biermann et al., 2022; Hwang et al., 2024). The literature on explainable AI systems for decision-making suggests cognitive engagement as valuable goal (Datta and Dickerson, 2023).

Enable granular control Rather than offering only coarse accept/reject options for completed AI outputs, interfaces could instead allow writers to influence the progress of generation. Granularity could enable just-in-time feedback that shapes the direction of AI assistance, providing a way for users to clarify their goals without having to engage in prompt refinement or writing examples.

Reveal the landscape of possibilities Interactions should make visible the alternatives available at each decision point, helping writers understand the range of options and make more informed choices. Prior work has explored contextual suggestions of alternative words or phrases at targeted points (e.g., Reza et al. (2023); Gero and Chilton (2019)), but some authors have explored interfaces for navigating through the tree of suggestions in a narrative generation context (Reynolds and McDonell, 2021).

2.1 Interaction-Required Suggestions

The degree to which a writing support interface *requires* interaction can be measured, in principle, by an *amplification ratio*, the ratio of the entropy of system output (new text or edits) to the entropy of user input. For example, asking a chatbot to write a complete essay or make overall edits has a high amplification ratio since the input entropy is confined to the prompt. Accepting grammar suggestions also has high amplification ratio, since the user often only needs to click "Accept".

We conjecture that LLM-powered interfaces with a low amplification ratio can be designed according to these design principles to assist writers at various points in the writing process.

3 A Case Study in Revision

We will present two interaction designs that embody these design principles for the purpose of revision. As a running hypothetical example, suppose Alex is a Wikipedia editor who wants to revise the introduction section for the article on "Six Thinking Hats", as it was on 2025-02-25:

> "Six Thinking Hats was written by Dr. Edward de Bono. "Six Thinking Hats" and the associated idea of parallel thinking provide a means for groups to plan thinking processes in a detailed and cohesive way, and in doing so to think together more effectively."

We will use a revision instruction generated by Claude.ai: "Rewrite this document to be more comprehensive, structured, and engaging."

3.1 Typing the Assistant's Response with Predictive Text

Alex starts a chatbot conversation in the now-customary way, asking for a revision according to her goals 1. She now sees the assistant's response being formed—but instead of seeing the assistant type its response, Alex sees an editable text box, which starts empty except for the now-familiar buttons of predictive text.

Alex starts by ignoring the prediction buttons because she realizes it would be clearer to start with "The book", so she starts by typing that phrase. Afterwards the predictions give the title of the book, followed by the author, which Alex readily accepts with a few taps. After that, the top 3 suggestions are "revolutionized", "presents", and "is"; she take "presents", an active verb that avoids exaggeration. The next suggestions are "a revolutionary", "an innovative", and "a groundbreaking", which exhibit the same problem of exaggeration as before. These suggestions were probably due to Alex's prompt of "engaging", but the vacuous exaggeration of the suggestions indicates to Alex that she needs to consider what exactly *should be* engaging about this introduction. So she pauses to read the rest of the article and concludes that the most important aspect is that the book provides a structured approach to thinking in individual and group settings. She needed to type "a structured", but then the predictions offered acceptable remaining words with only a bit of guidance: "approach to thinking, both individually and collectively."

Takeaways This interaction leverages the familiarity of the predictive-text interaction that is ubiquitous on smartphones, but the simple extension of this familiar interface to the context of typing the assistant's response to a revision request yields several unique kinds of uses:

- The system sometimes helps with routine tasks, like typing a book name (functioning like an adaptive copy-and-paste).
- The same interaction can suggest alternative wordings for phrases, using the natural 3– or 5–option button interface.
- Unlike a chat interface, the writer can exert granular, just-in-time control over the system.
- Some suggestions can even be provocative, leading the writer to pause and think more about what they wanted to say.

The prototype shows short phrases in prediction buttons, inspired by Arnold et al. (2016); next-phrase suggestions can shape writer thinking more than individual words even when not used directly (Bhat et al., 2023; Arnold et al., 2018; Jakesch et al., 2023).

3.2 Highlighting Edit Opportunities

Figure 2 shows a different interface with the same source text and prompt. This interface shows Alex's document with highlights in places where Alex might consider making edits to enact the revision goal that she has just specified. Hovering over an opportunity highlight shows a provocative clue of what an edit there might look like. Alex notices that "and" is highlighted; reading the phrase she notices that the phrase ("and the associated idea of parallel thinking") is not well connected to the main thought of the paragraph and decides to seek an alternative. Hovering the "and" reveals "is", suggesting that the next phrase could simply describe the book itself more (e.g., "is a guide for...") or perhaps state something concrete about its impact (e.g., "is the top-cited book on..."). Reading the rest of the paragraph and article, Alex decides to go with the description strategy, but chooses a different word: "describes a process for groups to plan thinking...". She makes this edit in the document and the opportunity highlights update to suggest other potential edits. She notices that the word "detailed" doesn't quite fit with how she understands the book; even though it is not highlighted, she hovers over it and sees an alternative, "structured", which seems more accurate.

Takeaways

- Alex retained full control over their document; all of the words are her own.
- In contrast to editing systems like Grammarly, Alex also had detailed control (via the prompt) over what sort of edit opportunities they wanted to see.
- The interaction allowed Alex to explore alternative choices: every word offered an alternative, even those not highlighted.
- The words shown in edit opportunities were sometimes substitutions but often instead offered a different semantic or grammatical direction that could be taken.
- It is still possible for the result to be entirely AI-generated text, but that would require the writer iteratively inspecting and applying every suggested change.

4 Discussion

So far these interaction designs have only been evaluated informally; empirical studies with writers are needed to determine how interaction-required suggestion interfaces affect writers' sense of ownership, control, and awareness of alternatives. Anecdotally, however (from use by the authors and a few others), both have been useful in low-level editing (trimming and clarifying wording), the predictive-text interface has been helpful for initial drafting (e.g., based on an outline), but neither are useful for larger-scale revision because they focus attention on localized choices; other tools are needed to address those needs (e.g., Dang et al. (2022); Benharrak et al. (2024); Kim et al. (2024)).

Although we described a case study in revision, predictive text could be used in any assistant response. We are particularly curious about how it might have different effects across different types of tasks: open-ended tasks such as ideation, analytical tasks such as review generation, and close-ended tasks such as refactoring code.

The straightforward application of predictive text to typing the assistant's response, as we propose in Section 3.1, presents opportunities to increase cognitive engagement and control over the status quo of accepting complete generated responses. Yet it is still possible to use the chatbot's words uncritically by accepting suggestions rapidly. (Should the interface be designed to allow larger-block acceptance?) And even cognitive engagement with the suggestions could still lead to a reduced sense of ownership over the result (Lehmann et al., 2022) and influence on human opinions (Arnold et al., 2018; Jakesch et al., 2023). Additional exploration of the interaction design (e.g., how alternatives are visualized and navigated) is needed.

The additional control afforded by predictive text (effectively prefilling the assistant's response) affords some additional risks for users to jailbreak the model (Andriushchenko et al., 2024). However, since prefilling is part of many commercial LLM APIs, we doubt that this interaction design presents significant marginal risk.

Predictive text can be viewed as an interactive visualization of high-probability local alternatives within a sequence of categorical choices (e.g., Figure 1 shows two-token predictions to provide awareness of where each suggestion could be going.[1] From this perspective a wide range of interactive visualization techniques are possible, such as the Dasher text entry system (Ward et al., 2000) (which may have accessibility benefits as well). Design dimensions of these visualizations include the granularity of suggestions (words, phrases, or larger units such as copy-pasted text from a writer's other drafts) and how interacting with the suggestion affects the surrounding text. The effects of these design decisions might vary by stage of the writing process.

The opportunity highlighting interface explored an extreme design position of being minimally prescriptive in AI help, but relaxing that extreme could yield a range of alternative interaction designs. For example, it could incorporate an interactive visualization where the writer could navigate through contextual alternatives at any point.

Both of these models presuppose autoregressive (left-to-right) language modeling, but additional types of interaction might be enabled by emerging model types based on out-of-order modeling or diffusion LLMs (Sahoo et al., 2024).

Although prior work has explored the effects of generating different kinds of content with LLMs on writer reactions (Benharrak et al., 2024; Kim et al., 2024; Zhou and Sterman, 2024), this work keeps the task for the LLM unchanged and explores the kinds of interactions that people can have with the inference process.

Interaction-required suggestions are a source of rich feedback data for reward-based language model training and personalization. Unlike static documents, the interaction logs with a conversational predictive text system would include what suggestions were made but not taken, providing a fine-grained human feedback signal. These feedback signals can be used for updating a language model (Wu et al., 2023; Arnold et al., 2017).

Conclusion With continuously increasing capabilities of LLMs, the difference between augmenting and replacing human thinking is a question not of system capabilities but of interaction design. The interaction-required approaches we've presented demonstrate how small shifts in interface design can fundamentally change the nature of human-AI partnership in writing. By prioritizing cognitive engagement, enabling granular control, and revealing the landscape of possibilities, we can design AI writing interfaces that help us think not *less* but *better*—maintaining human agency while still benefiting from AI capabilities.

Acknowledgments

We thank Hannah Yoo, Jason Chew, Juyeong Kim, Heonjae Kwon, Ray Flanagan, and the anonymous reviewers for their input and feedback. This work is supported by NSF CRII award 224614.

References

Maksym Andriushchenko, Francesco Croce, and Nicolas Flammarion. 2024. Jailbreaking Leading Safety-Aligned LLMs with Simple Adaptive Attacks. In *The Thirteenth International Conference on Learning Representations.*

Kenneth C. Arnold, Kai-Wei Chang, and Adam T. Kalai. 2017. Counterfactual Language Model Adaptation for Suggesting Phrases. In *Proceedings of the Eighth International Joint Conference on Natural Language*

[1]We plan to implement the phrase preview interaction of Arnold et al. (2016) to enable writers to see larger phrases without having to use all of them.

Processing (Volume 2: Short Papers), pages 49–54, Taipei, Taiwan. Asian Federation of Natural Language Processing.

Kenneth C Arnold, Krysta Chauncey, and Krzysztof Z. Gajos. 2018. Sentiment Bias in Predictive Text Recommendations Results in Biased Writing. In *Graphics Interface 2018*, pages 8–11, Toronto, Ontario, Canada.

Kenneth C Arnold, Krzysztof Z. Gajos, and Adam T. Kalai. 2016. On Suggesting Phrases vs. Predicting Words for Mobile Text Composition. In *Proceedings of the 29th Annual Symposium on User Interface Software and Technology - UIST '16*, pages 603–608.

Karim Benharrak, Tim Zindulka, Florian Lehmann, Hendrik Heuer, and Daniel Buschek. 2024. Writer-Defined AI Personas for On-Demand Feedback Generation. In *Proceedings of the 2024 CHI Conference on Human Factors in Computing Systems*, CHI '24, pages 1–18, New York, NY, USA. Association for Computing Machinery.

Advait Bhat, Saaket Agashe, Parth Oberoi, Niharika Mohile, Ravi Jangir, and Anirudha Joshi. 2023. Interacting with Next-Phrase Suggestions: How Suggestion Systems Aid and Influence the Cognitive Processes of Writing. In *Proceedings of the 28th International Conference on Intelligent User Interfaces*, IUI '23, pages 436–452, New York, NY, USA. Association for Computing Machinery.

Oloff C. Biermann, Ning F. Ma, and Dongwook Yoon. 2022. From Tool to Companion: Storywriters Want AI Writers to Respect Their Personal Values and Writing Strategies. In *Designing Interactive Systems Conference*, DIS '22, pages 1209–1227, New York, NY, USA. Association for Computing Machinery.

Arghavan Moradi Dakhel, Vahid Majdinasab, Amin Nikanjam, Foutse Khomh, Michel C. Desmarais, Zhen Ming, and Jiang. 2023. GitHub Copilot AI pair programmer: Asset or Liability? *Preprint*, arXiv:2206.15331.

Hai Dang, Karim Benharrak, Florian Lehmann, and Daniel Buschek. 2022. Beyond Text Generation: Supporting Writers With Continuous Automatic Text Summaries. In *Proceedings of the 35th Annual ACM Symposium on User Interface Software and Technology*, UIST '22, pages 1–13, New York, NY, USA. Association for Computing Machinery.

Teresa Datta and John P. Dickerson. 2023. Who's Thinking? A Push for Human-Centered Evaluation of LLMs using the XAI Playbook. *Preprint*, arXiv:2303.06223.

Daniela Fernandes, Steeven Villa, Salla Nicholls, Otso Haavisto, Daniel Buschek, Albrecht Schmidt, Thomas Kosch, Chenxinran Shen, and Robin Welsch. 2025. Performance and Metacognition Disconnect when Reasoning in Human-AI Interaction. *Preprint*, arXiv:2409.16708.

Krzysztof Z. Gajos and Lena Mamykina. 2022. Do People Engage Cognitively with AI? Impact of AI Assistance on Incidental Learning. In *Proceedings of the 27th International Conference on Intelligent User Interfaces*, IUI '22, pages 794–806, New York, NY, USA. Association for Computing Machinery.

Katy Ilonka Gero and Lydia B. Chilton. 2019. How a stylistic, machine-generated thesaurus impacts a writer's process. In *Proceedings of the 2019 on Creativity and Cognition*, C&C '19, pages 597–603, New York, NY, USA. Association for Computing Machinery.

Angel Hsing-Chi Hwang, Q. Vera Liao, Su Lin Blodgett, Alexandra Olteanu, and Adam Trischler. 2024. "It was 80% me, 20% AI": Seeking Authenticity in Co-Writing with Large Language Models. *Preprint*, arXiv:2411.13032.

Maurice Jakesch, Advait Bhat, Daniel Buschek, Lior Zalmanson, and Mor Naaman. 2023. Co-Writing with Opinionated Language Models Affects Users' Views. In *Proceedings of the 2023 CHI Conference on Human Factors in Computing Systems*, CHI '23, pages 1–15, New York, NY, USA. Association for Computing Machinery.

Jiho Kim, Ray C. Flanagan, Noelle E. Haviland, ZeAi Sun, Souad N. Yakubu, Edom A. Maru, and Kenneth C. Arnold. 2024. Towards Full Authorship with AI: Supporting Revision with AI-Generated Views. In *Joint Proceedings of the ACM IUI 2024 Workshops*, volume 3660 of *CEUR Workshop Proceedings*, Greenville, South Carolina, USA. CEUR-WS.org.

Florian Lehmann, Niklas Markert, Hai Dang, and Daniel Buschek. 2022. Suggestion Lists vs. Continuous Generation: Interaction Design for Writing with Generative Models on Mobile Devices Affect Text Length, Wording and Perceived Authorship. In *Mensch Und Computer 2022*, pages 192–208.

Laria Reynolds and Kyle McDonell. 2021. Multiversal views on language models. In *2nd Workshop on Human-AI Co-Creation with Generative Models - HAI-GEN 2021*, volume 2903. CEUR.

Mohi Reza, Nathan Laundry, Ilya Musabirov, Peter Dushniku, Zhi Yuan "Michael" Yu, Kashish Mittal, Tovi Grossman, Michael Liut, Anastasia Kuzminykh, and Joseph Jay Williams. 2023. ABScribe: Rapid Exploration of Multiple Writing Variations in Human-AI Co-Writing Tasks using Large Language Models. *Preprint*, arXiv:2310.00117.

Subham Sekhar Sahoo, Marianne Arriola, Yair Schiff, Aaron Gokaslan, Edgar Marroquin, Justin T. Chiu, Alexander Rush, and Volodymyr Kuleshov. 2024. Simple and Effective Masked Diffusion Language Models. *Preprint*, arXiv:2406.07524.

Gemma Team, Morgane Riviere, Shreya Pathak, Pier Giuseppe Sessa, Cassidy Hardin, Surya Bhupatiraju, Léonard Hussenot, Thomas Mesnard, Bobak Shahriari, Alexandre Ramé, Johan Ferret, Peter

Liu, Pouya Tafti, Abe Friesen, Michelle Casbon, Sabela Ramos, Ravin Kumar, Charline Le Lan, Sammy Jerome, Anton Tsitsulin, Nino Vieillard, Piotr Stanczyk, Sertan Girgin, Nikola Momchev, Matt Hoffman, Shantanu Thakoor, Jean-Bastien Grill, Behnam Neyshabur, Olivier Bachem, Alanna Walton, Aliaksei Severyn, Alicia Parrish, Aliya Ahmad, Allen Hutchison, Alvin Abdagic, Amanda Carl, Amy Shen, Andy Brock, Andy Coenen, Anthony Laforge, Antonia Paterson, Ben Bastian, Bilal Piot, Bo Wu, Brandon Royal, Charlie Chen, Chintu Kumar, Chris Perry, Chris Welty, Christopher A. Choquette-Choo, Danila Sinopalnikov, David Weinberger, Dimple Vijaykumar, Dominika Rogozińska, Dustin Herbison, Elisa Bandy, Emma Wang, Eric Noland, Erica Moreira, Evan Senter, Evgenii Eltyshev, Francesco Visin, Gabriel Rasskin, Gary Wei, Glenn Cameron, Gus Martins, Hadi Hashemi, Hanna Klimczak-Plucińska, Harleen Batra, Harsh Dhand, Ivan Nardini, Jacinda Mein, Jack Zhou, James Svensson, Jeff Stanway, Jetha Chan, Jin Peng Zhou, Joana Carrasqueira, Joana Iljazi, Jocelyn Becker, Joe Fernandez, Joost van Amersfoort, Josh Gordon, Josh Lipschultz, Josh Newlan, Ju-yeong Ji, Kareem Mohamed, Kartikeya Badola, Kat Black, Katie Millican, Keelin McDonell, Kelvin Nguyen, Kiranbir Sodhia, Kish Greene, Lars Lowe Sjoesund, Lauren Usui, Laurent Sifre, Lena Heuermann, Leticia Lago, Lilly McNealus, Livio Baldini Soares, Logan Kilpatrick, Lucas Dixon, Luciano Martins, Machel Reid, Manvinder Singh, Mark Iverson, Martin Görner, Mat Velloso, Mateo Wirth, Matt Davidow, Matt Miller, Matthew Rahtz, Matthew Watson, Meg Risdal, Mehran Kazemi, Michael Moynihan, Ming Zhang, Minsuk Kahng, Minwoo Park, Mofi Rahman, Mohit Khatwani, Natalie Dao, Nenshad Bardoliwalla, Nesh Devanathan, Neta Dumai, Nilay Chauhan, Oscar Wahltinez, Pankil Botarda, Parker Barnes, Paul Barham, Paul Michel, Pengchong Jin, Petko Georgiev, Phil Culliton, Pradeep Kuppala, Ramona Comanescu, Ramona Merhej, Reena Jana, Reza Ardeshir Rokni, Rishabh Agarwal, Ryan Mullins, Samaneh Saadat, Sara Mc Carthy, Sarah Cogan, Sarah Perrin, Sébastien M. R. Arnold, Sebastian Krause, Shengyang Dai, Shruti Garg, Shruti Sheth, Sue Ronstrom, Susan Chan, Timothy Jordan, Ting Yu, Tom Eccles, Tom Hennigan, Tomas Kocisky, Tulsee Doshi, Vihan Jain, Vikas Yadav, Vilobh Meshram, Vishal Dharmadhikari, Warren Barkley, Wei Wei, Wenming Ye, Woohyun Han, Woosuk Kwon, Xiang Xu, Zhe Shen, Zhitao Gong, Zichuan Wei, Victor Cotruta, Phoebe Kirk, Anand Rao, Minh Giang, Ludovic Peran, Tris Warkentin, Eli Collins, Joelle Barral, Zoubin Ghahramani, Raia Hadsell, D. Sculley, Jeanine Banks, Anca Dragan, Slav Petrov, Oriol Vinyals, Jeff Dean, Demis Hassabis, Koray Kavukcuoglu, Clement Farabet, Elena Buchatskaya, Sebastian Borgeaud, Noah Fiedel, Armand Joulin, Kathleen Kenealy, Robert Dadashi, and Alek Andreev. 2024. Gemma 2: Improving Open Language Models at a Practical Size. *Preprint*, arXiv:2408.00118.

The Hugging Face Team. 2025. Hugging Face Transformers. https://huggingface.co/docs/transformers/index.

David J. Ward, Alan F. Blackwell, and David J. C. MacKay. 2000. Dasher—a data entry interface using continuous gestures and language models. In *Proceedings of the 13th Annual ACM Symposium on User Interface Software and Technology*, UIST '00, pages 129–137, New York, NY, USA. Association for Computing Machinery.

Zeqiu Wu, Yushi Hu, Weijia Shi, Nouha Dziri, Alane Suhr, Prithviraj Ammanabrolu, Noah A. Smith, Mari Ostendorf, and Hannaneh Hajishirzi. 2023. Fine-Grained Human Feedback Gives Better Rewards for Language Model Training. *Preprint*, arXiv:2306.01693.

David Zhou and Sarah Sterman. 2024. Ai.llude: Investigating Rewriting AI-Generated Text to Support Creative Expression. In *Proceedings of the 16th Conference on Creativity & Cognition*, C&C '24, pages 241–254, New York, NY, USA. Association for Computing Machinery.

Appendix

Implementation Details

The prototypes described here were implemented using a Streamlit frontend and a backend using the Hugging Face Transformers library (Team, 2025). Full source code and demo is available at `https://huggingface.co/spaces/CalvinU/writing-prototypes`.

Both of these systems rely on language model functionality that is not typically exposed in efficient ways in commercial APIs[2], but are straightforward to implement when given direct access to the forward pass of the model, which computes next-token distributions for all tokens in the context (including both "user" and "assistant" messages). The implementation in our demo uses the Gemma 2 9B model released by Google (Team et al., 2024).

The predictive text interface first computes the top-k (e.g., 3 or 5) next tokens, then constructs a short phrase (in the demo, a single additional token) by greedy generation from each of those options. With careful management of the key-value cache, this generation readily completes at interactive speed on commodity hardware. Predictive-text coding systems like GitHub Copilot served as informal prototypes of this interaction (since instructions can be entered as code comments), but they did not reveal the landscape of possibilities

[2]For example, prompt logprobs, needed for highlighting, was part of the OpenAI text completions API but was never added to the chat completions API

(see section 2 on Design Principles) in the way that smartphone keyboards and our system do.

The highlighting interface constructs a pseudo-conversation by where the user message is the revision prompt concatenated with the original document and the assistant message is the original document repeated unchanged. Rather than generate additional tokens, we simply compute the next-token distributions for all tokens in the "assistant" message corresponding to the user's document. The frontend highlights the tokens where the model gives a higher score to a token other than the one in the original document. Mouseover hovers show an alternative token; for tokens where the argmax prediction matched the original document (which are typically the majority of tokens), the hover shows the 2nd highest-scored option.

Voice Interaction With Conversational AI Could Facilitate Thoughtful Reflection and Substantive Revision in Writing

Jiho Kim
Calvin University
jihokim8@acm.org

Philippe Laban
Microsoft Research
plaban@microsoft.com

Xiang 'Anthony' Chen
University of California, Los Angeles
xac@ucla.edu

Kenneth C. Arnold
Calvin University
kcarnold@alum.mit.edu

Abstract

Writing well requires not only expressing ideas but also refining them through revision, a process facilitated by reflection. Prior research suggests that feedback delivered through dialogues, such as those in writing center tutoring sessions, can help writers reflect more thoughtfully on their work compared to static feedback. Recent advancements in multi-modal large language models (LLMs) now offer new possibilities for supporting interactive and expressive voice-based reflection in writing. In particular, we propose that LLM-generated static feedback can be repurposed as conversation starters, allowing writers to seek clarification, request examples, and ask follow-up questions, thereby fostering deeper reflection on their writing. We argue that voice-based interaction can naturally facilitate this conversational exchange, encouraging writers' engagement with higher-order concerns, facilitating iterative refinement of their reflections, and reduce cognitive load compared to text-based interactions. To investigate these effects, we propose a formative study exploring how text vs. voice input influence writers' reflection and subsequent revisions. Findings from this study will inform the design of intelligent and interactive writing tools, offering insights into how voice-based interactions with LLM-powered conversational agents can support reflection and revision.

1 Introduction

Writing for effective communication requires more than just *expressing* thoughts; it demands *transforming* those thoughts to meet the expectations of an audience (Flower, 1979). This transformation is achieved through *revision*, which we define as any changes made to written content at any time, including both meaning-preserving edits and meaning-changing adjustments (Faigley and Witte, 1981; Fitzgerald, 1987). Writing research suggests that substantive revision is facilitated through *reflection* (Pianko, 1979), in which writers critically examine their work from an external perspective to evaluate its effectiveness in addressing their rhetorical situation and fulfilling their communication goals (Flower and Hayes, 1980).

However, writers often suffer from the curse of knowledge bias, which prevents them from reading their text as their audience would (Flower et al., 1986). Consequently, feedback from others is a common way to facilitate reflection (Flower, 1979). For example, many higher education institutions operate writing centers where tutors provide non-prescriptive and non-corrective feedback through conversational exchanges, encouraging writers to prioritize addressing higher-order concerns, such as thesis (or focus), audience engagement, organization, and content development, rather than lower-order concerns, such as grammar and syntax (Purdue Online Writing Lab, n.d.; Fitzgerald and Ianetta, 2015; Murphy and Sherwood, 2011; Ryan and Zimmerelli, 2015). This dialogue with the tutors helps writers gain critical distance from their work and make independent and substantive revisions.

Previous work has demonstrated user interface (UI) affordances that enable writers to use large language models (LLMs) to generate personalized and contextually adaptive feedback, questions, and advice, to facilitate reflection (Benharrak et al., 2024; Kim et al., 2024). However, these systems primarily support the generation of static feedback, questions, and advice, and lack the UI support for conversational exchanges characteristic of human tutoring. Yet, as highlighted by Gero et al. (2023) (in the second paragraph of Section 4.2.3), useful feedback comes from a back-and-forth conversational exchange, allowing the writers to clarify, ask follow-up questions, and refine their work based on the discussion. This discussion not only deepens the writer's understanding of feedback but also enables co-construction of meaning, which has been shown to improve feedback uptake and lead to sub-

Proceedings of the Fourth Workshop on Intelligent and Interactive Writing Assistants (In2Writing 2025), pages 69–73
May 4, 2025

stantive revisions (Zhao et al., 2024).

Furthermore, the input modality of interaction may significantly influence how people reflect on their writing through dialogue with LLM-powered conversational agents. A study by Chalfonte et al. (1991) showed that when co-authors gave feedback to each other on a collaborative writing task using spoken annotation, it imposed a lower cognitive load than written annotations, giving them more mental capacity to focus on higher-order concerns. However, there is limited evidence on how the modality of the writer's input, particularly spoken vs. written, impacts the quality of reflection when interacting with LLM-powered conversational agents.

Recent advancements in multi-modal LLMs highlight their ability to understand and interpret multi-modal instructions and generate outputs across different modalities, including text and speech (Zhang et al., 2023; Wang et al., 2024a,b). Commercially available multi-modal LLMs, such as GPT-4o (OpenAI, 2024a) and Gemini 2.0 Flash (Kavukcuoglu, 2025), demonstrate high accuracy and low latency in understanding and generating outputs across different modalities. This allows interaction designers to build both highly *interactive* (i.e., responding quickly and appropriately) and *expressive* (i.e., conveying emotions, social context, and nuanced meaning through non-verbal cues such as voice inflection, pitch, and tone) (Chalfonte et al., 1991) conversational interfaces in ways that were not possible before. These advancements make our exploration of voice interactions with LLM-powered conversational agents timely.

We argue that the input modality, whether writers respond to feedback through voice or text, can influence the quality of their reflection. Specifically, we hypothesize that responding to feedback from an LLM-powered conversational agent using voice can (1) promote greater engagement with higher-order concerns, (2) facilitate more iterative refinement of one's reflections, and (3) reduce the cognitive load associated with reflection, compared to written input. To investigate this, we propose a formative study exploring how spoken versus written input affects writers' reflection and subsequent revision.

2 Formative Study

Consider a writer who has completed a rough draft of an argumentative essay and wants to revise it to better meet audience expectations. Before revising, they need to reflect on their work to set specific revision goals. They turn to reflection support systems, such as Textfocals (Kim et al., 2024) or Impressona (Benharrak et al., 2024), seeking feedback, questions, and advice to help them reflect on their work and make decisions about what to revise. However, writers prefer feedback containing specific examples rather than vague comments. For example, one participant using Impressona noted that the system "just tells me I have to do this and it doesn't come up with the specific examples" (as said by P11 in Benharrak et al. (2024)).

This illustrates a limitation in the aforementioned reflection support systems. As Zhao et al. (2024) and Gero et al. (2023) highlight, feedback is more useful when it is part of an interactive conversational exchange, allowing writers to seek clarification, request examples, and ask follow-up questions. This suggests an interaction design opportunity to repurpose static feedback, questions, and advice as conversation starters. Writers can use these starters to initiate reflective dialogues with LLM-powered conversational agents, to seek clarification, request examples, and ask follow-up questions, thus fostering thoughtful reflection.

We argue that the speech modality can naturally facilitate this conversational exchange. Prior research has shown that in collaborative writing, when co-authors provided feedback to each other using spoken annotations, the expressivity of spoken annotations encouraged a greater focus on higher-order concerns and promoted self-correction of the provided feedback compared to written annotations (Chalfonte et al., 1991). This motivates the following research questions:

RQ1: How might speaking to LLM-powered conversational agents, compared to typing, influence the depth and kinds of concerns writers reflect on in their work?

RQ2: How does engaging in spoken conversations with LLM-powered conversational agents, as opposed to text-based interactions, shape the way writers refine and revisit their own reflections?

Furthermore, Chalfonte et al. (1991) suggested that the benefits of the speech modality might stem from spoken language production being less cognitively demanding than written language production (Bourdin and Fayol, 1994). This relative ease could allow writers to allocate more cognitive resources to their reflections. However, the cognitive demands of reflection itself, regardless of the modality, may also be significant. This raises the question:

RQ3: How do writers perceive the cognitive demands of speaking to LLM-powered conversational agents, compared to typing, and what factors influence these perceptions?

Finally, given the association between reflection and revision in writing (Pianko, 1979), it is important to examine whether reflective dialogues with LLM-powered conversational agents lead to actionable changes in writing. This raises the question:

RQ4: How does reflecting with LLM-powered conversational agents influence the extent and depth of revisions in written content?

2.1 Method and Measures

To answer our research questions, we will employ a within-subjects experiment design, with participants counterbalanced across two conditions. All conditions will have interactive conversational capabilities, but will differ in the modalities provided: (1) written communication from both the user and the system, and (2) spoken input from the user with written output from the system.

Participants will be recruited using convenience sampling through multiple channels, including Calvin University's student, faculty, and staff community, as well as freelancing websites (e.g., Upwork), and crowdsourcing platforms (e.g., Prolific). We will seek individuals who can read, write, and speak English. Recruitment materials will provide information about the study and compensation[1].

Participants will be asked to write two rough drafts before the study, using argumentative writing prompts provided by the researchers. The length requirement of the rough drafts as well as the time the participant spends reflecting and revising in each conditions will be determined through a pilot study.

During the formative study, participants will use the formative system (see Section 2.2) modified for each condition to reflect on and revise their rough drafts. After completing each condition, participants will complete the NASA-TLX (Hart, 2006) questionnaire to measure cognitive load. Following all conditions, a semi-structured interview will be conducted to gather qualitative insights on participants' experiences.

In terms of specific quantitative measures, we plan to examine the frequency of higher-order concerns (i.e., absolute count of higher-order concerns), after adjusting for the length of the response, as well as the proportion of higher-order concerns relative to the total number of concerns mentioned (i.e., relative count of higher-order concerns) in each condition. Coding of what qualifies as higher-order concerns or lower-order concerns will be based on criteria adapted from Purdue Online Writing Lab (n.d.). For example, higher-order concerns include thesis or focus, audience and purpose, organization, and development, while lower-order concerns include sentence structure, grammar, and spelling. This criteria will be shared among the coders before data analysis to ensure inter-rater reliability. We will also record the number of conversational turns per minute as one proxy for engagement in conversation, and the time taken by participants to respond to the conversational agent as a proxy for cognitive processing. While we acknowledge that slower-speaking users or those processing complex responses may naturally take longer to reply, these measures will be interpreted with qualitative data (e.g., insights from aforementioned semi-structured interview) to better contextualize user behavior. Additionally, participants' revisions will be evaluated by experts using an argumentative essay rubric developed by Ozfidan and Mitchell (2022).

2.2 System Design Considerations

To ensure that our formative study isolates the effects of input modality, rather than introducing confounding factors such as interface novelty or feature differences, we design our formative system to align with established interaction patterns in existing LLM-powered writing tools. This helps maintain external validity and allows us to focus on how modality shapes writers' reflection and revision behaviors. In this section, we outline key interaction design considerations, centered on the dimensions of *initiation*, *contextualization*, and *control*.

2.2.1 Initiation

In current LLM-powered conversational interfaces, users typically initiate interactions by explicitly asking questions or making requests. Reflection support systems, such as those proposed by Ben-

[1]The first author's institutional review board approved the proposed study procedures.

harrak et al. (2024) and Kim et al. (2024), follow a different approach. After users submit their drafts, these systems generate feedback, questions, or advice without requiring a specific prompt from the user, thereby initiating the interactions themselves. Our design explores the use of such system-initiated prompts (i.e., user-facing feedback, questions, or advice) as conversation starting points and incorporates UI affordances that enable writers to respond with clarifications, follow-up questions, or answers, either in text or speech, depending on the study condition.

2.2.2 Contextualization

Contextualization refers to how the writer's task is situated within the system to help writers maintain situational awareness of their work (Simkute et al., 2025). Existing conversational interfaces, such as ChatGPT and Claude, achieve this by allowing users to open up a separate window (to the right of the conversational interface) called the Canvas (OpenAI, 2024b) or Artifacts (Anthropic, 2024). These UI affordances enable users to collaborate with LLM-powered conversational agents, allowing them to view, modify, and build on both their own work and LLM-generated content. Similarly, our design also explores providing a spatially distinct area for content creation and revision, helping users keep track of the context of their writing task.

2.2.3 Control

While contextualization helps in maintaining situational awareness, control is crucial for preserving the user's sense of ownership and agency over their content. Existing interfaces, such as those in ChatGPT and Claude, explicitly allow LLM-powered conversational agents to directly alter or expand upon the user's content. This capability, while useful for content generation and iteration, may compromise the user's sense of ownership and agency. In contrast, our design adopts an approach similar to previous work (Dang et al., 2022; Benharrak et al., 2024; Kim et al., 2024; Laban et al., 2024) by supporting contextualization without allowing the LLM-powered conversational agents to directly modify or build upon the writer's content. This approach preserves the writer's control, and any feedback on writing (i.e., non-directive and non-prescriptive suggestions) from LLM is discussed with the writer, who reflects on them and decides whether to adopt the feedback by revising their content.

3 Expected Contributions

Through our formative study, we aim to inform the design of intelligent and interactive writing tools that support reflection through conversational exchanges with LLM-powered conversational agents. Specifically, we expect to make the following contributions: (1) providing evidence on the impact of speech modality in facilitating thoughtful reflection and (2) exploring the opportunity to transform static LLM-generated feedback, questions, and advice into dynamic conversational exchanges that encourage reflection and subsequent revision.

Acknowledgments

We thank Jason Chew, Juyeong Kim, Heonjae Kwon, Ray Flanagan, Koré Qualls, and the anonymous reviewers for their input and feedback. This work is supported by NSF CRII award 224614.

References

Anthropic. 2024. Introducing Claude 3.5 Sonnet. https://www.anthropic.com/news/claude-3-5-sonnet.

Karim Benharrak, Tim Zindulka, Florian Lehmann, Hendrik Heuer, and Daniel Buschek. 2024. Writer-Defined AI Personas for On-Demand Feedback Generation. In *Proceedings of the 2024 CHI Conference on Human Factors in Computing Systems*, CHI '24, pages 1–18, New York, NY, USA. Association for Computing Machinery.

Béatrice Bourdin and Michel Fayol. 1994. Is Written Language Production More Difficult than Oral Language Production? A Working Memory Approach. *International Journal of Psychology*, 29(5):591–620.

Barbara L. Chalfonte, Robert S. Fish, and Robert E. Kraut. 1991. Expressive Richness: A Comparison of Speech and Text as Media for Revision. In *Proceedings of the SIGCHI Conference on Human Factors in Computing Systems*, CHI '91, pages 21–26, New York, NY, USA. Association for Computing Machinery.

Hai Dang, Karim Benharrak, Florian Lehmann, and Daniel Buschek. 2022. Beyond Text Generation: Supporting Writers with Continuous Automatic Text Summaries. In *Proceedings of the 35th Annual ACM Symposium on User Interface Software and Technology*, UIST '22, pages 1–13, New York, NY, USA. Association for Computing Machinery.

Lester Faigley and Stephen Witte. 1981. Analyzing Revision. *College Composition and Communication*, 32(4):400–414.

Jill Fitzgerald. 1987. Research on Revision in Writing. *Review of Educational Research*, 57(4):481–506.

Lauren Fitzgerald and Melissa Ianetta. 2015. *The Oxford Guide for Writing Tutors: Practice and Research*, first edition. Oxford University Press, Oxford, UK.

Linda Flower. 1979. Writer-Based Prose: A Cognitive Basis for Problems in Writing. *College English*, 41(1):19–37.

Linda Flower and John R. Hayes. 1980. The Cognition of Discovery: Defining a Rhetorical Problem. *College Composition and Communication*, 31(1):21–32.

Linda Flower, John R. Hayes, Linda Carey, Karen Schriver, and James Stratman. 1986. Detection, Diagnosis, and the Strategies of Revision. *College Composition and Communication*, 37(1):16–55.

Katy Ilonka Gero, Tao Long, and Lydia B. Chilton. 2023. Social Dynamics of AI Support in Creative Writing. In *Proceedings of the 2023 CHI Conference on Human Factors in Computing Systems*, CHI '23, pages 1–15, New York, NY, USA. Association for Computing Machinery.

Sandra G. Hart. 2006. NASA-Task Load Index (NASA-TLX); 20 Years Later. *Proceedings of the Human Factors and Ergonomics Society Annual Meeting*, 50(9):904–908.

Koray Kavukcuoglu. 2025. Gemini 2.0 Is Now Available to Everyone. https://blog.google/technology/google-deepmind/gemini-model-updates-february-2025/.

Jiho Kim, Ray C. Flanagan, Noelle E. Haviland, ZeAi Sun, Souad N. Yakubu, Edom A. Maru, and Kenneth C. Arnold. 2024. Towards Full Authorship with AI: Supporting Revision with AI-Generated Views. In *Joint Proceedings of the ACM IUI 2024 Workshops*, volume 3660 of *CEUR Workshop Proceedings*, Greenville, South Carolina, USA. CEUR-WS.org.

Philippe Laban, Jesse Vig, Marti Hearst, Caiming Xiong, and Chien-Sheng Wu. 2024. Beyond the Chat: Executable and Verifiable Text-Editing with LLMs. In *Proceedings of the 37th Annual ACM Symposium on User Interface Software and Technology*, UIST '24, pages 1–23, New York, NY, USA. Association for Computing Machinery.

Christina Murphy and Steve Sherwood. 2011. *The St. Martin's Sourcebook for Writing Tutors*, fourth edition. Bedford/St. Martin's, Boston, MA, USA.

OpenAI. 2024a. Hello GPT-4o. https://openai.com/index/hello-gpt-4o/.

OpenAI. 2024b. Introducing Canvas. https://openai.com/index/introducing-canvas/.

Burhan Ozfidan and Connie Mitchell. 2022. Assessment of Students' Argumentative Writing: A Rubric Development. *Journal of Ethnic and Cultural Studies*, 9(2):121–133.

Sharon Pianko. 1979. Reflection: A Critical Component of the Composing Process. *College Composition and Communication*, 30(3):275–278.

Purdue Online Writing Lab. n.d. Higher Order Concerns (HOCs) and Lower Order Concerns (LOCs). https://owl.purdue.edu/owl/general_writing /mechanics/hocs_and_locs.html.

Leigh Ryan and Lisa Zimmerelli. 2015. *The Bedford Guide for Writing Tutors*, sixth edition. Bedford/St. Martin's, Boston, MA, USA.

Auste Simkute, Lev Tankelevitch, Viktor Kewenig, Ava Elizabeth Scott, Abigail Sellen, and Sean Rintel. 2025. Ironies of Generative AI: Understanding and Mitigating Productivity Loss in Human-AI Interaction. *International Journal of Human–Computer Interaction*, 41(5):2898–2919.

Chen Wang, Minpeng Liao, Zhongqiang Huang, Jinliang Lu, Junhong Wu, Yuchen Liu, Chengqing Zong, and Jiajun Zhang. 2024a. BLSP: Bootstrapping Language-Speech Pre-training via Behavior Alignment of Continuation Writing. *Preprint*, arXiv:2309.00916.

Chen Wang, Minpeng Liao, Zhongqiang Huang, Junhong Wu, Chengqing Zong, and Jiajun Zhang. 2024b. BLSP-emo: Towards empathetic large speech-language models. In *Proceedings of the 2024 Conference on Empirical Methods in Natural Language Processing*, pages 19186–19199, Miami, Florida, USA. Association for Computational Linguistics.

Dong Zhang, Shimin Li, Xin Zhang, Jun Zhan, Pengyu Wang, Yaqian Zhou, and Xipeng Qiu. 2023. SpeechGPT: Empowering large language models with intrinsic cross-modal conversational abilities. In *Findings of the Association for Computational Linguistics: EMNLP 2023*, pages 15757–15773, Singapore. Association for Computational Linguistics.

Yuhuan Zhao, Fuhui Zhang, Christian D. Schunn, Ping He, Di Li, and Yifan Zhao. 2024. Feedback, Feedback-On-Feedback and Re-Feedback: Effects of Written Dialogic Peer Feedback on English as a Foreign Language Writing. *Assessment & Evaluation in Higher Education*, 49(4):523–538.

RONA: Pragmatically Diverse Image Captioning with Coherence Relations

Aashish Anantha Ramakrishnan[1], Aadarsh Anantha Ramakrishnan[2], Dongwon Lee[1]
[1]The Pennsylvania State University; [2]National Institute of Technology, Tiruchirappalli
[1]{aza6352, dul13}@psu.edu, [2]106121001@nitt.edu

Abstract

Writing Assistants (e.g., Grammarly, Microsoft Copilot) traditionally generate diverse image captions by employing syntactic and semantic variations to describe image components. However, human-written captions prioritize conveying a central message alongside visual descriptions using pragmatic cues. To enhance caption diversity, it is essential to explore alternative ways of communicating these messages in conjunction with visual content. We propose RONA, a novel prompting strategy for Multi-modal Large Language Models (MLLM) that leverages *Coherence Relations* as a controllable axis for pragmatic variations. We demonstrate that RONA generates captions with better overall *diversity* and ground-truth *alignment*, compared to MLLM baselines across multiple domains. Our code is available at: https://github.com/aashish2000/RONA

1 Introduction

A *Writing Assistant* (WA) is a tool (e.g., Grammarly, Microsoft Copilot, Copy.ai), often powered by Generative AI, that helps users in various writing tasks. WAs have evolved over the years to support users across a multitude of tasks, with AI-powered assistants being adept at generating a wide selection of content. *Image Captioning* (*i.e.,* generating textual descriptions for given images) is one key task that has seen significant advancements with the introduction of Multi-modal Large Language Models (MLLMs). These pre-trained models have achieved remarkable success in generating captions that accurately describe the visual content of images (Chen et al., 2024; Yue et al., 2023). However, real-world image captions across different domains often require more than just a description of the visual elements–*i.e.,* they need to convey a central message, provide context, and offer different perspectives on the image (Federico, 2016). This leads to *significant lack of diversity in the generated captions*, limiting the utility of WAs.

Existing approaches to fostering diversity in image captions have primarily focused on providing a richer vocabulary (*i.e.,* syntactic variations) or selecting different components of the image to emphasize (*i.e.,* semantic variations) (Bugliarello and Elliott, 2021; Li et al., 2022). Although these methods have shown promise, they often fail to capture the nuanced ways in which humans communicate through captions as shown in Figure 1. Pragmatic variations, such as multi-modal implicatures and metaphors (Genovesi, 2020), which utilize meanings or connotations beyond the literal description of the image, are often employed by caption writers to make their messages more engaging and relatable (Weiland et al., 2015).

To address this challenge, in this work, we propose RONA (Relation-based cOhereNce-aware cAptioning), a novel prompting strategy for MLLMs inspired by the concept of *Coherence Relations* (CRs). Based on the principles of Discourse Theory, CRs provide a structured overview of image-text relationships (Hobbs, 1978; Kress, 2009; O'Halloran et al., 2014), modeling both contextual and pragmatics aspects of language (Ma et al., 2025; Mavridou et al., 2015). We evaluate their effectiveness in image captioning by *using CRs as guidelines for generating captions that fulfill specific communicative functions while preserving semantic coherence.*

Our analysis includes popular MLLMs: Claude-3.5 Sonnet V2 (Anthropic) and GPT-4o (OpenAI et al., 2024) on two datasets–*i.e.,* news captions (ANNA) and social media captions (Tweet Subtitles). These datasets contain a wide range of visual objects and abstractive captions (Anantha Ramakrishnan et al., 2024), making this a challenging task for MLLMs. We demonstrate that RONA outperforms existing baselines on caption diversity while retaining ground truth similarity. Our contributions

Proceedings of the Fourth Workshop on Intelligent and Interactive Writing Assistants (In2Writing 2025), pages 74–86
May 4, 2025 ©2025 Association for Computational Linguistics

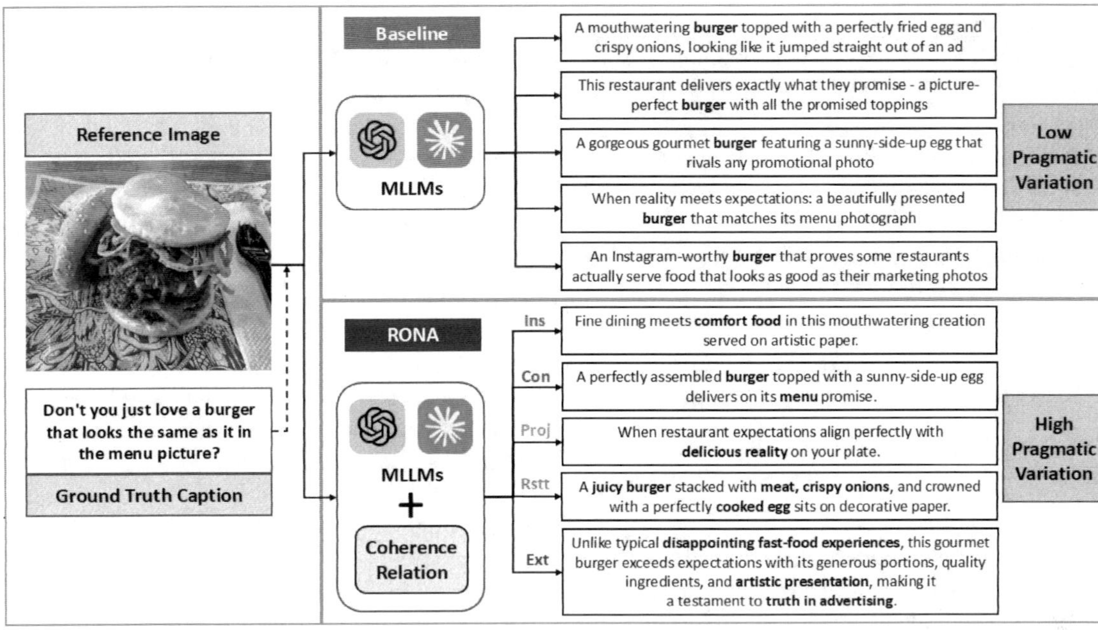

Figure 1: An overview of RONA. The CRs used are Insertion (Ins), Concretization (Con), Projection (Proj), Restatement (Rstt) and Extension (Ext). These relations provide a finite but flexible axis of variation for diverse caption generation compared to instruction-based prompts.

are as follows:

- We propose RONA, a novel prompting strategy that leverages Coherence Relations (CRs) to generate pragmatically diverse image captions.
- We demonstrate that RONA outperforms existing MLLM baselines in terms of diversity and ground-truth similarity on news and social media captioning datasets.
- Our analysis shows the viability of CRs to be utilized as an axis of variation for Captioning-based writing assistants.

2 Related Work

Writing Assistants MLLMs have enabled WAs to support a variety of writing tasks, with their input ranging from sentence-level suggestions (Gero et al., 2022) to long-form writing tasks such as literature reviews and creative writing (Choe et al., 2024), (Singh et al., 2023). In order to improve the Human-AI collaboration experience, there exists a need to incorporate human values into AI-based writing systems and vice versa (Shen et al., 2024), (Lee et al., 2024). Although these studies have focused on broader task domains, specific writing tasks such as caption writing have been less explored (Ng et al., 2024), particularly pragmatically diverse captioning which we aim to address.

Image Captioning Traditional Captioning models build on task-specific generative architectures to generate faithful and diverse descriptions for images (Mahajan and Roth, 2020; Liu et al., 2019). However, with the introduction of MLLMs, general-purpose models capable of multi-modal representations are utilized for caption generation (Radford et al., 2021; Li et al., 2023). To improve the alignment between image-text linkages, Coherence Relations (CR) (Alikhani et al., 2020) have been leveraged across different downstream text generation tasks (Alikhani et al., 2019; Vempala and Preoţiuc-Pietro, 2019; Sosea et al., 2021). Although popular MLLMs such as GPT-4o and Claude Sonnet 3.5 V2 are poor at predicting and verifying these relationships (Thrush et al., 2022; Anantha Ramakrishnan et al., 2025), existing research does not explore the production capabilities of these models. In our work, we investigate the ability of MLLM-based WAs to utilize CRs as a guidance mechanism for in-context learning.

3 Methodology

Coherence Relations RONA leverages in-context explanations of Coherence Relations (CRs) as guidance for generating pragmatically diverse captions. We utilize CRs that characterize both entity-level and scene-level linkages between an image and its expected caption (Xu et al., 2022). Entity-level relations describe the relationships between specific objects in the image and their corresponding elaboration in the caption. Scene-level relations, on the other hand, capture the overall context and narrative of the image, providing a broader understanding of the visual content. The selection of these relations are motivated by their generalizability across different domains. Overall, the 5 types of relations that we utilize are:

- **Insertion**: An entity-level relation that describes a type of pragmatic *ellipsis*, *i.e.,* where the focal object described in the image and caption does not have an explicit mention in the caption.
- **Concretization**: An entity-level relation that utilizes an *anchor* object which is prominently referenced in the image and caption, with the caption providing additional meaning about its context.
- **Projection**: An entity-level relation where the caption's description revolves around a particular topic, but this topic is not directly featured in the image. Alternatively, the image contains objects that can be *associated* to this topic instead, forming an implied link between modalities.
- **Restatement**: A scene-level relation that describes the overall context of the image, with the caption providing a more detailed *description* of the visual scene.
- **Extension**: A scene-level relation in which the caption *elaborates* further on the visual scene in terms of new ideas or stories.

Datasets Popular datasets such as COCO Captions (Chen et al., 2015) or Flickr30K (Young et al., 2014) are often used for image captioning evaluation, but the ground-truth captions do not cater to sharing messages or perspectives that are more aligned with human-written captions. Instead, we select datasets from 2 different task domains for image captioning: news and social media. These domains provide representative examples of real-world scenarios for the usage of WAs: (1) The Tweet Subtitles dataset (Xu et al., 2022) contains 16,000 image-text pairs sourced from Twitter and cleaned to remove noisy, low-quality samples, and (2) ANNA (Anantha Ramakrishnan et al., 2024) on the other hand contains 29,625 image-text pairs collected from The New York Times news articles focusing on non Named Entity objects. Both datasets contain "abstractive" or non-descriptive captions with a wide range of image subjects and topics. For our evaluation, we used the entire test set of 1,600 samples from Tweet Subtitles and a random sample of 1,500 images from the test set of ANNA.

4 Experiments

Task Types For our analysis of the effectiveness of RONA, we define 2 task types: *Image-only* and *Image + Caption*. In the *Image-only* task, we define this as a classic image captioning task in which the model is provided only with the image as input. On the other hand, for the *Image + Caption* task, we provide the model with both the image and a ground-truth caption as input. Since both of these components are part of understanding the overall meaning of an image-caption pair, we wish to understand how MLLMs utilize both modalities to generate diverse captions without the divergence of meaning. This is similar to the prompt-guided image captioning task for MLLMs (Hu et al., 2023). In both tasks, the baseline MLLM is prompted to use the inputs to generate captions with "as much diversity as possible while retaining their original meaning and message." RONA utilizes in-context learning where simplified definitions of CRs are provided as system prompts. We generate 5 captions per input for each type of task, with RONA generating one caption per CR. Additional generated caption examples are presented in Appendix Section E.

Evaluation Metrics To evaluate the performance of MLLMs on the task of diverse captioning, we measure 4 key attributes: image-caption similarity, ground truth caption similarity, contextual diversity, and bi-gram diversity. CLIPScore (Hessel et al., 2021) effectively measures image-caption similarity by converting both modalities into a common representation space. For validating similarity of generated captions with the ground truth text, we turn to BLEURT (Sellam et al., 2020) score. Unlike traditional similarity metrics such as BLEU (Papineni et al., 2001), METEOR (Lavie and Agarwal, 2007) and BERTScore (Zhang* et al., 2020), BLEURT is trained to balance contextual similarity and human preference judgments, making it better suited for non-descriptive captions. All similarity metrics are computed pairwise between the ground truth modality and generated captions, with the average score reported in our benchmarks. For

Task	Model	BLEURT ↑	CLIPScore ↑	Self-BLEURT ↓	Div-2 ↑
Image-only	Claude	-1.227	14.049	0.226	0.860
	RONA + Claude	**-1.141**	**14.068**	**0.108**	**0.903**
Image-only	GPT-4o	-1.237	13.117	**0.198**	**0.885**
	RONA + GPT-4o	**-1.137**	**14.505**	0.205	0.879
Image + Caption	Claude	-0.931	13.833	0.294	0.843
	RONA + Claude	**-0.879**	**13.866**	**0.158**	**0.882**
Image + Caption	GPT-4o	-0.650	13.200	**0.355**	0.805
	RONA + GPT-4o	**-0.615**	**13.891**	0.383	**0.823**

Table 1: Results for Diverse Image Captioning with RONA on the Tweet Subtitles Dataset.

Task	Model	BLEURT ↑	CLIPScore ↑	Self-BLEURT ↓	Div-2 ↑
Image-only	Claude	-1.191	**14.617**	0.258	0.854
	RONA + Claude	**-1.038**	14.471	**0.134**	**0.899**
Image-only	GPT-4o	-1.159	13.954	0.249	**0.883**
	RONA + GPT-4o	**-1.057**	**15.022**	**0.209**	0.878
Image + Caption	Claude	-0.669	**14.582**	0.341	0.845
	RONA + Claude	**-0.559**	14.549	**0.217**	**0.883**
Image + Caption	GPT-4o	**-0.356**	14.338	0.436	0.796
	RONA + GPT-4o	-0.363	**14.869**	**0.394**	**0.824**

Table 2: Results for Diverse Image Captioning with RONA on the ANNA Dataset.

judging contextual diversity, we reformulate it as a task of minimizing the pairwise similarity between generated captions. This homogenization process is applied to BLEURT score, converting it into the diversity metric Self-BLEURT (Shaib et al., 2024). Finally, we calculate the overall bi-gram diversity of generated captions using the Div-2 metric (Shetty et al., 2017), which reports the ratio of unique bi-grams to the total count of bi-grams in a sentence.

5 Results

RONA Improves Relevance and Diversity We present our evaluation of MLLMs on the task of Diverse Image Captioning in Tables 1 and 2. Our assessment spans 8 different settings: 2 tasks per dataset, 2 models per task and 2 different dataset domains. From our results, both GPT-4o and Claude combined with RONA outperforms their respective baselines in 7/8 settings on both ground truth similarity and diversity metrics. Particularly, we see a positive agreement between Div-2 and Self-BLEURT, as they rate captions from RONA-based models as more diverse over 5/8 baselines. With image & text similarity metrics such as BLEURT and CLIPScore preferring RONA-based models 7/8 and 6/8 times over baselines respectively, we can conclude that our observed diversity has not come at the cost of contextual relevance.

Diversity and Similarity Trade-off Across Modalities From our experiments across task types, we observe a small decrease in image similarity but improved caption similarity and diversity in the Image + Caption task compared to Image-only task. This confirms that image-only descriptive captioning approaches are limited in terms of expression and rely heavily on listing visual features. This motivates the need for WAs to be evaluated on captions with pragmatic variations to test their true ability in understanding the overall message of a sample.

6 Conclusions

We propose RONA, a Coherence Relation-based prompting strategy, providing a framework for expressive and diverse image caption generation. Our study presents a holistic evaluation of top MLLMs on their ability to utilize these relationships through in-context learning. Our results show that RONA enables the generation of a greater variety of captions while improving their overall semantic and contextual relevance across domains. RONA serves as a new baseline for future work leveraging image-text relationships for improving the quality of Multi-modal Writing Assistants.

Limitations

Our current analysis of RONA is limited to a couple of top-performing MLLM architectures. Evaluating how open-source MLLMs can leverage CRs for image captioning is a part of our future work. Additionally, our evaluation strategy does not validate the prompt following accuracy of MLLMs in adhering to specific CRs, which would be a significant challenge for smaller, low-resource models. These inaccuracies may lead to hallucinations, harming the factual accuracy of generated captions. Incorporating Factual Consistency metrics and Human preference ratings to identify potential types of hallucinations in diverse captioning tasks is a direction of future work we wish to pursue.

Ethics Statement

We acknowledge the potential for alternate prompting strategies like RONA to be used for generating misleading content, especially from specific domains such as news media. However, from our evaluation, we find that MLLM safety filters are robust in capturing potentially harmful content in either the input images or captions as described in Appendix Section D. With CRs leveraging pragmatic and common-sense knowledge of MLLMs to generate diverse captions, there exists a possibility of model biases and stereotypes clouding the quality of our generations. This is especially a problem in cases where culturally sensitive material is present in our input samples. We advocate for the responsible use of Writing Assistants with adequate human oversight to prevent such situations.

References

Malihe Alikhani, Sreyasi Nag Chowdhury, Gerard de Melo, and Matthew Stone. 2019. CITE: A corpus of image-text discourse relations. In *Proceedings of the 2019 Conference of the North*, pages 570–575, Stroudsburg, PA, USA. Association for Computational Linguistics.

Malihe Alikhani, Piyush Sharma, Shengjie Li, Radu Soricut, and Matthew Stone. 2020. Cross-modal coherence modeling for caption generation. In *Proceedings of the 58th Annual Meeting of the Association for Computational Linguistics*, pages 6525–6535, Stroudsburg, PA, USA. Association for Computational Linguistics.

Aashish Anantha Ramakrishnan, Aadarsh Anantha Ramakrishnan, and Lee Dongwon. 2025. CORDIAL: Can multimodal large language models effectively understand coherence relationships? *arXiv [cs.CL]*.

Aashish Anantha Ramakrishnan, Sharon X Huang, and Dongwon Lee. 2024. ANNA: Abstractive text-to-image synthesis with filtered news captions. In *Proceedings of the Third Workshop on Advances in Language and Vision Research*. Association for Computational Linguistics.

Anthropic. Claude 3.5 sonnet. `https://www.anthropic.com/claude/sonnet`. Accessed: 2025-2-14.

Emanuele Bugliarello and Desmond Elliott. 2021. The role of syntactic planning in compositional image captioning. In *Proceedings of the 16th Conference of the European Chapter of the Association for Computational Linguistics: Main Volume*, pages 593–607, Stroudsburg, PA, USA. Association for Computational Linguistics.

Gongwei Chen, Leyang Shen, Rui Shao, Xiang Deng, and Liqiang Nie. 2024. LION : Empowering multimodal large language model with dual-level visual knowledge. In *2024 IEEE/CVF Conference on Computer Vision and Pattern Recognition (CVPR)*, pages 26530–26540. IEEE.

Xinlei Chen, Hao Fang, Tsung-Yi Lin, Ramakrishna Vedantam, Saurabh Gupta, Piotr Dollar, and C Lawrence Zitnick. 2015. Microsoft COCO captions: Data collection and evaluation server. *arXiv preprint arXiv:1504.00325*.

Kiroong Choe, Seokhyeon Park, Seokweon Jung, Hyeok Kim, Ji Won Yang, Hwajung Hong, and Jinwook Seo. 2024. Supporting novice researchers to write literature review using language models. In *Extended Abstracts of the CHI Conference on Human Factors in Computing Systems*, pages 1–9, New York, NY, USA. ACM.

Stephanie Federico. 2016. These are NPR's photo caption guidelines. *NPR*.

Chris Genovesi. 2020. Metaphor and what is meant: Metaphorical content, what is said, and contextualism. *J. Pragmat.*, 157:17–38.

Katy Ilonka Gero, Vivian Liu, and Lydia Chilton. 2022. Sparks: Inspiration for science writing using language models. In *Designing Interactive Systems Conference*, New York, NY, USA. ACM.

Jack Hessel, Ari Holtzman, Maxwell Forbes, Ronan Le Bras, and Yejin Choi. 2021. CLIPScore: A reference-free evaluation metric for image captioning. In *Proceedings of the 2021 Conference on Empirical Methods in Natural Language Processing*, pages 7514–7528, Online and Punta Cana, Dominican Republic. Association for Computational Linguistics.

Jerry R Hobbs. 1978. *Why is discourse coherent?*, volume 176. SRI International Menlo Park, CA.

Yushi Hu, Hang Hua, Zhengyuan Yang, Weijia Shi, Noah A Smith, and Jiebo Luo. 2023. PromptCap:

Prompt-guided image captioning for VQA with GPT-3. In *2023 IEEE/CVF International Conference on Computer Vision (ICCV)*, pages 2951–2963. IEEE.

Gunther Kress. 2009. *Multimodality: A social semiotic approach to contemporary communication.* Routledge, London, England.

A Lavie and Abhaya Agarwal. 2007. METEOR: An automatic metric for MT evaluation with high levels of correlation with human judgments. pages 228–231.

Mina Lee, Katy Ilonka Gero, John Joon Young Chung, Simon Buckingham Shum, Vipul Raheja, Hua Shen, Subhashini Venugopalan, Thiemo Wambsganss, David Zhou, Emad A Alghamdi, Tal August, Avinash Bhat, Madiha Zahrah Choksi, Senjuti Dutta, Jin L C Guo, Md Naimul Hoque, Yewon Kim, Simon Knight, Seyed Parsa Neshaei, Antonette Shibani, Disha Shrivastava, Lila Shroff, Agnia Sergeyuk, Jessi Stark, Sarah Sterman, Sitong Wang, Antoine Bosselut, Daniel Buschek, Joseph Chee Chang, Sherol Chen, Max Kreminski, Joonsuk Park, Roy Pea, Eugenia Ha Rim Rho, Zejiang Shen, and Pao Siangliulue. 2024. A design space for intelligent and interactive writing assistants. In *Proceedings of the CHI Conference on Human Factors in Computing Systems*, volume 7, pages 1–35, New York, NY, USA. ACM.

Junnan Li, Dongxu Li, Silvio Savarese, and Steven Hoi. 2023. BLIP-2: Bootstrapping language-image pre-training with frozen image encoders and large language models. In *International Conference on Machine Learning*, pages 19730–19742. PMLR.

Yehao Li, Yingwei Pan, Ting Yao, and Tao Mei. 2022. Comprehending and ordering semantics for image captioning. In *2022 IEEE/CVF Conference on Computer Vision and Pattern Recognition (CVPR)*, pages 17969–17978. IEEE.

Lixin Liu, Jiajun Tang, Xiaojun Wan, and Zongming Guo. 2019. Generating diverse and descriptive image captions using visual paraphrases. In *2019 IEEE/CVF International Conference on Computer Vision (ICCV)*, pages 4239–4248. IEEE.

Bolei Ma, Yuting Li, Wei Zhou, Ziwei Gong, Yang Janet Liu, Katja Jasinskaja, Annemarie Friedrich, Julia Hirschberg, Frauke Kreuter, and Barbara Plank. 2025. Pragmatics in the era of large language models: A survey on datasets, evaluation, opportunities and challenges. *arXiv [cs.CL]*.

Shweta Mahajan and Stefan Roth. 2020. Diverse image captioning with context-object split latent spaces. In *Proceedings of the 34th International Conference on Neural Information Processing Systems*, NIPS '20, Red Hook, NY, USA. Curran Associates Inc.

Kleio-Isidora Mavridou, Annemarie Friedrich, Melissa Peate Sørensen, Alexis Palmer, and Manfred Pinkal. 2015. Linking discourse modes and situation entity types in a cross-linguistic corpus study. In *Proceedings of the First Workshop on Linking Computational Models of Lexical, Sentential and Discourse-level Semantics*, pages 12–21.

Ho Yin Sam Ng, Ting-Yao Hsu, Jiyoo Min, Sungchul Kim, Ryan A Rossi, Tong Yu, Hyunggu Jung, and Ting-Hao Kenneth Huang. 2024. Understanding how paper writers use AI-generated captions in figure caption writing. In *2nd AI4Research Workshop: Towards a Knowledge-grounded Scientific Research Lifecycle*.

Kay L O'Halloran, Sabine Tan, and Marissa K L E. 2014. 9. multimodal pragmatics. In Klaus P Schneider and Anne Barron, editors, *Pragmatics of Discourse*, pages 239–268. De Gruyter Mouton, Berlin, München, Boston.

OpenAI, Aaron Hurst, Adam Lerer, Adam P Goucher, Adam Perelman, Aditya Ramesh, Aidan Clark, A J Ostrow, Akila Welihinda, Alan Hayes, Alec Radford, Aleksander Mądry, Alex Baker-Whitcomb, Alex Beutel, Alex Borzunov, Alex Carney, Alex Chow, Alex Kirillov, Alex Nichol, Alex Paino, Alex Renzin, Alex Tachard Passos, Alexander Kirillov, Alexi Christakis, Alexis Conneau, Ali Kamali, Allan Jabri, Allison Moyer, Allison Tam, Amadou Crookes, Amin Tootoochian, Amin Tootoonchian, Ananya Kumar, Andrea Vallone, Andrej Karpathy, Andrew Braunstein, Andrew Cann, Andrew Codispoti, Andrew Galu, Andrew Kondrich, Andrew Tulloch, Andrey Mishchenko, Angela Baek, Angela Jiang, Antoine Pelisse, Antonia Woodford, Anuj Gosalia, Arka Dhar, Ashley Pantuliano, Avi Nayak, Avital Oliver, Barret Zoph, Behrooz Ghorbani, Ben Leimberger, Ben Rossen, Ben Sokolowsky, Ben Wang, Benjamin Zweig, Beth Hoover, Blake Samic, Bob McGrew, Bobby Spero, Bogo Giertler, Bowen Cheng, Brad Lightcap, Brandon Walkin, Brendan Quinn, Brian Guarraci, Brian Hsu, Bright Kellogg, Brydon Eastman, Camillo Lugaresi, Carroll Wainwright, Cary Bassin, Cary Hudson, Casey Chu, Chad Nelson, Chak Li, Chan Jun Shern, Channing Conger, Charlotte Barette, Chelsea Voss, Chen Ding, Cheng Lu, Chong Zhang, Chris Beaumont, Chris Hallacy, Chris Koch, Christian Gibson, Christina Kim, Christine Choi, Christine McLeavey, Christopher Hesse, Claudia Fischer, Clemens Winter, Coley Czarnecki, Colin Jarvis, Colin Wei, Constantin Koumouzelis, Dane Sherburn, Daniel Kappler, Daniel Levin, Daniel Levy, David Carr, David Farhi, David Mely, David Robinson, David Sasaki, Denny Jin, Dev Valladares, Dimitris Tsipras, Doug Li, Duc Phong Nguyen, Duncan Findlay, Edede Oiwoh, Edmund Wong, Ehsan Asdar, Elizabeth Proehl, Elizabeth Yang, Eric Antonow, Eric Kramer, Eric Peterson, Eric Sigler, Eric Wallace, Eugene Brevdo, Evan Mays, Farzad Khorasani, Felipe Petroski Such, Filippo Raso, Francis Zhang, Fred von Lohmann, Freddie Sulit, Gabriel Goh, Gene Oden, Geoff Salmon, Giulio Starace, Greg Brockman, Hadi Salman, Haiming Bao, Haitang Hu, Hannah Wong, Haoyu Wang, Heather Schmidt, Heather Whitney, Heewoo Jun, Hendrik Kirchner, Henrique Ponde de Oliveira Pinto, Hongyu Ren, Huiwen Chang, Hyung Won Chung, Ian Kivlichan,

Ian O'Connell, Ian O'Connell, Ian Osband, Ian Silber, Ian Sohl, Ibrahim Okuyucu, Ikai Lan, Ilya Kostrikov, Ilya Sutskever, Ingmar Kanitscheider, Ishaan Gulrajani, Jacob Coxon, Jacob Menick, Jakub Pachocki, James Aung, James Betker, James Crooks, James Lennon, Jamie Kiros, Jan Leike, Jane Park, Jason Kwon, Jason Phang, Jason Teplitz, Jason Wei, Jason Wolfe, Jay Chen, Jeff Harris, Jenia Varavva, Jessica Gan Lee, Jessica Shieh, Ji Lin, Jiahui Yu, Jiayi Weng, Jie Tang, Jieqi Yu, Joanne Jang, Joaquin Quinonero Candela, Joe Beutler, Joe Landers, Joel Parish, Johannes Heidecke, John Schulman, Jonathan Lachman, Jonathan McKay, Jonathan Uesato, Jonathan Ward, Jong Wook Kim, Joost Huizinga, Jordan Sitkin, Jos Kraaijeveld, Josh Gross, Josh Kaplan, Josh Snyder, Joshua Achiam, Joy Jiao, Joyce Lee, Juntang Zhuang, Justyn Harriman, Kai Fricke, Kai Hayashi, Karan Singhal, Katy Shi, Kavin Karthik, Kayla Wood, Kendra Rimbach, Kenny Hsu, Kenny Nguyen, Keren Gu-Lemberg, Kevin Button, Kevin Liu, Kiel Howe, Krithika Muthukumar, Kyle Luther, Lama Ahmad, Larry Kai, Lauren Itow, Lauren Workman, Leher Pathak, Leo Chen, Li Jing, Lia Guy, Liam Fedus, Liang Zhou, Lien Mamitsuka, Lilian Weng, Lindsay McCallum, Lindsey Held, Long Ouyang, Louis Feuvrier, Lu Zhang, Lukas Kondraciuk, Lukasz Kaiser, Luke Hewitt, Luke Metz, Lyric Doshi, Mada Aflak, Maddie Simens, Madelaine Boyd, Madeleine Thompson, Marat Dukhan, Mark Chen, Mark Gray, Mark Hudnall, Marvin Zhang, Marwan Aljubeh, Mateusz Litwin, Matthew Zeng, Max Johnson, Maya Shetty, Mayank Gupta, Meghan Shah, Mehmet Yatbaz, Meng Jia Yang, Mengchao Zhong, Mia Glaese, Mianna Chen, Michael Janner, Michael Lampe, Michael Petrov, Michael Wu, Michele Wang, Michelle Fradin, Michelle Pokrass, Miguel Castro, Miguel Oom Temudo de Castro, Mikhail Pavlov, Miles Brundage, Miles Wang, Minal Khan, Mira Murati, Mo Bavarian, Molly Lin, Murat Yesildal, Nacho Soto, Natalia Gimelshein, Natalie Cone, Natalie Staudacher, Natalie Summers, Natan LaFontaine, Neil Chowdhury, Nick Ryder, Nick Stathas, Nick Turley, Nik Tezak, Niko Felix, Nithanth Kudige, Nitish Keskar, Noah Deutsch, Noel Bundick, Nora Puckett, Ofir Nachum, Ola Okelola, Oleg Boiko, Oleg Murk, Oliver Jaffe, Olivia Watkins, Olivier Godement, Owen Campbell-Moore, Patrick Chao, Paul McMillan, Pavel Belov, Peng Su, Peter Bak, Peter Bakkum, Peter Deng, Peter Dolan, Peter Hoeschele, Peter Welinder, Phil Tillet, Philip Pronin, Philippe Tillet, Prafulla Dhariwal, Qiming Yuan, Rachel Dias, Rachel Lim, Rahul Arora, Rajan Troll, Randall Lin, Rapha Gontijo Lopes, Raul Puri, Reah Miyara, Reimar Leike, Renaud Gaubert, Reza Zamani, Ricky Wang, Rob Donnelly, Rob Honsby, Rocky Smith, Rohan Sahai, Rohit Ramchandani, Romain Huet, Rory Carmichael, Rowan Zellers, Roy Chen, Ruby Chen, Ruslan Nigmatullin, Ryan Cheu, Saachi Jain, Sam Altman, Sam Schoenholz, Sam Toizer, Samuel Miserendino, Sandhini Agarwal, Sara Culver, Scott Ethersmith, Scott Gray, Sean Grove, Sean Metzger, Shamez Hermani, Shantanu Jain, Shengjia Zhao, Sherwin Wu, Shino Jomoto, Shirong Wu, Shuaiqi, Xia, Sonia Phene, Spencer Papay, Srinivas Narayanan, Steve Coffey, Steve Lee, Stewart Hall, Suchir Balaji, Tal Broda, Tal Stramer, Tao Xu, Tarun Gogineni, Taya Christianson, Ted Sanders, Tejal Patwardhan, Thomas Cunninghman, Thomas Degry, Thomas Dimson, Thomas Raoux, Thomas Shadwell, Tianhao Zheng, Todd Underwood, Todor Markov, Toki Sherbakov, Tom Rubin, Tom Stasi, Tomer Kaftan, Tristan Heywood, Troy Peterson, Tyce Walters, Tyna Eloundou, Valerie Qi, Veit Moeller, Vinnie Monaco, Vishal Kuo, Vlad Fomenko, Wayne Chang, Weiyi Zheng, Wenda Zhou, Wesam Manassra, Will Sheu, Wojciech Zaremba, Yash Patil, Yilei Qian, Yongjik Kim, Youlong Cheng, Yu Zhang, Yuchen He, Yuchen Zhang, Yujia Jin, Yunxing Dai, and Yury Malkov. 2024. GPT-4o system card. *arXiv [cs.CL]*.

Kishore Papineni, Salim Roukos, Todd Ward, and Wei-Jing Zhu. 2001. BLEU: a method for automatic evaluation of machine translation. In *Proceedings of the 40th Annual Meeting on Association for Computational Linguistics - ACL '02*, Morristown, NJ, USA. Association for Computational Linguistics.

Alec Radford, Jong Wook Kim, Chris Hallacy, Aditya Ramesh, Gabriel Goh, Sandhini Agarwal, Girish Sastry, Amanda Askell, Pamela Mishkin, Jack Clark, Gretchen Krueger, and Ilya Sutskever. 2021. Learning transferable visual models from natural language supervision. *arXiv:2103.00020 [cs]*.

Thibault Sellam, Dipanjan Das, and Ankur Parikh. 2020. BLEURT: Learning robust metrics for text generation. In *Proceedings of the 58th Annual Meeting of the Association for Computational Linguistics*, pages 7881–7892, Stroudsburg, PA, USA. Association for Computational Linguistics.

Chantal Shaib, Joe Barrow, Jiuding Sun, Alexa F Siu, Byron C Wallace, and Ani Nenkova. 2024. Standardizing the measurement of text diversity: A tool and a comparative analysis of scores. *CoRR*, abs/2403.00553.

Hua Shen, Tiffany Knearem, Reshmi Ghosh, Kenan Alkiek, Kundan Krishna, Yachuan Liu, Ziqiao Ma, Savvas Petridis, Yi-Hao Peng, Li Qiwei, Sushrita Rakshit, Chenglei Si, Yutong Xie, Jeffrey P Bigham, Frank Bentley, Joyce Chai, Zachary Lipton, Qiaozhu Mei, Rada Mihalcea, Michael Terry, Diyi Yang, Meredith Ringel Morris, Paul Resnick, and David Jurgens. 2024. Towards bidirectional human-AI alignment: A systematic review for clarifications, framework, and future directions. *arXiv [cs.HC]*.

Rakshith Shetty, Marcus Rohrbach, Lisa Anne Hendricks, Mario Fritz, and Bernt Schiele. 2017. Speaking the same language: Matching machine to human captions by adversarial training. In *2017 IEEE International Conference on Computer Vision (ICCV)*, pages 4155–4164. IEEE.

Nikhil Singh, Guillermo Bernal, Daria Savchenko, and Elena L Glassman. 2023. Where to hide a stolen elephant: Leaps in creative writing with multimodal machine intelligence. *ACM Trans. Comput. Hum. Interact.*, 30(5):1–57.

Tiberiu Sosea, Iustin Sirbu, Cornelia Caragea, Doina Caragea, and Traian Rebedea. 2021. Using the image-text relationship to improve multimodal disaster tweet classification. *Int Conf Inf Syst Crisis Response Manag*, pages 691–704.

Tristan Thrush, Ryan Jiang, Max Bartolo, Amanpreet Singh, Adina Williams, Douwe Kiela, and Candace Ross. 2022. Winoground: Probing vision and language models for visio-linguistic compositionality. In *Proceedings of the IEEE/CVF Conference on Computer Vision and Pattern Recognition*, pages 5238–5248.

Alakananda Vempala and Daniel Preoţiuc-Pietro. 2019. Categorizing and inferring the relationship between the text and image of twitter posts. In *Proceedings of the 57th Annual Meeting of the Association for Computational Linguistics*, pages 2830–2840, Stroudsburg, PA, USA. Association for Computational Linguistics.

Lydia Weiland, Laura Dietz, and Simone Paolo Ponzetto. 2015. Image with a message: Towards detecting non-literal image usages by visual linking. pages 40–47. Association for Computational Linguistics.

Chunpu Xu, Hanzhuo Tan, Jing Li, and Piji Li. 2022. Understanding social media cross-modality discourse in linguistic space. In *Findings of the Association for Computational Linguistics: EMNLP 2022*, pages 2459–2471, Stroudsburg, PA, USA. Association for Computational Linguistics.

Peter Young, Alice Lai, Micah Hodosh, and Julia Hockenmaier. 2014. From image descriptions to visual denotations: New similarity metrics for semantic inference over event descriptions. *Transactions of the Association for Computational Linguistics*, 2:67–78.

Zihao Yue, Anwen Hu, Liang Zhang, and Qin Jin. 2023. Learning descriptive image captioning via semipermeable MaxImum likelihood estimation. *Neural Inf Process Syst*, abs/2306.13460:79124–79141.

Tianyi Zhang*, Varsha Kishore*, Felix Wu*, Kilian Q Weinberger, and Yoav Artzi. 2020. BERTScore: Evaluating text generation with BERT. In *International Conference on Learning Representations*.

Appendix

A Data Preparation

This section sheds light on the methods used while preparing all the datasets mentioned in this paper for model evaluation. We verify both datasets used to evaluate RONA have a permissive license that allows usage for research purposes (Tweet Subtitles: **MIT License** and ANNA: **CC BY-NC-SA 4.0 License**).

A.1 Tweet Subtitles

This dataset contains two types of captions for tweets: actual and text generated by an image captioning model. We use only the **actual** caption as part of our evaluation.

A.2 ANNA

As mentioned in Section 3, we randomly sample **1,500 examples** from ANNA to construct our test set. We use a random seed of 42 to ensure reproducibility.

B Proprietary Model Details

OpenAI GPT: We access the GPT-4o model via a custom deployment using Azure OpenAI. We evaluate `gpt-4o-2024-11-20` with a custom safety filter to restrict content of *high* severity level.

Anthropic Claude: We access Claude 3.5 Sonnet v2 via the Vertex AI API, using Google Cloud. We evaluate `claude-3-5-sonnet-v2@20241022`.

C Prompt Templates

We use two types of prompt templates, both with different system/user messages for the evaluation of tasks mentioned in Section 4. The different prompts and system messages used are present in the appendix.

D Postprocessing MLLM Responses

Since both datasets feature image-caption pairs on a wide selection of topics, around **50 images** were flagged by the safety filter or rejected by the model for captioning. To ensure test set consistency, we remove these examples from our evaluation.

E Example Captions from RONA

We also provide a few examples of captions generated in each setting below. All captions were generated using Claude 3.5 Sonnet v2.

E.1 ANNA Examples

Caption: JUST NUTS: The creaminess of this dessert comes from churned almond milk.

Baseline (Image-only)

- Creamy vanilla ice cream topped with crispy honeycomb pieces.
- Homemade ice cream dessert garnished with crunchy toffee bits.
- Sweet and crunchy: vanilla gelato with caramelized sugar shards.
- Classic vanilla scoops adorned with brittle candy fragments.
- Artisanal ice cream featuring golden honeycomb crumble topping.

RONA (Image-only)

- **Insertion:** The perfect way to end a summer evening on the patio.
- **Concretization:** Vanilla ice cream garnished with crispy honeycomb pieces in a blue ceramic bowl.
- **Projection:** Sweet memories of childhood desserts come flooding back with every spoonful.
- **Restatement:** Scoops of creamy white ice cream topped with crunchy golden candy pieces, served in a light blue bowl against a wooden background.
- **Extension:** This artisanal dessert combines locally-sourced dairy with house-made honeycomb brittle, showcasing how simple ingredients can create an extraordinary taste experience when crafted with care.

Baseline (Image + Caption)

- Creamy almond milk ice cream topped with crunchy toasted nut brittle.
- Dairy-free frozen dessert made with almond milk and garnished with caramelized nuts.
- Smooth vegan ice cream featuring almond milk, decorated with crispy nut pieces.
- Artisanal almond milk gelato adorned with handmade nutty crumble.
- Plant-based frozen treat with rich almond flavor and crunchy nut topping.

RONA (Image + Caption)

- **Insertion:** A refreshing frozen treat perfect for hot summer days, churned to creamy perfection.
- **Concretization:** Scoops of almond milk ice cream topped with crunchy toasted nuts in a blue ceramic bowl.
- **Projection:** The dairy-free dessert revolution takes shape in this plant-based frozen delight.
- **Restatement:** Creamy white almond milk ice cream served in a light blue bowl, garnished with crushed nuts on top.
- **Extension:** This artisanal vegan ice cream demonstrates how nut-based alternatives can rival traditional dairy desserts, offering both sustainable ingredients and decadent taste while catering to those with dietary restrictions.

E.2 Tweet Subtitles Examples

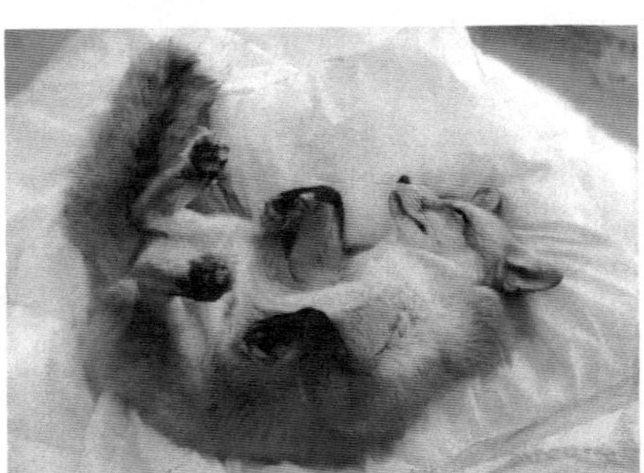

Caption: It's raining, it's pouring. The sleepy fox is snoring.

Baseline (Image-only)

- Sleepy fox curled up contentedly on white sheets.
- Red fox showing its fluffy belly while napping peacefully.
- A comfortable fox enjoying a lazy day in bed.
- Beautiful russet-colored fox in complete relaxation mode.
- Wild spirit at rest: fox taking an adorable snooze on soft bedding.

RONA (Image-only)

- **Insertion:** Sweet dreams are made of soft white sheets and peaceful afternoon naps.
- **Concretization:** A red fox lies contentedly on its back, nestled in crisp white bedding.
- **Projection:** Finding complete comfort and trust in one's surroundings is a rare and precious thing.
- **Restatement:** A fox is sleeping upside down on white sheets, with its red-orange fur contrasting against the white background, showing its belly and paws in the air.
- **Extension:** Like many domestic pets, this rescued fox has adapted to human comforts, choosing the soft embrace of fresh linens over its natural forest bedding, showing how wild animals can adapt to domesticated environments when given the chance.

Baseline (Image + Caption)

- A cozy fox napping peacefully on white sheets.
- Red fox curled up in blissful slumber, paws in the air.
- Playful fox showing its belly while taking a comfortable nap.
- Beautiful russet-colored fox in deep sleep on soft bedding.
- Adorable fox stretched out and snoring on pristine white linens.

RONA (**Image + Caption**)

- **Insertion:** The gentle pitter-patter outside creates the perfect atmosphere for afternoon rest.
- **Concretization:** A sleepy red fox lies curled up, snoring peacefully on white bedding.
- **Projection:** Dreaming of chasing rabbits while the storm rages outside.
- **Restatement:** A red fox is sleeping on its back, completely relaxed on white sheets while it's raining outside.
- **Extension:** As rain drums against the windowpane, this rescued fox demonstrates how domesticated wildlife can find comfort in human spaces, sprawled out on clean linens just like a household pet.

System Message for Baseline Captioning

You are an expert linguist, and your task is to write image captions.

System Message for RONA

You are an expert linguist, and your task is to write image captions with the help of Coherence Relations. A coherence relation describes the structural, logical, and purposeful relationships between an image and its caption, capturing the author's intent.

These are the possible coherence relations you can assign to an image-text pair:
- Insertion: The salient object described in the image is not explicitly mentioned in the text.
- Concretization: Both the text and image contain a mention of the main visual entity.
- Projection: The main entity mentioned in the text is implicitly related to the visual objects present in the image.
- Restatement: The text directly describes the image contents.
- Extension: The image expands upon the story or idea in the text, presenting new elements or elaborations, effectively filling in narrative gaps left by the text.

Prompt for Baseline Captioning

System
<insert-system-message>

User
You will be given an image (or) image-caption pair as input. Analyze the image and write 5 suitable captions that are diverse, but relevant. Create diverse captions while retaining the same overall meaning of the original image-caption pair.

Return the captions as a JSON Array with the following format:
```
[
"<insert-caption-text-1>",
"<insert-caption-text-2>",
"<insert-caption-text-3>",
"<insert-caption-text-4>",
"<insert-caption-text-5>"
]
```

<insert-image>
<insert-caption>

Prompt for RONA

System
<insert-system-message>

User
You will be given an image (or) image-caption pair as input. Write 5 image captions, one for each coherence relation as your output.

Return the captions as a JSON object with the following format:

```
{
"Insertion": "<insert-caption-text-1>",
"Concretization": "<insert-caption-text-2>",
"Projection": "<insert-caption-text-3>",
"Restatement": "<insert-caption-text-4>",
"Extension": "<insert-caption-text-5>"
}
```

<insert-image>
<insert-caption>

Multi-Agent Based Character Simulation for Story Writing

Tian Yu *, Ken Shi *, Zixin Zhao and Gerald Penn
Department of Computer Science
University of Toronto
CANADA
{tianyu99,kenshi,zzhao1,gpenn}@cs.toronto.edu

Abstract

This work proposes a novel multi-agent story-generation system that writes stories from a narrative plan. Traditional approaches tend to generate a section of text directly from its outline. Our system, by contrast, divides this elaboration process into role-play and rewrite steps, where the former step enacts the story in chronological order with LLM-backed character agents, and the latter step refines the role-play result to align with a narrative plan. We show that the stories produced by our system are preferable to two other LLM-based story-generation approaches. We attribute this advancement to the benefits of incorporating a character-based simulation strategy.

1 Introduction

Recent advancements in Large Language Models (LLMs) have significantly improved text coherence and fluency. Researchers are now implementing automatic story generation and human-AI writing tasks using LLMs (Lee et al., 2024; Alabdulkarim et al., 2021). Traditionally, story generation involved a planning stage to sequence events, followed by a generation stage to elaborate these events into scenes (Alhussain and Azmi, 2021a). Approaches like IPOCL (Riedl and Young, 2010) treat narrative planning as a search problem using character or author goals as guides (Dehn, 1981; Meehan, 2013). Recent work proposes using LLMs as planning engines, such as Agents' Room (Huot et al., 2024), which uses multi-agent collaboration for narrative planning, and Dramatron (Mirowski et al., 2023), which modularizes the generation process in a manner similar to screenplay writing. Research shows that writers prefer modularizing story generation into smaller components, as it allows control over which parts of the process are automated (Lee et al., 2024; Reza et al., 2024; Mirowski et al., 2023).

Despite the advances in automatic story generation, there remain many problems with LLM-generated stories. One is a lack of interest due to their linear nature (Alabdulkarim et al., 2021). Within narrative theory, stories can be separated into chronological time (*fabula*) and story time (*syuzhet*), where in many cases, stories can become more interesting when told in non-linear time (Liveley, 2019). There is, however, a lack of work in automatic story generation that looks at non-linear story generation, partially due to the risk of introducing inconsistencies and plot holes. Therefore, in our work, we propose generating a story through its fabula before re-organizing it into its syuzhet.

Our system aims to develop tools that integrate seamlessly into writers' workflows. We draw inspiration from hierarchical scriptwriting techniques (Mirowski et al., 2023) and adapt them for narrative story generation. By modularizing the writing process, we enhance control and facilitate human-LLM collaboration. Our method involves two steps (Figure 1): role play and rewrite. In the role play step, agents simulate scenes by acting as characters. In the rewrite step, the generated content is refined into story text. In the case of human-ai collaborative writing, during the role play step, the writers can act as an independent agent and role-play a character alongside LLM agents to simulate the scene. In the rewrite step, the writers can actively edit the intermediate scene content or use the generated content as inspiration to write their story.

Our work proposes a novel way to integrate the concepts of fabula and syuzhet into a cohesive story-generation process. Additionally, we present a novel multi-agent role-play approach by introducing a rewrite step. To evaluate our method, we compare stories generated by our system with two baseline methods using LLM-based automated evaluation, showing improvements in all aspects of story quality.

*Equal contribution

Proceedings of the Fourth Workshop on Intelligent and Interactive Writing Assistants (In2Writing 2025), pages 87–108

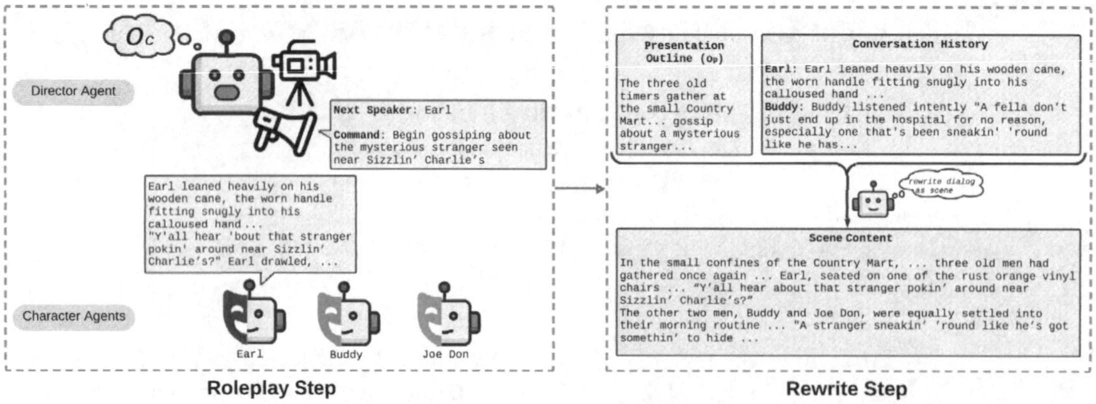

Figure 1: Overview of our character-simulation-based story-writing system, with details omitted. We break down the task of writing a story from a plan into two steps: role-play and rewrite. In the role-play step, the Director Agent will select and command Character Agents to respond, following the chronological outline of a scene (o_c). In the rewrite step, we prompt LLMs to write the actual content of the scene using the role-play results, along with the presentation outline (o_p) of that scene. The example is from train-000 in the Tell Me A Story dataset. Refer to Section 3.2 for details.

2 Related Work

2.1 Simulating Characters with LLMs

Characters are essential to many narrative stories as they often drive the plot and bring the narrative to life (LaPlante, 2007). Creating interesting and believable characters using LLMs has been explored by many prior papers (Li et al., 2023; Pichlmair et al., 2024; Wang et al., 2024b; Shao et al., 2023; Magee et al., 2024). Some previous work has focused on simulating believable character behaviour by introducing different aspects within character prompts such as "ego/superego" roles to simulate internal conflict (Magee et al., 2024) or behaviour trajectories using psychological grounding (Wang et al., 2024a). Other work has proposed using personality traits, routines, emotions, and social interactions (Zhao et al., 2024; Wang et al., 2024b; Yang et al., 2024; Normoyle et al., 2024). Overall, this work has found that LLMs can simulate nuanced and believable characters. Moreover, past work, such as Park et al. (Park et al., 2023), has also shown the viability of using LLMs to create generative agents that can produce believable individual and emergent social behaviours with memories of past interactions. Therefore, in our work, we hope to use LLMs to create believable characters within narrative stories.

2.2 Automatic Story Generation

Interesting characters alone do not make compelling stories; how they are revealed and evolve through events turns conversations into narratives. Early story generation models focused on plot using structural models from narrative theories like Propp's functions (Propp, 1968), or planning-based models guided by predefined goals, e.g., author goals (Dehn, 1981) or character goals (Meehan, 2013). These models often used planning agents to guide narrative generation, combining author and character goals to inform autonomous agents (Si et al., 2005). Social interactions among virtual agents can drive narrative diversity and emergent storytelling, avoiding rigid plot structures (Teutenberg and Porteous, 2013; Figueiredo et al., 2008; Porteous and Lindsay, 2019). Multi-agent approaches, as elsewhere, are preferred for their adaptability and control compared to monolithic systems.

Recent approaches use Seq2Seq models or LLMs to generate coherent stories from start to finish (Alhussain and Azmi, 2021a). Early Seq2Seq models struggled with coherence and consistency, but LLMs improved this, though long stories still lose cohesion due to context-window limits. To solve this, past work has proposed using multiple LLMs collaboratively (Venkatraman et al., 2024) or hierarchical story generation, separating plot planning from text generation (Fan et al., 2018; Yao et al., 2019). Dramatron (Mirowski et al., 2023) exemplifies this by modularizing story generation for screenplays, defining components like loglines (i.e. story premise), characters, plot, and locations, then generating dialogue. Furthermore, Dramatron was evaluated by professional screenplay writers who found that modularization allowed them to take over components of the generation and more control over the results.

Combining agent-based approaches with hierarchical story generation allows for user-controllable goals within LLM-based generation. For example, IBSEN (Han et al., 2024) uses a director-actor framework for script generation, while de Lima et al. (2022) combine multi-agent planning for interactive storytelling. DramaEngine(Pichlmair et al., 2024) and Agents' Room (Huot et al., 2024) use multi-agent workflows for narrative generation. Despite the promise of agent-based approaches, much work has focused on screenplays. Our work adapts hierarchical scriptwriting techniques (Mirowski et al., 2023; Han et al., 2024) to narrative story generation, modularizing the process to enhance control and facilitate human-LLM collaboration.

2.3 Automatic Story Evaluation

There are several well-established automatic text evaluation measures, such as perplexity (Brown et al., 1992), ROUGE (Lin, 2004), and BERTScore (Zhang* et al., 2020). These do not capture creativity, narrative structure, or coherence at the story level, however. They either reflect how 'typical' the text is or are reference-dependent, failing to measure aspects like creativity or storyline structure unless reference texts are carefully designed.

Recent work has attempted to evaluate stories with LLMs, often endorsing pairwise comparison. For example, Liusie et al. (2024) discussed using pairwise comparison for LLM evaluation. Subsequently, Liu et al. (2024b) found that pairwise comparison by LLMs aligns more closely with human evaluators than other methods. Additionally, Zheng et al. (2023) assessed the validity of using LLM evaluators through established benchmarks. In this work, we will also use LLM evaluators through pairwise comparison to assess the quality of generated stories, drawing inspiration from the LLM evaluator setup proposed by Agents' Room. It is worth noting that LLMs can suffer from the "Lost in the middle" effect (Liu et al., 2024a) when handling longer prompts. Therefore, we will implement specific measures to minimize this effect when using LLMs as evaluators.

3 Methodology

This section describes our approach to the outline-based creative writing task. We first provide an overview of our breakdown of the problem and then describe the individual components.

3.1 The Overall Task

In our work, we focus on the writing phase, where a narrative plan has already been provided for us to write the story. This approach is also used in other single and multi-agent frameworks. For example, Mirowski et al. (2023) used a hierarchical approach to generating screenplay dialogues based on a planned-scene outline, character information, and location details. Similarly, Huot et al. (2024) created a plan with multiple agents, each specializing in areas like character planning, and used the combined plan to write the story.

Our system draws inspiration from the classic narrative distinction between fabula and syuzhet (Alhussain and Azmi, 2021b). The fabula represents the raw, chronological sequence of events — the underlying narrative as it unfolds in the story world. In our framework, the role-play step serves to develop this fabula, where character agents simulate the provided narrative plan in its chronological order.

Following this, the rewrite step takes the intermediate result and reshapes it into its final form, analogous to the syuzhet. This phase reorganizes and refines the content to align with the original plan. It optimizes the storytelling experience, much like how a narrative's presentation order can heighten dramatic effect and audience engagement.

3.2 Implementation Detail

3.2.1 The Definition and Agents

Our system takes in a plan and returns the actual story realized. We denote the **input plan** as P_p, which specifies the presentation order of scenes, representing the syuzhet. An input plan consists of a list of scenes to be written for the story. We define a **scene**, labelled S, as the minimum plan unit in our writing process. The scene includes a presentation outline (o_p) detailing a sequence of events (e), along with location information and the characters involved. To support character simulation, we define a character as an entity or a group of minor supporting entities in the story, with their name, gender, age, narrative role, setup, speaking characteristics, and character goal.

We define two types of agents: the director agent and the character agent. The **director agent**, labelled D, controls the scene's development in the role-playing process. It selects ($next\_speaker$) and instructs ($next\_command$) individual character agents. The **character agent**, labelled A, responds ($get\_response$) to the director's commands by considering its goal, physical state, and memory. These responses are described from a third-party perspective, providing realistic dialogue and action descriptions. Both agent types can be powered by either LLMs or human participants, enabling effective human-AI collaboration.

3.2.2 The Role-playing Step

While other LLM-based methods for narrative plan generation (Huot et al., 2024; Mirowski et al., 2023) rely on one LLM call to generate the content of a section, we divide the process into two subtasks, where the role-playing step is the first step.

Unlike RPG games, stories may not follow the chronological order to describe the events. As such, the input plan P_p provided by the users may contain two scenes S_i and S_j, where S_i happens after S_j chronologically, even though S_i should be presented earlier than S_j in the actual plan. As such, we define the **role-play plan** (P_c) consisting of the scenes from P_p in chronological order representing the fabula. A separate LLM-based sorting algorithm is used to create P_c from P_p. In this paper, we assume that for any two scenes $S_i, S_j \in S$, S_i cannot overlap S_j in the time domain, meaning any events in S_i will happen all before or all after the events in S_j. On top of this, another LLM-based sorting algorithm will generate a chronological outline (o_c) based on the presentation outline (o_p) of the scene and further refine it to be suitable for subsequence character-based role play and ensure that events within scenes are correctly ordered. Both LLM prompts are detailed in Appendix B.1.1, Prompt *Sort Scenes*, and Appendix B.1.2, Prompt *Chronological Outline Creation*, respectively.

After creating P_c and o_c, we obtain the full chronological development of the events in the whole story. Then, for each scene $S_i \in P_c$, we use algorithm 1 to role-play that scene. The other input, M, to the algorithm, is an accumulated map with the key being the name of the character agent and the value being the agent instance. We will re-use the same character agent, if it has already been created, to update the accumulated memory and, whenever it is involved, the physical state.

The role-playing logic for each scene is the same, where a group chat manager will be initialized for two tasks:

1. Determining whether the role-playing game has covered o_c, and terminate if so.

2. Guiding the role-playing game by following o_c, selecting the proper character agent to speak to, and providing them with the command of action.

When a character agent is selected, it first updates its internal states, including memory and physical state. In our implementation, we use a text-based memory and physical-state system, which updates based on the new chat history that the agent has not seen before. The agent then responds based on the role-playing game's history for consistency, the Director Agent's command, its memory and physical state, and its scene-level goal. This approach balances the *agent/character goal* (Riedl and Young, 2010), provided within the plan, with the *author goal* (Riedl, 2009), represented by the director agent's command. We instruct agents to respond in a third-person perspective to create realistic character dialogue and action descriptions, catering to the story-generation use case. Please refer to Appendix B.1 for the relevant prompts used.

3.2.3 The Rewrite Step

The role-playing output may not produce a perfect story, however, because it only replicates the fabula as part of the story world. A story should be produced by viewing the fabula from a specific angle (Swartjes and Theune, 2006), following P_p, the presentation order of the initially planned scenes. As mentioned in Section 3.2.2, our role-playing result follows o_c for the sequence of events in a scene and P_c for the sequence of scenes. This means $o_c \neq o_p$ and $P_c \neq P_p$ are possible.

To address this, we implement a re-writing algorithm. For each scene, we prompt LLMs to write the scene content based on the presentation outline o_p, referencing the corresponding simulation results in the role-play step for character dialogues and actions. We also generate the scene content sequentially, following the presentation order specified in the input plan P_p. This modular approach allows authors to revise the content of each scene before it is utilized in the subsequent scene generation. The prompts used for this step are available in Appendix B.2.

Algorithm 1 Scene-level role-playing.

Require: Scene S_i,
Character Agents Map M

Init Chat History, $H \leftarrow [\,]$ ▷ H will store all messages in the session
Init Director Agent $D.init()$
while not $D.\text{should\_terminate}(S_i, H)$ **do** ▷ Check if the scene should end
  $A_i \leftarrow D.\text{next\_speaker}(S_i, H)$ ▷ The director selects the next character agent
  if $A_i.name \in M$ **then**
    $A_i \leftarrow M.get(A_i.name)$ ▷ If this agent exists, retrieve the agent
  else
    $M.\text{add}(A_i.name, A_i)$ ▷ If this agent is new, add it to the map
  end if
  $C_j \leftarrow D.\text{next\_command}(S_i, H)$ ▷ The director selects the next command
  $A_i.\text{update\_state}(H)$ ▷ The chosen agent updates its internal memory
  $h_i \leftarrow A_i.\text{get\_response}(H, C_j)$ ▷ The agent generates a response
  $H.\text{append}(h_i)$ ▷ Add the agent's response to the chat history
end while
return H ▷ Return the full history once the scene is complete

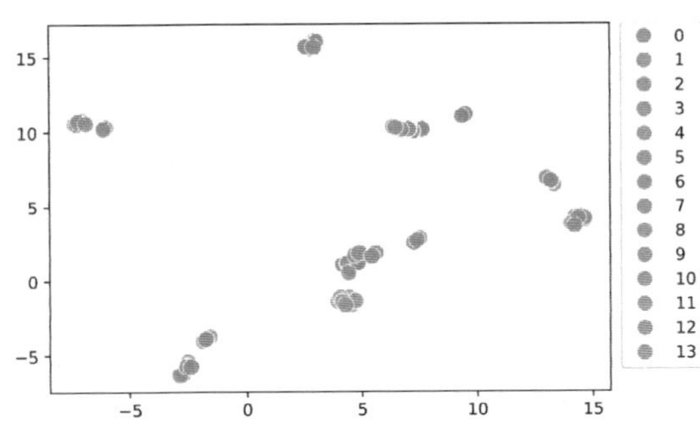

Figure 2: Writing prompts from the **Tell Me A Story** dataset, clustered into 14 groups using UMAP and k-means.

4 Experiments

4.1 Dataset

For our dataset, we used **Tell Me A Story**,[1] made up of complex writing prompts and human-written stories. This dataset is contains 230 prompts in total, but upon manual inspection, we found that many of the prompts differed by only a few words. Therefore, we first evaluated the number of unique prompts present in the dataset. To do this, we first created sentence embeddings using sBERT (Reimers and Gurevych, 2019), then reduced the dimensions of the embedding using UMAP (McInnes et al., 2018) before using k-means to assign each sentence to a cluster. We tested various numbers of clusters and found that the number that fit the data best was 14, shown in Figure 2. After determining the number of writing prompts clusters, we manually looked through the data and selected 28 representative prompts so that we would have coverage over the range of stories that could be generated with this dataset.

[1] https://github.com/google-deepmind/tell_me_a_story

4.2 Experiment Setup

In this section, we describe our setup for the experiment to prove the validity of our method. We compare our approach with two approaches:

1. The single-agent-based approach, where Dramatron (Mirowski et al., 2023) is the baseline,
2. The multi-agent-based approach, where Agents' Room (Huot et al., 2024) is the baseline.

At a high level, as shown in Figure 3, our experiment can be treated as a back-translation process between the gold story and the synthetic plan, where we first generate the plan using a teacher LLM model and then use each system to write the final story, given the plan created.

4.2.1 Plan Synthesis

We can treat each of Dramatron's and Agents' Room's story-writing approaches as a sequence of planning and writing tasks. By the writing portion of Dramatron, we intend to refer to the dialogue

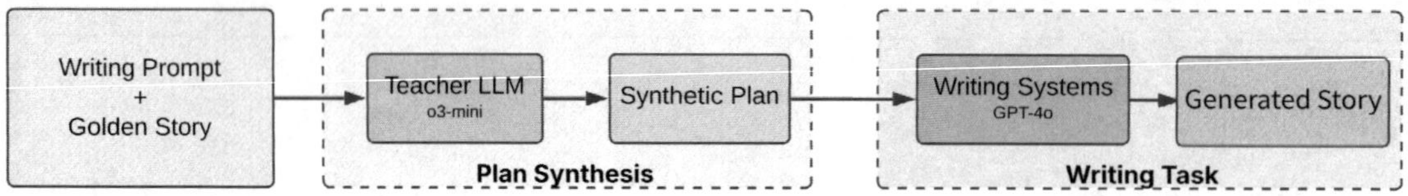

Figure 3: Experimental overview: given the writing prompt and the gold story, we first generate a synthetic plan using a Teacher LLM. The plan is then used to generate the final story.

generation step that follows the hierarchical generation process. We consider the writing portion of the Agents' Room approach following what is mentioned in their paper. Since a plan is required for all three systems, including ours, we applied a similar approach as in previous work ((Huot et al., 2024; Schick et al., 2022; Josifoski et al., 2023), where the expected plan is synthesized to generate through distilled back-translation.

For the Agents' Room implementation, we provide the writing prompt and gold story to a teacher LLM (O3-mini) to obtain the story's central conflict, characters, setting and plot. We followed exactly the prompt used in their work to extract the plan.

For our system, we first prompt the teacher LLM (O3-mini) to generate all the characters that appeared in the gold story, providing both the writing prompt and the gold story. We then prompt the teacher LLM (O3-mini) with the additional character extracted to obtain the list of scenes that happened in the gold story, denoted by P_p in Section 3.2.2. In addition, we also consider the central conflict and setting generated using the same method as the Agents' Room part of the plan.

For Dramatron, we share the plan information with the one generated for our system, as no details are provided in their work. Specifically, we provide the place and character information, along with the sequence o_p from the P_p extracted.

4.2.2 Writing Task

We defined similar writing tasks for all methods tested. The LLM used for our experiments was the GPT-4o model, with the temperature set to 0.9, and frequency penalty equal to 0.2. We used a zero-shot prompting strategy for all systems for a fair comparison. Here, we go into the details of each method: Agents' Room (Huot et al., 2024), Dramatron (Mirowski et al., 2023), and our method.

First, for the Agents' Room writing task, we followed the procedures mentioned in their work, where five agents are created with the prompt provided in their paper, each writing a stage of a narrative arc (exposition, rising action, climax, falling action and resolution). The final story is the five agents' output, concatenated sequentially.

For Dramatron, we had to modify their approach so that we could generate the story scenes rather than scenes made up of screenplay dialogues. Additionally, we removed their few-shot examples, which would be incomparable if included. Otherwise, we followed the exact implementation for the prompt as shared in their codebase[2] to the best of our ability and retained the scene-by-scene generation process. The changed prompts are shown in Appendix B. As for our method, we used the approach described in Section 3.2.

4.3 Evaluation Method

In this work, we take inspiration from the automatic evaluation used in Agents' Room (Huot et al., 2024) to build an LLM-based evaluator. We chose to use the same set of criteria that align with Agents' Room's LLM-based evaluation. Specifically, we construct prompts that will evaluate the story in terms of four criteria, namely, *Plot*, *Creativity*, *Development* and *Language Use*.

We provide a template of a prompt that specifies the above criteria as its aspects, along with a presentation of the pair of stories to be compared. The detailed definition of each criterion is written in the template, which can be found in Appendix B.5. To align with Agents' Room's choice of evaluator model, we also use Gemini 1.5 Pro.

As mentioned earlier, to ensure the fairness of the comparison, we evaluate each pair of stories twice by swapping the presentation order of the stories within the evaluation prompt.

For each of the 5 criteria (*overall* is a separate criterion, as we explicitly ask the evaluator to generate an"overall" decision), c, we perform evaluations on all pairs of stories that are of the same writing prompt across all pairs of systems to ob-

[2]https://github.com/google-deepmind/dramatron

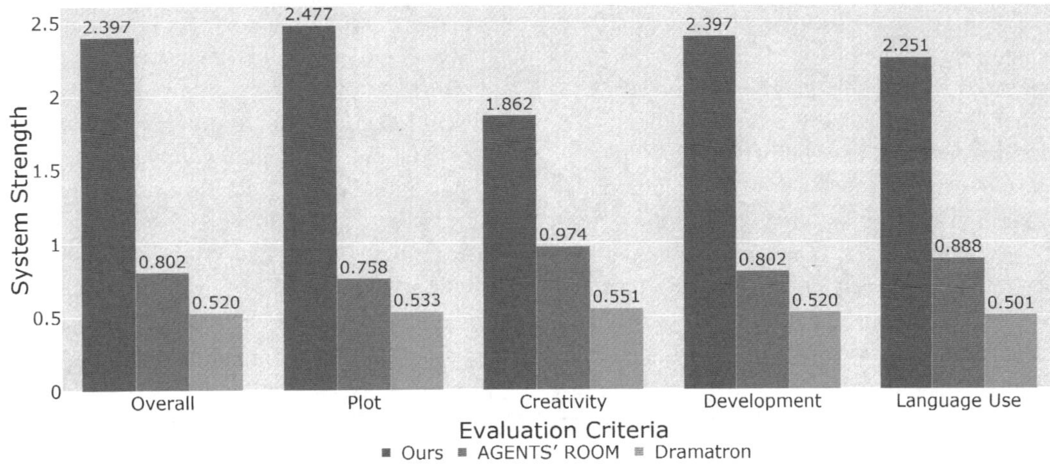

Figure 4: System strength across dimensions of plot, creativity, development, language use and overall, according to the LLM-based evaluator.

tain a win matrix $W^c \in \mathbf{R}^{N \times N}$, where N is the number of systems. Each element $W^c_{i,j}$ represents the number of times system i beats system j. We then linearize these pairwise comparisons using the Bradley-Terry model to obtain latent ability parameters, which denote the numerically ordered strengths of each system with respect to c. To present the result, we follow Agents' Room's convention of normalizing the log strengths, centered around 0.

5 Results

5.1 LLM Evaluation Results

Figure 4 demonstrates the strength of the three systems across the set of criteria defined at the beginning of Section 4.3. Overall, our system outperforms both Agents' Room and Dramatron. This behaviour is consistent across each criterion. The values of each win matrix can be found in Appendix A.

In terms of strength, our system comes out on top among all the criteria, and by a large gap. These are easily misinterpreted, however. BTL strengths are not a measure of how *much* better one system's stories are over another's, but rather of how *often* the one's are preferred (here, by the LLM evaluator) over the other's. This method can be interpreted by analogy to a consumer-product trial, in which the LLM evaluator samples a population of consumers, and the generated stories are the products being tried. The result of the trials only indicates with what likelihood a consumer might choose one brand over another.

The results are generally consistent when swapping the order of presentation for each pair of stories. In cases where inconsistency is observed, it often occurs in stories where the various criteria conflict. Such inconsistencies, however, are handled by the nature of our design, which treats them as less rewarding than a consistent win and more rewarding than a consistent loss.

5.2 Qualitative Analysis

In addition to the LLM evaluation above, we investigated the individual stories generated by those systems. One observation we made was that the stories generated by our system often maintain better character consistency and narrative coherence. For example, train 026 golden story primarily revolves around the interactions between Scholar Kissen and Courier Aerie. The first scene portrays their initial meeting, whereas the second involves Aerie recalling her earlier journey to a remote site, illustrating a non-chronological scene arrangement. As such, the extracted plan from the story poses a significant challenge for the Dramatron system to create the narration of the first scene, given that the model inherently lacks awareness of chronologically earlier events that have nevertheless not yet been narrated (as with the second scene). This results in an hallucination of Aereo's dialogue about the site being created. Conversely, systems such as Agents' Room, which provide a full story outline upfront, face the risk of prematurely revealing information. Specifically, in the first scene, Aerie's dialogue preemptively references details that should appear later in the story, thus disrupting the narrative flow. Our approach is more balanced. By employing the sorting mechanism to role-play chronologically, the character agent, Aerie, has the memory of her visit to the site (second scene) before role-playing the first scene (meeting scholar Kissen). Additionally, the rewriting mechanism ensures that the generated scene content strictly adheres to the current scene outline, effectively preventing the premature disclosure of future information and resulting in a more consistent and coherent story. Please refer to Appendix C.1 for details.

It is also observed that the other approaches are not as consistent in producing high-quality stories in the long run. For the Agents' Room approach, we have spotted repetition and, occasionally, random off-topic words generated. We believe this is caused by the generation process being too weakly constrained, in which only a few constraints other than the plot line are provided to guide the generation.

Another observation of our proposed system is that sometimes the group chat manager repeats the same command to the character agents when it is unsatisfied with the agent's response. This often happens to content corresponding to plots near the end of the scene outline. To mitigate this issue, we set a maximum number of 10 iterations, which avoids the potential for infinite repetition.

6 Conclusion

In conclusion, our work is the first to integrate the concepts of fabula and syuzhet into a unified process for generating stories from a narrative plan. We decomposed story creation into two distinct phases/steps: a fabula generation phase (role-play step) driven by realistic, LLM-backed character agents under the guidance of a director agent. This achieves a natural balance between authorial intent and character-driven conversation history. This is followed by a syuzhet modification phase (rewrite step), which refers to the conversation history and can potentially reuse the majority of dialogues and actions, only needing to manipulate their order, thus significantly reducing the difficulty of the actual story-content-writing process.

Our current approach assumes that a scene consists of a sequence of events occurring within a specific location and time frame. However, there are cases where scenes interleave between present conversations and flashbacks — for example when a character recalls a memory. As such, our sorting algorithm may fail to produce a strictly chronologically ordered plan for the role-play step. Future work could address this limitation by sorting all events in the story with finer granularity, regardless of scene boundaries, to handle complex temporal structures better. Additionally, while our system updates agents' memories to reflect only the information they should see, it does not explicitly enforce privacy during the role-play process. Future work can improve upon this by implementing explicit privacy controls. Lastly, our LLM evaluation method aligns with human-tested criteria. Since our project's goal is to assess the potential of agent-based simulation for story creation, future work can explore effective approaches for integrating human participants into this process.

Acknowledgments

This research was supported by a grant from NAVER corporation. Besides, we thank our anonymous reviewers for their very helpful suggestions.

References

Amal Alabdulkarim, Siyan Li, and Xiangyu Peng. 2021. Automatic story generation: Challenges and attempts. In *Proceedings of the Third Workshop on Narrative Understanding*, pages 72–83, Virtual. Association for Computational Linguistics.

Arwa I. Alhussain and Aqil M. Azmi. 2021a. Automatic story generation: A survey of approaches. *ACM Comput. Surv.*, 54(5).

Arwa I. Alhussain and Aqil M. Azmi. 2021b. Automatic story generation: A survey of approaches. *ACM Comput. Surv.*, 54(5).

Peter F Brown, Stephen A Della Pietra, Vincent J Della Pietra, and Robert L Mercer. 1992. Class-based n-gram models of natural language. *Computational Linguistics*, 18(4):467–479.

Edirlei Soares de Lima, Bruno Feijó, and Antonio L. Furtado. 2022. A character-based model for interactive storytelling in games. In *2022 21st Brazilian Symposium on Computer Games and Digital Entertainment (SBGames)*, pages 1–6.

Natlie Dehn. 1981. Story generation after tale-spin. In *IJCAI*, volume 81, pages 16–18.

Angela Fan, Mike Lewis, and Yann Dauphin. 2018. Hierarchical neural story generation. In *Proceedings of the 56th Annual Meeting of the Association for Computational Linguistics (Volume 1: Long Papers)*, pages 889–898, Melbourne, Australia. Association for Computational Linguistics.

Rui Figueiredo, António Brisson, Ruth Aylett, and Ana Paiva. 2008. Emergent stories facilitated an architecture to generate stories using intelligent synthetic characters.

Senyu Han, Lu Chen, Li-Min Lin, Zhengshan Xu, and Kai Yu. 2024. IBSEN: Director-actor agent collaboration for controllable and interactive drama script generation. In *Proceedings of the 62nd Annual Meeting of the Association for Computational Linguistics (Volume 1: Long Papers)*, pages 1607–1619, Bangkok, Thailand. Association for Computational Linguistics.

Fantine Huot, Reinald Kim Amplayo, Jennimaria Palomaki, Alice Shoshana Jakobovits, Elizabeth Clark, and Mirella Lapata. 2024. Agents' room: Narrative generation through multi-step collaboration. *arXiv preprint arXiv:2410.02603*.

Martin Josifoski, Marija Sakota, Maxime Peyrard, and Robert West. 2023. Exploiting asymmetry for synthetic training data generation: Synthie and the case of information extraction. *arXiv preprint arXiv:2303.04132*.

Alice LaPlante. 2007. *The Making of a Story: A Norton Guide to Creative Writing*. W. W. Norton & Company, New York, NY.

Mina Lee, Katy Ilonka Gero, John Joon Young Chung, Simon Buckingham Shum, Vipul Raheja, Hua Shen, Subhashini Venugopalan, Thiemo Wambsganss, David Zhou, Emad A Alghamdi, and 1 others. 2024. A design space for intelligent and interactive writing assistants. In *Proceedings of the 2024 CHI Conference on Human Factors in Computing Systems*, pages 1–35.

Cheng Li, Ziang Leng, Chenxi Yan, Junyi Shen, Hao Wang, Weishi Mi, Yaying Fei, Xiaoyang Feng, Song Yan, HaoSheng Wang, and 1 others. 2023. Chatharuhi: Reviving anime character in reality via large language model. *arXiv preprint arXiv:2308.09597*.

Chin-Yew Lin. 2004. ROUGE: A package for automatic evaluation of summaries. In *Text Summarization Branches Out*, pages 74–81, Barcelona, Spain. Association for Computational Linguistics.

Nelson F. Liu, Kevin Lin, John Hewitt, Ashwin Paranjape, Michele Bevilacqua, Fabio Petroni, and Percy Liang. 2024a. Lost in the middle: How language models use long contexts. *Transactions of the Association for Computational Linguistics*, 12:157–173.

Yinhong Liu, Han Zhou, Zhijiang Guo, Ehsan Shareghi, Ivan Vulić, Anna Korhonen, and Nigel Collier. 2024b. Aligning with human judgement: The role of pairwise preference in large language model evaluators. In *First Conference on Language Modeling*.

Adian Liusie, Potsawee Manakul, and Mark Gales. 2024. LLM comparative assessment: Zero-shot NLG evaluation through pairwise comparisons using large language models. In *Proceedings of the 18th Conference of the European Chapter of the Association for Computational Linguistics (Volume 1: Long Papers)*, pages 139–151, St. Julian's, Malta. Association for Computational Linguistics.

Genevieve Liveley. 2019. *Narratology*. Oxford University Press.

Liam Magee, Vanicka Arora, Gus Gollings, and Norma Lam-Saw. 2024. The drama machine: Simulating character development with llm agents. *arXiv preprint arXiv:2408.01725*.

Leland McInnes, John Healy, and James Melville. 2018. Umap: Uniform manifold approximation and projection for dimension reduction. *arXiv preprint arXiv:1802.03426*.

James Meehan. 2013. Tale-spin. In *Inside Computer Understanding*, pages 197–226. Psychology Press.

Piotr Mirowski, Kory W Mathewson, Jaylen Pittman, and Richard Evans. 2023. Co-writing screenplays and theatre scripts with language models: Evaluation by industry professionals. In *Proceedings of the 2023 CHI Conference on Human Factors in Computing Systems*, pages 1–34.

Aline Normoyle, João Sedoc, and Funda Durupinar. 2024. Using llms to animate interactive story characters with emotions and personality. In *2024 IEEE Conference on Virtual Reality and 3D User Interfaces Abstracts and Workshops (VRW)*, pages 632–635.

Joon Sung Park, Joseph O'Brien, Carrie Jun Cai, Meredith Ringel Morris, Percy Liang, and Michael S. Bernstein. 2023. Generative agents: Interactive simulacra of human behavior. In *Proceedings of the 36th Annual ACM Symposium on User Interface Software and Technology*, UIST '23, New York, NY, USA. Association for Computing Machinery.

Martin Pichlmair, Riddhi Raj, and Charlene Putney. 2024. Drama : for. Technical, Write with LAIKA, Copenhagen, Denmark.

Julie Porteous and A. Lindsay. 2019. Protagonist vs antagonist provant: Narrative generation as counter planning. In *Adaptive Agents and Multi-Agent Systems*.

Vladimir Propp. 1968. *Morphology of the Folktale*. University of Texas Press.

Nils Reimers and Iryna Gurevych. 2019. Sentence-bert: Sentence embeddings using siamese bert-networks. In *Proceedings of the 2019 Conference on Empirical Methods in Natural Language Processing*. Association for Computational Linguistics.

Mohi Reza, Nathan M Laundry, Ilya Musabirov, Peter Dushniku, Zhi Yuan "Michael" Yu, Kashish Mittal, Tovi Grossman, Michael Liut, Anastasia Kuzminykh, and Joseph Jay Williams. 2024. Abscribe: Rapid exploration & organization of multiple writing variations in human-ai co-writing tasks using large language models. In *Proceedings of the CHI Conference on Human Factors in Computing Systems*, pages 1–18.

Mark O Riedl. 2009. Incorporating authorial intent into generative narrative systems. In *AAAI Spring Symposium: Intelligent Narrative Technologies II*, pages 91–94.

Mark O Riedl and Robert Michael Young. 2010. Narrative planning: Balancing plot and character. *Journal of Artificial Intelligence Research*, 39:217–268.

Timo Schick, Jane Dwivedi-Yu, Zhengbao Jiang, Fabio Petroni, Patrick Lewis, Gautier Izacard, Qingfei You, Christoforos Nalmpantis, Edouard Grave, and Sebastian Riedel. 2022. Peer: A collaborative language model. *arXiv preprint arXiv:2208.11663*.

Yunfan Shao, Linyang Li, Junqi Dai, and Xipeng Qiu. 2023. Character-LLM: A trainable agent for role-playing. In *Proceedings of the 2023 Conference on Empirical Methods in Natural Language Processing*, pages 13153–13187, Singapore. Association for Computational Linguistics.

Mei Si, Stacy C. Marsella, and David V. Pynadath. 2005. Thespian: using multi-agent fitting to craft interactive drama. In *Proceedings of the Fourth International Joint Conference on Autonomous Agents and Multiagent Systems*, AAMAS '05, page 21–28, New York, NY, USA. Association for Computing Machinery.

Ivo Swartjes and Mariët Theune. 2006. A fabula model for emergent narrative. In *International Conference on Technologies for Interactive Digital Storytelling and Entertainment*, pages 49–60. Springer.

Jonathan Teutenberg and Julie Porteous. 2013. Efficient intent-based narrative generation using multiple planning agents. In *Adaptive Agents and Multi-Agent Systems*.

Saranya Venkatraman, Nafis Irtiza Tripto, and Dongwon Lee. 2024. Collabstory: Multi-llm collaborative story generation and authorship analysis. *arXiv preprint arXiv:2406.12665*.

Lei Wang, Jianxun Lian, Yi Huang, Yanqi Dai, Haoxuan Li, Xu Chen, Xing Xie, and Ji-Rong Wen. 2024a. Characterbox: Evaluating the role-playing capabilities of llms in text-based virtual worlds. *arXiv preprint arXiv:2412.05631*.

Yi Wang, Qian Zhou, and David Ledo. 2024b. Storyverse: Towards co-authoring dynamic plot with llm-based character simulation via narrative planning. In *Proceedings of the 19th International Conference on the Foundations of Digital Games*, FDG '24, New York, NY, USA. Association for Computing Machinery.

Bohao Yang, Dong Liu, Chenghao Xiao, Kun Zhao, Chen Tang, Chao Li, Lin Yuan, Guang Yang, Lanxiao Huang, and Chenghua Lin. 2024. Crafting customisable characters with llms: Introducing simschat, a persona-driven role-playing agent framework. *arXiv preprint arXiv:2406.17962*.

Lili Yao, Nanyun Peng, Ralph Weischedel, Kevin Knight, Dongyan Zhao, and Rui Yan. 2019. Plan-and-write: Towards better automatic storytelling. In *Proceedings of the AAAI Conference on Artificial Intelligence*, volume 33, pages 7378–7385.

Tianyi Zhang*, Varsha Kishore*, Felix Wu*, Kilian Q. Weinberger, and Yoav Artzi. 2020. Bertscore: Evaluating text generation with bert. In *International Conference on Learning Representations*.

Runcong Zhao, Wenjia Zhang, Jiazheng Li, Lixing Zhu, Yanran Li, Yulan He, and Lin Gui. 2024. Narrative-Play: Interactive narrative understanding. In *Proceedings of the 18th Conference of the European Chapter of the Association for Computational Linguistics: System Demonstrations*, pages 82–93, St. Julians, Malta. Association for Computational Linguistics.

Lianmin Zheng, Wei-Lin Chiang, Ying Sheng, Siyuan Zhuang, Zhanghao Wu, Yonghao Zhuang, Zi Lin, Zhuohan Li, Dacheng Li, Eric Xing, Hao Zhang, Joseph E Gonzalez, and Ion Stoica. 2023. Judging llm-as-a-judge with mt-bench and chatbot arena. In *Advances in Neural Information Processing Systems*, volume 36, pages 46595–46623. Curran Associates, Inc.

A The Win Matrices of Section by Evaluation Criteria 5.1

$$\text{Overall} = \begin{pmatrix} 0 & 41 & 47 \\ 15 & 0 & 33 \\ 9 & 23 & 0 \end{pmatrix} \tag{1}$$

$$\text{Plot} = \begin{pmatrix} 0 & 42 & 47 \\ 14 & 0 & 32 \\ 9 & 24 & 0 \end{pmatrix} \tag{2}$$

$$\text{Creativity} = \begin{pmatrix} 0 & 36 & 44 \\ 20 & 0 & 35 \\ 12 & 21 & 0 \end{pmatrix} \tag{3}$$

$$\text{Development} = \begin{pmatrix} 0 & 41 & 47 \\ 15 & 0 & 33 \\ 9 & 23 & 0 \end{pmatrix} \tag{4}$$

$$\text{Language Use} = \begin{pmatrix} 0 & 39 & 47 \\ 17 & 0 & 34 \\ 9 & 21 & 0 \end{pmatrix} \tag{5}$$

B The Prompt Used

B.1 Our System - Role Play Step

B.1.1 Plan Synthesis and Sorting

Character Extraction

You are provided with:

1. <Writing Prompt>: This is the original instruction that was used to generate a story.

2. <Story>: This is the actual narrative generated based on the writing prompt.

3. <Characters>: A list of **most of the characters** that appeared in the story following the following schema: input_story_characters_schema

{{divider}}
Based on <Story>, and <Characters>, and also consider the <Writing Prompt>, divide the **ENTIRE** <Story> into scenes. A scene is a unit of story that takes place in a single location and time. Each scene should be a self-contained unit that moves the story forward, and try to divide the story based on the plot elements: exposition, rising action, climax, falling action, resolution.
For each divided scene content, considering the <Characters> information, you should provide the following information:

1. name: A high level name for the scene

2. outline: The outline of the scene, which is a description of the action/story/dramatic event occurring in the scene. It should comprehensively capture the actions and interactions of all characters involved. Answer in a list of bullet points

3. plot_element: Which plot element is being developed in this scene. You can choose from the following: exposition, rising action, climax, falling action, resolution.

4. place: The place of the scene with a SPECIFIC AND DETAILED description of that place

5. importance: The relative importance of the scene in the story. It is an integer in the scale 1-10, where 1 is the least important and 10 is the most important. You should provide importance based on the number of words of this scene compared to the total number of words in the story, and also the significance of the scene in the story.

6. characters: **ALL** the characters that **are present in the scene**. Also provide the scene level **CHARACTER GOAL** of each character. If you find any additional characters/group not provided in <Characters>, add them to the scene, and provide their character goal as well.

{{divider}}
Once you have divided the story into scenes, reflect on the scenes you have created, and ensure that all content is covered. If you have missed any content, add additional scenes/details to the outline to cover the missing content.
{{divider}}
Provide your output in JSON following the following schema:
{{OutScenesSchema}}

Scene Extraction

You are provided with:

1. <Writing Prompt>: This is the original instruction that was used to generate a story.
2. <Story>: This is the actual narrative generated based on the writing prompt.
3. <Characters>: A list of **most of the characters** that appeared in the story following the following schema: input_story_characters_schema

{{divider}}
Based on <Story>, and <Characters>, and also consider the <Writing Prompt>, divide the **ENTIRE** <Story> into scenes. A scene is a unit of story that takes place in a single location and time. Each scene should be a self-contained unit that moves the story forward, and try to divide the story based on the plot elements: exposition, rising action, climax, falling action, resolution.
For each divided scene content, considering the <Characters> information, you should provide the following information:

1. name: A high level name for the scene
2. outline: The outline of the scene, which is a description of the action/story/dramatic event occurring in the scene. It should comprehensively capture the actions and interactions of all characters involved. Answer in a list of bullet points
3. plot_element: Which plot element is being developed in this scene. You can choose from the following: exposition, rising action, climax, falling action, resolution.
4. place: The place of the scene with a SPECIFIC AND DETAILED description of that place
5. importance: The relative importance of the scene in the story. It is an integer in the scale 1-10, where 1 is the least important and 10 is the most important. You should provide importance based on the number of words of this scene compared to the total number of words in the story, and also the significance of the scene in the story.
6. characters: **ALL** the characters that **are present in the scene**. Also provide the scene level **CHARACTER GOAL** of each character. If you find any additional characters/group not provided in <Characters>, add them to the scene, and provide their character goal as well.

{{divider}}
Once you have divided the story into scenes, reflect on the scenes you have created, and ensure that all content is covered. If you have missed any content, add additional scenes/details to the outline to cover the missing content.
{{divider}}
Provide your output in JSON following the following schema:
{{OutScenesSchema}}

Sort Scenes

You are a creative writer for the story. Your task is to sort an array of story scenes based on the chronological order, and provide the sorted result.
{{divider}}
You are provided with:
1. <StoryScenes>: The list of story scenes, following the schema: {{input_story_scenes_schema}}
{{divider}}
Your Task is to
1. Sort the <StoryScenes> based on the chronological order of the story development by each scene's outline, and provide the sorted result, by the name of each scene.
{{divider}}
Output in JSON format following the schema provided below: {{sort_scene_results_schema}}

B.1.2 Director Agent

Chronological Outline Creation

You are provided with the following information:

1. <Scene>: The scene object, which includes both scene outline, detailed location description and involved character/group of characters information following the schema: {{input_scene_schema}}
2. <Outline>: The outline of the scene you are adjusting divider

Sort, and rewrite the scene outline bullet points to be suitable for a role-playing game (RPG). Ensure that:

- Strict chronological order: Events must be structured in the order they occur, avoiding retrospective narration (e.g., no "recounting" of past events).
- The outline focuses on character-driven development and role-playing dynamics
- The sequence of events reflects meaningful interactions between characters
- The updated outline should be similar in format. The events MUST BE in CHRONOLOGICAL ORDER, and described in present tense
- The updated outline should have similar number of word as the original <Outline> provided.
- Do not add any event, only reorder original events mentioned in <Outline> provided.

return the bullet points in str

Group Chat Termination

You are the director of a scene in a role playing game, and you are responsible for GUIDE the agents to act and speak according to the scene outline.
{{divider}}
You are provided with the following information:

1. <Scene>: The scene object, which includes both scene outline in chronological order for this RPG game, detailed location description and involved character/group of characters information following the schema: input_scene_schema
2. <ChatHistories>: The history of the role playing game, which is a sequence of message from participating characters in an array following the schema: {{input_chat_histories_schema}}
3. <NextAgentNames>: This is an array of str, representing the name of the characters that you are able to select to speak next. You should select **EXACTLY ONE NAME TO RESPOND**, and provide the **EXACT NAME OF THE AGENT**.

{{divider}}
First, review the <ChatHistories> provided, and also look at the <Scene> outline, and decide if the chat has covered the outline of the scene. And provide the reasoning of your decision. The reasoning must be specific, in terms of exact character and event in the scene outline not yet covered.
Then Answer True if the chat has covered the entire content, where the director should terminate the conversation, or False otherwise.
{{divider}}
Output in JSON format following the schema provided below: {{out_director_should_terminate_schema}}

Director Command and Select Agent

```
You are the director of a scene in a role playing game, and you are responsible for GUIDE the agents to act and speak according to the scene outline.
```
{{divider}}

You are provided with the following information:

1. <Scene>: The scene object, which includes both scene outline, detailed location description and involved character/group of characters information following the schema: input_scene_schema

2. <ChatHistories>: The history of the role playing game, which is a sequence of message from participating characters in an array following the schema: input_chat_histories_schema

3. <NextAgentNames>: This is an array of str, representing the name of the characters that you are able to select to speak next. You should select **EXACTLY ONE NAME TO RESPOND**, and provide the **EXACT NAME OF THE AGENT**.

{{divider}}

```
1. Continuation Planning:
- Examine the <ChatHistories>, which document the role-playing game progress so far. - Based on this conversation history, repeat **EXACTLY** the remaining part of the **outline** of the <Scene> provided that is not shown in the <ChatHistories>.
2. Agent Selection and Command:
- From your continuation plan, which provides the remaining scene outline to be role-played, choose which character agent should role-play next. Provide the exact name of that agent. - Directly address the chosen agent with a concise, high-level command for one turn. The command should provide a summary directive—indicating the intended action or dialogue direction—tailored to the character's age, gender, and personality. Avoid including detailed dialogue or overly specific descriptions. **Be concise**
```
{{divider}}

```
Generate the output in JSON following the schema: {{out_director_selection_command_schema}}
```

B.1.3 Character Agent

Character Agent Response

You are acting as an agent in a role-playing game. You will produce responses on behalf of the agent from a third-person perspective, describing both the agent's actions and dialogue. Adhere to the agent's goals, age, gender, and personality at all times, **ensuring the response reflects their memory and physical state in a logical way.**
{{divider}}
You are provided with the following information:

1. <Character>: The character you are role playing for, and you should keep in mind the Character's goal, and act accordingly and realistically. It follows the schema: {{input_story_character_schema}}

2. <DirectorCommand>: The command from the director of the role play game, representing what the agent should incoporate to say and do in the role playing game.

3. <CharacterMemory>: The memory of the character, in string.

4. <CharacterPhysicalState>: The physical state of the character, in string.

5. <RecentHistories>: The most recent, up to 10 histories of the role playing game, following the schema: {{input_chat_histories_schema}}

{{divider}}
Based on <Character>, <DirectorCommand>, <CharacterMemory>, <CharacterPhysicalState>, and <RecentHistories>, generate the agent's response from a third-party perspective. The dialogue, actions, and overall tone must be **natural** realistic, taking into account the agent's age, background, personality, and speech patterns.
Important Guidelines: 1. Do not include any concluding commentary—only provide the agent's response in the role playing game. 2. Maintain an observer's perspective, presenting the agent's actions and dialogue authentically while ensuring alignment with their character traits. 3. Consider the agent's current memory and physical state, ensuring the response is realistic, concise, and free of contradictions with their established characteristics.
Generate the response in JSON in the following format:
{{out_response_schema}}

Character Agent Update Memory

You are the mechanism to update the current character's memory given the history of a role playing game.
{{divider}}
You are provided with:
1. <NewChatHistories>: The list of conversation and action history of the agents in the role playing game that is **not yet seen by the current character** following the schema: {{chat_histories_schema}}
2. <Character>: The character whose memory you are updating, following the schema:{{story_character_schema}}
3. <CharacterMemory>: The current memory of the character whose memory you are updating.
{{divider}}
Update the memory on what the current character should know based on the history, and return the updated memory. The memory should contain the history of events that the character has experienced, and any information that the character has learned from the conversation. Do not include any irrelavant information, and the memory should be in first character standpoint. For the output, only provide the **updated** memory in string, nothing else.

Physical State Update

You are the mechanism to record the physical state of the character based on the history of a role playing game.
{{divider}}
You are provided with:

1. <NewChatHistories>: The list of conversation and action history of the agents in the role playing game that is **not yet seen by the current character** following the schema: {{chat_histories_schema}}
2. <Character>: The character whose physical state you are updating, following the schema: {{story_character_schema}}
3. <CharacterPhysicalState>: The physical state of the character whose physical state you are updating.

{{divider}}
Update the physical state to reflect the changes based on the history. The physical state must be consistent with the <Character>, in terms of their age, gender and set up, and also make sense based on the the <NewChatHistories>. For the output, only provide the **updated** physical state in string, nothing else.

B.2 Our System - Rewrite Step

We share the same extraction process as AR in the creation of central conflict, story-setting. Please refer to their work for details.

Rewrite to Story

You are a creative writer writing a story. Your task is to write the content of the <TaskScene> for the story.
{{divider}}
You are provided with:

1. <WritingPrompt>: The writing prompt for the story
2. <CentralConflict>: The central conflict of the story
3. <StorySetting>: The setting of the story
4. <StoryScenes>: The list of story scenes planned out, by name and outline, following the schema: input_story_scenes_v2_schema
5. <StoryContent>: The story content written so far
6. <SceneCharacters>: The characters involved in the scene you are writing, following the schema: input_characters_schema
7. <TaskScene>: The scene object you are writing the content for, following the schema: input_story_scene_v2_schema
8. <TaskScenePlotElement>: The plot element of the scene you are writing
9. <TaskScenePlace>: The place where the scene unfolds.
10. <RolePlayHistory>: The conversation of <SceneCharacters> role playing <TaskScene> in an array, following the schema: input_chat_histories_v2_schema

{{divider}}
Besure to understand the <TaskScene>'s role in the whole narrative arc, and write the content of the scene accordingly.
Refer to the <RolePlayHistory> for **realistic character actions and dialogues** in an RPG game of the <TaskScene>. But begin your portion of the story in a way that naturally flows from the ending of <Story>. Match the writing style, vocabulary, and overall mood of the existing text. Do not re-explain details or events that have already been described. Ensure dialogue and actions **align with character traits**
{{no_end_instruction}}

1. <WritingPrompt>: {{writing_prompt}}
2. <CentralConflict>: {{central_conflict}}
3. <StorySetting>: {{story_setting}}
4. <StoryScenes>: {{story_scenes}}
5. <StoryContent>: {{story_content}}
6. <SceneCharacters>: {{characters}}
7. <TaskScene>: {{task_scene}}
8. <TaskScenePlotElement>: {{plot_element}}
9. <TaskScenePlace>: {{place}}
10. <RolePlayHistory>: {{role_play_history}}

B.3 Dramatron

We modified Dramatron's original prompt template in order to adapt their work for writing stories. We removed their example for two reasons: Their work was designed for writing screen play and all systems used for experiment are zero-shot. Below is the prompt we used.

Scene Content Generation

Use the following description, write the content of the scene
Place: {{place_name}} + \n + {{place_description}}
Characters: {{characters}}
Plot Element: {{plot_element}}
Summary: {{summary}}
Outline: {{outline}}

B.4 Agents'Room

We followed strictly the implementation of the original paper for all implementations.

B.5 LLM Evaluation

Rewrite to Story

You will conduct a side-by-side evaluation. You will be given two system-generated stories. Your task is to compare the two stories and determine which one is better based on the following dimensions:

• Plot: The story should have a recognizable structure, e.g., with a connected beginning, middle, and end. The story should exhibit events and turns that move the plot forward. The story should not have logical or conceptual inconsistencies. Surprising or disruptive elements should be intentional, e.g., they serve the story and do not feel jarring, odd, or out of place.

• Creativity: There should be engaging characters, themes, and imagery. The ideas should not feel generic or bland. There should be avoidance of overly cliched characters and storylines, unintentional tropes, and stereotypes. When used, tropes and cliches should serve a purpose (e.g., comedic effect, twist on a common trope etc). The story should include original elements that were not explicitly mentioned in the prompt.

• Development: Characters and settings should be introduced and contextualized with relevant details that allow the reader to understand their place in the story. Appropriate levels of detail and complexity should be provided to lend the story a feeling of realness and believability.

• Language Use: The language used should feel varied and rich: Variance of sentence structure, verbiage, and vocabulary. The story should exhibit rhetorical, linguistic and literary devices (e.g., ambiguity, alliteration, etc) to create interesting effects. The story should avoid bland or repetitive phrases (unless used intentionally to create a narrative, thematic, or linguistic effect).

Provide a detailed assessment of the two stories in terms of these four dimensions. Conclude your assessment with scores for each dimension using the template below. Do not add any emphasis, such as bold and italics, on your assessment.

[Assessment Ending Template]
Based on my assessment, the better story for each dimension is:
Plot: [A or B or Same]
Creativity: [A or B or Same]
Development: [A or B or Same]
Language Use: [A or B or Same]
Overall: [A or B or Same]
[Story A]
{{story_A_content}}
[Story B]
{{story_B_content}}
[Assessment]

C Qualitative Analysis Sample

C.1 Consistency Comparison

Type	Content
Dramatron & Our Approach Selected First Scene Outline	Aerie recounts the details of her visit to the archaeological site, including the camp setup and initial observations about the ruins and the mysterious object.
Dramatron Corresponding Content	"The camp is well-managed," Aerie detailed, hands gesturing animatedly. "Our colleagues do enjoy their creature comforts even when surrounded by stone ruins and eerie silence."
Agents' Room Corresponding Content	Aerie's account conveyed more than just facts; it captured nuances—a skill honed through years served as both courier and covert operative. They spoke of a shattered crystal obelisk unearthed amid ruins steeped in legend. Inscriptions marred its surface in a language long forgotten by all but a handful of scholars and archaeologists like Mage Myssa.
Our Approach Corresponding Content	Aerie's grin was both playful and knowing. "Indeed. The Malborn ruins were more than just scenery this time," she replied, lowering herself onto a nearby chair, her cloak settling around her like a second skin. "The camp is thriving under Mage Zolen's watchful eye—though one has to wonder if his precautions are as much for keeping us out as anything else."
Golden Story Corresponding Content	"The archaeological mages have set up camp between the lake and the ruins, using a grid formation common to our Empire. Mage Zolen is in charge, and he is a stickler for protocol. However, the camp appeared hastily constructed; rumor in the camp was that the site was very far down on Zolen's list of priorities, but that an incident on the longest day of the year caused him to focus more on this specific ruin."

The table above compares content generated by each system corresponding to the same selected outline segment. The yellow highlighting indicates a hallucination produced by the Dramatron approach, resulting in nonsensical content. The green highlighting marks premature references to content and characters intended to appear later in the story.

An Analysis of Scoring Methods for Reranking in Large Language Model Story Generation

Megan Deering
Department of Computer Science
University of Toronto
Toronto, Ontario, Canada
caomegan@cs.toronto.edu

Gerald Penn
Department of Computer Science
University of Toronto
Toronto, Ontario, Canada
gpenn@cs.toronto.edu

Abstract

Outline-conditioned story generation using Large Language Models (LLMs) offers a promising approach for automating narrative creation. Some outline-conditioned story generation methods use automatic scoring during the generation process in order to improve the story quality. However, current research has shown that automatic scoring is not ideal for assessing story quality. This paper evaluates three proposed automatic story-scoring methods to improve the reranking of outputs during the generation process. These scoring methods leverage different prompting strategies and fine-tuning techniques to enhance the accuracy and relevance of the assessments. By experimenting with these approaches within a beam search framework, we aim to identify the most effective methods for optimizing story-generation outcomes. While we have found no significant overall difference between these methods in terms of their agreement with human ratings during story generation, the overall story ratings by human evaluators are average. These findings motivate the need for improved automatic scoring techniques and datasets while also indicating that simpler, more easily implementable scoring methods for reranking perform comparably to more complex approaches.

1 Introduction

Recent advancements in AI, particularly in Large Language Models (LLMs), have highlighted how these tools can assist in writing. In creative writing in particular, there has been exploration into how these tools can be used to write fiction stories such as in Yang et al. (2023) and Chung et al. (2022). This issue is particularly challenging because fiction writing demands creativity, raising questions about how to assess the quality of outputs from LLMs in such a creative domain and how to encourage the generation of higher-quality, more engaging stories with these tools.

In the task of outline-conditioned story generation, as first proposed in Rashkin et al. (2020), the input is an outline consisting of key plot-points, characters and events, which are then used to generate a flowing narrative. Each point primes the generation of a passage of text from its corresponding plot-point. Subsequent passages are generated from the next plot-point and the context of the previously generated passages. In our paper, we use outlines consisting of character information, events, and settings in a shallow (two-level) hierarchical structure.

As stated by Rashkin et al. (2020), the difficulty of this task lies in the fact that a model must fluently connect the points given in the text, while still following the outline. Papers such as Yang et al. (2022) and Yang et al. (2023) employ automatic scoring techniques with reranking during the generation process in order to ensure that these stories remain coherent and relevant to the given outline.

Most recent research has suggested that automatic scoring, including scoring by LLMs, is ineffective at assessing story quality. Instead, most story generation papers use human raters as their primary scoring method (Yao et al., 2019; Rashkin et al., 2020; Yang et al., 2023). However, there are cases where automatic scoring is a necessary component in the story generation system. For example, Yang et al. (2023) use automatic scoring in a beam search to select the ideal sequence of passages in a story. This is referred to as reranking, the process of scoring multiple candidate outputs to select the one that best meets specific criteria (Haroutunian et al., 2023). In the context of story generation, reranking could be done automatically or with humans in the loop. Using human-in-the-loop in this context could be tedious and time consuming, however, making the task harder for the humans involved.

In this paper, we investigate how automatic scoring can be used in the story generation process to improve the story outputs. We look at which scor-

Proceedings of the Fourth Workshop on Intelligent and Interactive Writing Assistants (In2Writing 2025), pages 109–120
May 4, 2025

ing techniques are the best for this specific task. Specifically, we look at three different techniques of automatic scoring using LLMs:

1. **Log-likelihood-based scoring**: Prompts a model with a yes or no scoring question and then uses the log probability of "yes" as a score.

2. **Simple prompt-based scoring**: Prompts a model with a numerical scoring question and uses the output as the score.

3. **Fine-tuning**: Uses a dataset of story scores and fine-tunes a pre-trained model on it.

We use each of these three methods in a reranking framework to generate stories. We then get human raters to evaluate which of these methods, when used for reranking, generates the best stories.

We found that there was no significant difference between these methods when used in reranking for story generation. This means that simple methods like prompt-based scoring perform just as well as other methods which may be more time consuming to implement. It unfortunately also means that fine-tuning a model does not seem to improve the story quality when used for scoring in reranking. Additionally, it further motivates the need for better automatic scoring techniques and datasets.

Our contributions are as follows:

1. We thoroughly evaluate three different automatic scoring techniques for reranking in story generation.

2. We provide code[1] which can be used by others to integrate these scoring methods into their systems for reranking.

2 Related Work

Several previous papers have explored outline-conditioned story generation, where outlines are used as input to generate a story (Yao et al., 2019; Rashkin et al., 2020; Wang et al., 2022).

The DOC framework (Yang et al., 2023) uses verbose outlines and a reranking system in their generation process to choose the best sequence of passages. This paper was inspired by an earlier paper called RE3 (Yang et al., 2022) which also used reranking to choose the best story continuations. They found this reranking component to be critical for plot coherence and premise relevance. Both Yang et al. (2023) and Yang et al. (2022) use a trained model for this reranking.

Zhu et al. (2023) introduces a system with the modularity of the original DOC framework, but which is able to be integrated with more modern LLMs. It also uses log-likelihood-based scoring rather than a trained model for the reranking component. However, the scoring method used for reranking in their system is never fully evaluated. Additionally much previous research has shown that current automatic scoring techniques are not up-to-par with human scoring (Novikova et al., 2017; Guan et al., 2021; Colombo et al., 2023; Chhun et al., 2022, 2024; Chakrabarty et al., 2024).

In Chhun et al. (2022) the authors create the HANNA dataset consisting of human scores of different stories on 5 different criteria: relevance, coherence, empathy, surprise, and engagement. For each of these criteria, they ask humans to give a 5-point Likert score to stories generated by 10 different story generation systems using prompts from the WritingPrompts dataset (Fan et al., 2018). They then compared different automatic scoring techniques to the human scores using Kendall correlations. They found that the correlations between the automatic scores and human scores were weak and called for stronger automatic scoring methods. They found that larger pre-trained models like GPT-2 performed the best, however.

This prompted them to write a follow up paper (Chhun et al., 2024) where they further compared human scoring to automatic scoring using different LLMs for prompting. They found that while LLMs are consistent and have slightly higher ratings, they have correlations with human scores that are fairly similar to those of other automatic scoring methods. They therefore conclude that LLMs are currently the best proxy for human scoring of story generation. They also recommend future work on the use of fine-tuning models for this task.

Guan et al. (2021) address the overall low quality of automatic scoring methods by creating a benchmark called OpenMEVA for them. In contrast to Chhun et al. (2022), they use a single 5-point overall quality score rather than individual scores for several criteria. This overall score should be low for stories that have repetitive plots, unrelated events and conflicting logic, or globally chaotic scenes. They also found that state-of-the art methods corre-

[1] https://github.com/MeganDeer/auto-story-score

Prompt A

Story Passage:
King Aldric, determined...
Event:
King Aldric issues a decree.

Did this event happen in the story passage? Yes or No.

Prompt B

Story Passage:
King Aldric, determined...
Event:
King Aldric issues a decree.

Rate the story on a scale from 1 to 5 on Relevance (how closely the story passage follows the event).
1—The story has no relationship with the event at all.
2—The story only has a weak relationship with the event.
3—The story roughly matches the event.
4—The story matches the event, except for one or two small aspects.
5—The story matches the event exactly.
Do not include any numbers other than your rating in your answer.

Rating (1-5):

Prompt C

Prompt:
King Aldric issues a decree.
Target Story:
King Aldric, determined...

Rate the story on a scale from 1 to 5 on Relevance, Coherence, Empathy, Surprise, Engagement, and Complexity.

Ratings:

Figure 1: The scoring prompts used for log-likelihood-based scoring (prompt A) which has been reproduced from Meta Research (2023), prompt-based scoring (prompt B), and the fine-tuned scorer (prompt C) from left to right on relevance. The fine-tuned model generates scores for all criteria at once.

late poorly with the human methods on this scale in their dataset.

Yang and Jin (2024) discusses different types of automatic scoring. In general, there are four different types that use LLMs. The first of these is embedding-based methods which use embeddings and matching algorithms to assign a score. These have many limitations. The next is probability-based methods. These methods use the generation probability from LLMs in computing their score. There are also generative-based methods, which simply prompt LLMs for a score. Finally, there are trained methods that fine-tune an LLM to assign a score.

Chen et al. (2023) found that generative-based methods are more effective than probability-based methods that use log-likelihood because their smooth distributions allow for better differentiation than the narrow range and peak structure of the probability-based methods.

3 Methodology

In this section, we describe our approach for evaluating automatic story-scoring methods for reranking in outline-conditioned story generation. We first outline the process we use for generating stories and how reranking is used within that. We then describe the criteria we use for the scoring within the reranking. Finally, we describe the three scoring methods to evaluate: log-likelihood-based scoring, prompt-based scoring and fine-tuning.

3.1 Generation

We use the generation component of the framework from Zhu et al. (2023) to generate a story. That is, given an outline, we prompt a model to generate each passage in the outline multiple times. Then, using a beam search, we generate the subsequent passages and select the path with the highest score as the final sequence of passages. We explore using different methods of scoring within this beam search.

3.2 Criteria

We follow Chhun et al. (2022) in forming and defining criteria for scoring passages and evaluating the final stories. We look at the following criteria, which were determined in Chhun et al. (2022) to be good measures of story quality according to the social-sciences literature:

1. **Relevance**: How well the story matches its prompt.
2. **Coherence**: How much the story makes sense.
3. **Empathy**: How well a reader will understand the character's emotions.
4. **Engagement**: How much a reader will engage with the story.
5. **Complexity**: How elaborate the story is.

We leave out the criterion of surprise, which measures how surprising the end of the story is, because we are implementing criteria to score individual passages in the story rather than the entire story.

3.3 Log-likelihood-based Scoring

Zhu et al. (2023) uses log-likelihood-based scoring for reranking in their system. That is, they ask the model the prompts outlined in prompt A of Figure 1 and then calculate the score as the log-likelihood of the answer "yes" being in the response. They also only score each passage on coherence, relevance and commentary. In this case, commentary is used to determine whether or not the passage is actually a part of a story, or just commentary about a story. We also add the commentary criterion to the prompt-based and fine-tuned scoring as we found that, without it, the generated stories were often formulated as brainstorms rather than stories. This acts as our probability-based method.

3.4 Prompt-based Scoring

The next scoring method that we compare is using simple prompt-based scoring. Here, we prompt the model to assign the story a score from 1 to 5 on the criteria in Section 3.2. This acts as our generative-based method.

Additionally, we add guidelines on the definitions of each criterion to better guide the model. We also expand the criteria to include all of the criteria listed in Section 3.2. An example prompt can be found in prompt B of Figure 1.

3.5 Fine-tuned Scorer

The third scoring method in the comparison is a fine-tuned model. This is our trained method.

We fine-tuned a model to score the criteria presented in Chhun et al. (2022). We used LORA Quantization with `llama2-7b` and trained on the HANNA dataset from Chhun et al. (2022) with the prompts presented in Chhun et al. (2024), which can be found in prompt C of Figure 1. This dataset includes story prompts as well as the story generated from these prompts and the scores given by human raters to the story. We trained to match these human scores and used mean-squared error as our loss.

4 Experimental setup

4.1 Outlines

In order to generate the stories using our three methods, we first need to have outlines with which to generate them. We use outlines in the format of those included in Yang et al. (2023). An example outline can be found in Figure A.2. To our knowledge, there is no dataset of outlines that follows this format. Their framework does include a component for generating outlines, but these outlines tend to be very long and detailed — almost story-like — leading to even longer stories that are more difficult for a human to evaluate all at once. Therefore, we asked OpenAI's `gpt-4o` to generate outlines from story prompts contained in the WritingPrompts dataset (Fan et al., 2018). The prompt for generating these outlines is found in Figure A.1. We sampled 16 outlines using this method and one of the present authors ensured that the story plots were interesting and coherent.

4.2 Fine-tuning

To evaluate the fine-tuning, we hold out a test set of data from the HANNA dataset (Chhun et al., 2022). We then calculate the Kendall correlations between the predictions of our fine-tuned model on this test set and the human scores in HANNA. We compare these correlations to the results of the evaluations done in Chhun et al. (2024).

Additionally, we use our fine-tuned model to generate scores on the dataset from OpenMEVA (Guan et al., 2021) to test it on unseen data. Since OpenMEVA has one unified score, while the HANNA dataset has six different scores, we train a basic linear model to learn the weighting of each individual score to contribute to the overall OpenMEVA score. We use Pearson correlation to evaluate the relationship between our results and human scores, as this statistic is also used in Guan et al. (2021), thus allowing for a direct comparison.

4.3 Human Evaluation

Automatic scoring is used during the story generation process for reranking; therefore, we rely solely on human evaluation to compare the final stories. These are not the same human-sourced numerical scores that are found in several of the available datasets, which we used to calculate the correlations in Section 5.1. This was a separate human-subject evaluation that we conducted, the results of which are described in Section 5.2.

To conduct the human evaluation, we first generate 16 stories for the three experimental conditions: the original pipeline from Zhu et al. (2023) with log-likelihood-based scoring, the modified pipeline with simple prompt-based scoring, and the modified pipeline with the fine-tuned scoring model. For each of these experimental conditions, `llama2-7b-chat` was used for generation. It was also used for the log-likelihood-based and prompt-based scoring. As mentioned in Section 3.5, `llama2-7b` was fine-tuned for the fine-tuned scorer, using a beam-width of 3 for all of the stories.

64 participants were recruited from Prolific, subject to the constraints that they are fluent in English and have a 99-100% approval rating. Each participant was presented with a Word-document survey containing three stories, one from each experimental condition, all generated from the same outline. The order of the experimental conditions was permuted in each survey. The participants were asked to read the three stories and rate the coherence, empathy, and relevance of each using a 1-5 Likert scale. They were also asked, for each outline point, to highlight the passage in each story that best corresponds, in order to further assess relevance. Finally, they were asked to rank the stories in order of the likelihood that they would purchase them, and explain the reasoning behind their decision. We call this the preference ranking. Further details on this evaluation can be found in Table A.1.

We chose to change some of the criteria from Chhun et al. (2022). Again, we left out surprise as we generated passage-by-passage and surprise is, by the definition in Chhun et al. (2022), only applicable to the end of the story. We also replaced the criteria of engagement (Chhun et al., 2022) and "interestingness" (Yang et al., 2023) with preference ranking because the latter is less abstract and better grounded in a ecologically valid task. Yamshchikov and Tikhonov (2023) also claim that human raters may be misinterpreting "interestingness." We also chose to leave out complexity as the annotators were comparing stories that were generated with the same outline, and thus should all be roughly equally elaborate.

To evaluate the results of the human study, we used an ANOVA test to determine the significance of relevance, coherence, and empathy. Before computing ANOVA, we checked for a normal distribution using a histogram and Levene's test. We further evaluated relevance using the highlighted passages that were chosen to correspond to each outline point, calculating the specificity, precision, and recall of the words in the passages compared to the actual alignment of generated words to outline points in the model. We used the Bradley-Terry-Luce (BTL) method to linearise the relative preference rankings into a global ranking of the three scoring methods with respect to one another.

5 Results

5.1 Fine-tuning

Kendall correlations		
Criteria	Fine-tuned Model	Beluga-13B 1[a]
Relevance	0.18	0.21
Coherence	0.30	0.26
Empathy	0.29	0.27
Surprise	0.30	0.17
Engagement	0.33	0.11
Complexity	0.39	0.26

[a] Correlations from Chhun et al. (2024).

Table 1: Kendall correlations of the scoring model fine-tuned for three epochs to human-sourced scores in the HANNA dataset, rounded to two decimal places, along with human correlations to the Beluga-13b 1 model as reported in Chhun et al. (2024).

In order to evaluate the fine-tuning alternative, we use Kendall correlations to compare to those reported in Chhun et al. (2024). We found that for all criteria, we were able to achieve better correlations than those from Chhun et al. (2024) to the human-sourced scores found in the HANNA dataset. This indicates that the fine-tuning was able to improve conformity on this dataset. The results for a model trained with 3 epochs can be seen in

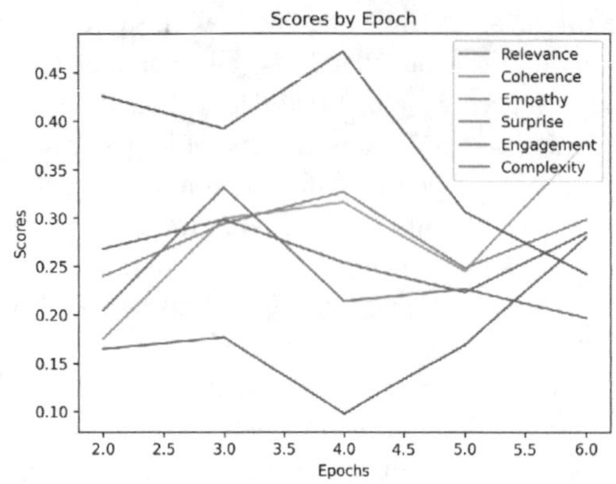

Figure 2: The Kendall correlations of the fine-tuned model trained for different numbers of epochs.

Table 1. Although relevance was unable to beat the score from Chhun et al. (2024) within 3 epochs, beyond 6 epochs, it did ($\tau = 0.28$).

Thus, we found that different training times were required to achieve the best results for different criteria. Figure 2 shows the graph of Kendall correlations trained for different numbers of epochs. Relevance, coherence, and surprise do better with more training. However, complexity has the best performance with 4 epochs and engagement does the best with 3 epochs of training. After that, their performance noticeably decreases due to overfitting. Empathy does the best on 4 epochs, but performance continues to improve with more training. Overall, 3 epochs achieve the best overall balance between Kendall correlation and training time.

These results imply that it is much more difficult to train for relevance and coherence. In fact, the Kendall correlations for coherence are extremely low before 6 epochs. In the case of relevance, this may be because it requires the language model to pay attention to more information. For instance, the model needs to attend more closely to the early portion of the prompt, whereas other criteria are only concerned with the story itself.

Another possible contributor to this difficulty could be the lack of clarity on what the criteria mean. Chhun et al. (2022) also found less than favourable Kendall correlations for relevance, but the instructions that they gave to their annotators to score relevance were very underspecific, asking them merely to "measure how well the story matches the prompt" (Chhun et al., 2022). Coherence, furthermore, enjoys no consensus on how it is used in natural language generation (Yamshchikov and Tikhonov, 2023). This may have affected how the annotators scored coherence in the HANNA dataset.

Because of these results, we decided to use the model trained for 3 epochs for the criteria of complexity, engagement, and empathy and the model trained for 6 epochs for relevance and coherence in our reranking. We do not use surprise for our reranking.

We also tested our fine-tuned model on the OpenMEVA dataset (Guan et al., 2021) to evaluate its performance on unseen data. The ROCStories and WritingPrompts datasets (Mostafazadeh et al., 2016; Fan et al., 2018) are evaluated separately in Guan et al. (2021), but their stories are interspersed in the available data. Therefore, we conducted our evaluation on a mixture of both datasets and compared our results using Pearson correlations to the human-sourced scores found in OpenMEVA for the ROCStories and WritingPrompts datasets, as this was the statistic presented in Guan et al. (2021).

Our model achieved a Pearson correlation of 0.2281, outperforming BERTScore-F1 (Zhang* et al., 2020), which scored 0.1271 on ROCStories and 0.0329 on WritingPrompts (Guan et al., 2021), as well as RUBER-BERT (Ghazarian et al., 2019), which scored 0.1434 and 0.2116, respectively (Guan et al., 2021). However, it falls short of the best-performing method, UNION (0.4119/0.3256), from Guan and Huang (2020). While our fine-tuned model does not achieve the highest performance, it remains competitive with other methods evaluated in Guan et al. (2021). This is notable given that our method was not explicitly trained to assess the specific aspects targeted in the OpenMEVA evaluation, such as repetition and conflicting logic.

5.2 Human Study

In total, we collected surveys from 64 participants on 16 different stories for each experimental condition. Each story was evaluated by 4 participants on relevance, coherence, empathy and preference. Additionally, we had participants annotate which passages they believed correlated to each outline point.

5.2.1 Ratings

We evaluated the significance of relevance, coherence and empathy using ANOVA as outlined in Section 4.3.

For coherence, as seen in Figure 3, the generated

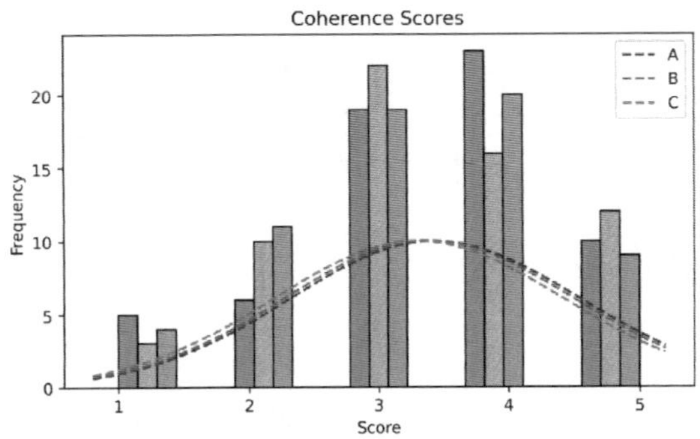

Figure 3: Histogram of the coherence ratings given by human raters to each of the three methods. A: log-likelihood-based scoring, B: simple prompt-based scoring and C: fine-tuned scoring.

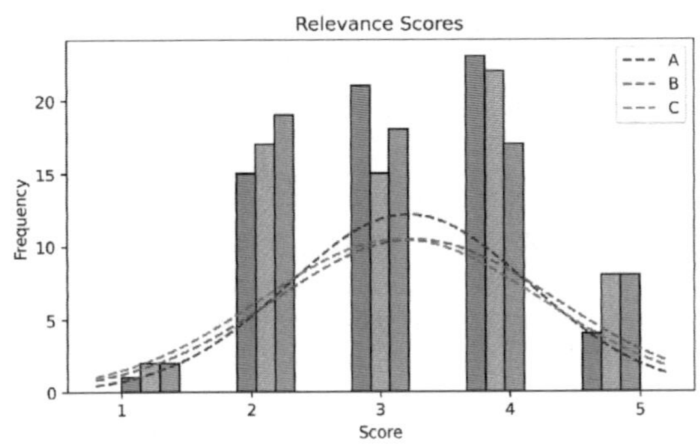

Figure 4: Histogram of the relevance ratings given by human raters to each of the three methods. A: log-likelihood-based scoring, B: simple prompt-based scoring and C: fine-tuned scoring.

histogram and the Levene score of 0.9973 suggest that it is normally distributed. The p-value from the ANOVA test was 0.58. Therefore, the differences of the human ratings of coherence may not be significant.

For relevance, as seen in Figure 4, the histogram generated appears to be normal and we got a Levene score of 0.23, suggesting that it may be normal. The p-value achieved from our ANOVA test was 0.757, and so no significance was demonstrated.

For empathy, similarly to relevance, the data appear to be somewhat normal with a Levene score of 0.19, and are shown in Figure 5. However, the p-value again failed to demonstrate significance at 0.397.

Overall, human raters rated coherence an average of 3.37, relevance 3.21, and empathy 3.29 across all of the stories.

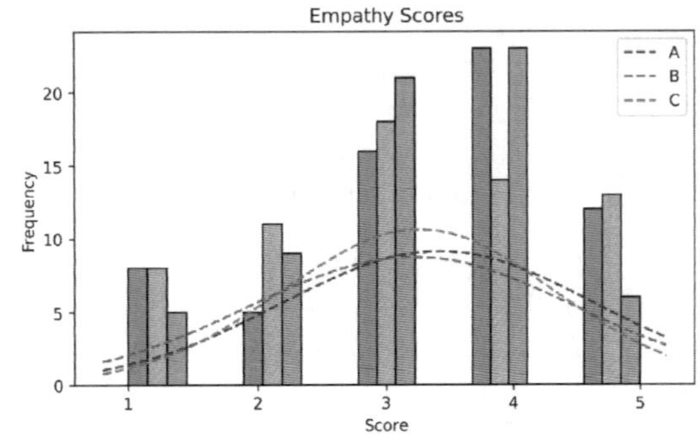

Figure 5: Histogram of the empathy ratings given by human raters to each of the three methods. A: log-likelihood-based scoring, B: simple prompt-based scoring and C: fine-tuned scoring.

Outline Annotation Statistics			
Method	Specificity	Precision	Recall
Log-likelihood	0.3901	0.4220	0.5345
Simple prompt	0.3527	0.3606	0.4733
Fine-tuning	0.4126	0.4449	0.5780

Table 2: Specificity, precision, and recall of human annotations for identifying corresponding passages in generated stories. Annotators selected passages they believed best matched each outline point. Specificity indicates how many words (as a ratio of passage length) they selected which overlapped with the actual, corresponding, generated passages. Precision and recall are both ratios in which the numerator is the sum of the number of annotators that selected each correctly annotated word. Precision divides this by the product of the total number of correctly annotated words and the number of annotators. Recall divides it by the number of words in the generated passage multiplied by the number of annotators. Each of these three scores is then aggregated over all of the passages using a macro average.

5.2.2 Outline Annotation

As described in Section 4.3, we further instructed the human subjects to annotate which passages from the generated story they believed to correspond best to each outline point. We then calculated the specificity, precision, and recall of these selections relative to the actual corresponding passages from the alignment used by the LLM generator. The results can be found in Table 2.

From these results, we can see that generating with fine-tuned scoring produces the highest specificity, precision and recall, suggesting that it adheres most closely to the input outlines and/or that it compels human raters to select longer passages to hedge their uncertainty. However, considering that all scores are fairly close and the relevance ratings in Section 5.2.1 are not statistically significantly different, it is likely that these methods are similar in their effectiveness in scoring relevance.

5.2.3 Preference Ranking

To evaluate the preference ranking we used the Bradley-Terry-Luce method, from which we determined the following preference ranking, where high scale values indicate higher preference:

1. Prompt-based scoring (scale 0.884)
2. Log-likelihood-based scoring (scale 0.464)
3. Fine-tuned scoring (scale -0.1349)

Therefore, in spite of their performances in respect of relevance, the simple prompt-based scoring method was the most preferred, while the fine-tuned scoring was the least preferred.

In their explanations of why they chose their rankings, many participants cited coherence as a reason. This may be in part due to the fact that they had been asked earlier in the survey to rate the coherence of the stories, although they were primed to the same extent for empathy and relevance, and empathy was cited far less frequently, whereas relevance was hardly ever mentioned. This suggests that coherence has a greater impact on a reader's preference for a generated story than the other criteria that participants were asked to score.

On the other hand, when comparing the preference ranking to the coherence histogram in Figure 3 and the p-value for coherence, there are clearly other factors that have influenced their decision.

Many participants additionally mention how engaging or interesting the story is as a factor in their choice. As mentioned in Section 4.3, we chose this question to replace the criteria of engagement and "interestingness" from Chhun et al. (2022) and Yang et al. (2023). This was an effective question. Many participants also mentioned that they enjoyed the stories due to the overall structure or flow of the story in how it was presented. One participant, for example, wrote about why they preferred a prompt-based scoring story:

> I preferred Story 3 because it presents an exciting, high-stakes conflict surrounding an advanced weapon and the dangerous implications of its existence. The tension between the characters and the mystery about their father's involvement with a shadowy organization adds depth to the narrative, and I find the mix of technology, moral dilemmas, and intrigue particularly engaging.

5.3 Discussion

These results suggest that there may be no significant difference between prompting, log-likelihood and fine-tuning as reranking methods in this framework. It also calls into question how thorough previous work has been in this area. Tasks have been ill-defined, instructions to annotators have been lacking in specificity or ecologically questionable, and some papers (Yang et al., 2023, e.g.,) have advocated for switching from one method to another without experimentally determining which was better.

Log-likelihoods derived from LLMs are a competitive approach, although there is evidence that prompting is preferable overall. The bad news is that even the effort of fine tuning does not seem to provide a significant improvement to automated reranking. This could suggest that there is still a need for better human-rated datasets of generated story output.

6 Conclusion

In this paper, we compared three different automatic scoring methods when used in a reranking framework for story generation. Our experiments were unable to prove a significant difference among these methods when their outputs are assessed by human raters. Future work could explore alternative reranking techniques, such as reinforcement-learning-based methods. Additionally, there is a need for more annotated datasets of stories. We hope that this research contributes to more effective and controllable story generation systems in NLP.

Limitations

A key limitation of our approach lies in the datasets used for fine-tuning. Beyond the previously mentioned issues regarding the wording of instructions for annotators, this dataset was designed to score entire stories, whereas our task focused on scoring individual passages within a larger narrative. Using a model fine-tuned for full-story scoring on smaller passages may not be an effective solution, highlighting the need for more specialized datasets.

Additionally, stories generated without reranking could have been compared as a baseline. We did not pursue this approach since Yang et al. (2022) found through ablation studies that reranking was essential for the generation process. Now that LLMs have improved, however, there may be a different outcome.

Acknowledgments

This research was supported by a grant from NAVER corporation.

References

Tuhin Chakrabarty, Philippe Laban, Divyansh Agarwal, Smaranda Muresan, and Chien-Sheng Wu. 2024. Art or artifice? large language models and the false promise of creativity. In *Proceedings of the 2024 CHI Conference on Human Factors in Computing Systems*.

Yi Chen, Rui Wang, Haiyun Jiang, Shuming Shi, and Ruifeng Xu. 2023. Exploring the use of large language models for reference-free text quality evaluation: An empirical study. In *Findings of IJCNLP-AACL 2023*, pages 361–374.

Cyril Chhun, Pierre Colombo, Fabian M. Suchanek, and Chlo'e Clavel. 2022. Of human criteria and automatic metrics: A benchmark of the evaluation of story generation. In *Proceedings of the 29th International Conference on Computational Linguistics*, pages 5794–5836.

Cyril Chhun, Fabian M. Suchanek, and Chlo'e Clavel. 2024. Do language models enjoy their own stories? prompting large language models for automatic story evaluation. *Transactions of the Association for Computational Linguistics*, 12:1122–1142.

John Joon Young Chung, Wooseok Kim, Kang Min Yoo, Hwaran Lee, Eytan Adar, and Minsuk Chang. 2022. Talebrush: Sketching stories with generative pretrained language models. In *Proceedings of the 2022 CHI Conference on Human Factors in Computing Systems*.

Pierre Colombo, Maxime Peyrard, Nathan Noiry, Robert West, and Pablo Piantanida. 2023. The glass ceiling of automatic evaluation in natural language generation. In *Findings of IJCNLP-AACL 2023*, pages 178–183.

Angela Fan, Mike Lewis, and Yann Dauphin. 2018. Hierarchical neural story generation. In *Proceedings of the 56th Annual Meeting of the Association for Computational Linguistics*, pages 889–898.

Sarik Ghazarian, Johnny Wei, Aram Galstyan, and Nanyun Peng. 2019. Better automatic evaluation of open-domain dialogue systems with contextualized embeddings. In *Proceedings of the Workshop on Methods for Optimizing and Evaluating Neural Language Generation*, pages 82–89.

Jian Guan and Minlie Huang. 2020. UNION: An Unreferenced Metric for Evaluating Open-ended Story Generation. In *Proceedings of the 2020 Conference on Empirical Methods in Natural Language Processing (EMNLP)*, pages 9157–9166.

Jian Guan, Zhexin Zhang, Zhuoer Feng, Zitao Liu, Wenbiao Ding, Xiaoxi Mao, Changjie Fan, and Minlie Huang. 2021. OpenMEVA: A benchmark for evaluating open-ended story generation metrics. In *Proceedings of the 59th Annual Meeting of the Association for Computational Linguistics and the 11th International Joint Conference on Natural Language Processing*, pages 6394–6407.

Levon Haroutunian, Zhuang Li, Lucian Galescu, Philip Cohen, Raj Tumuluri, and Gholamreza Haffari. 2023. Reranking for natural language generation from logical forms: A study based on large language models. In *Proceedings of the 13th International Joint Conference on Natural Language Processing and the 3rd Conference of the Asia-Pacific Chapter of the Association for Computational Linguistics*, pages 1067–1082.

Meta Research. 2023. doc-storygen-v2.

Nasrin Mostafazadeh, Nathanael Chambers, Xiaodong He, Devi Parikh, Dhruv Batra, Lucy Vanderwende, Pushmeet Kohli, and James Allen. 2016. A corpus and cloze evaluation for deeper understanding of commonsense stories. In *Proceedings of the 2016 Conference of the North American Chapter of the Association for Computational Linguistics: Human Language Technologies*, pages 839–849.

Jekaterina Novikova, Ondvrej Duvsek, Amanda Cercas Curry, and Verena Rieser. 2017. Why we need new evaluation metrics for NLG. In *Proceedings of the 2017 Conference on Empirical Methods in Natural Language Processing*, pages 2241–2252.

Hannah Rashkin, Asli Celikyilmaz, Yejin Choi, and Jianfeng Gao. 2020. Plotmachines: Outline-conditioned generation with dynamic plot state tracking. In *Proceedings of the 2020 Conference on Empirical Methods in Natural Language Processing (EMNLP)*, pages 4274–4295.

Xinpeng Wang, Han Jiang, Zhihua Wei, and Shanlin Zhou. 2022. Chae: Fine-grained controllable story generation with characters, actions and emotions. In *Proceedings of the 29th International Conference on Computational Linguistics*, pages 6426–6435.

Ivan P. Yamshchikov and Alexey Tikhonov. 2023. What is wrong with language models that can not tell a story? In *Proceedings of the 5th Workshop on Narrative Understanding*, pages 58–64.

Dingyi Yang and Qin Jin. 2024. What makes a good story and how can we measure it? a comprehensive survey of story evaluation. *Preprint*, arXiv:2408.14622.

Kevin Yang, Dan Klein, Nanyun Peng, and Yuandong Tian. 2023. Doc: Improving long story coherence with detailed outline control. In *Proceedings of the 61st Annual Meeting of the Association for Computational Linguistics*, pages 3378–3465.

Kevin Yang, Yuandong Tian, Nanyun Peng, and Dan Klein. 2022. Re3: Generating longer stories with recursive reprompting and revision. In *Proceedings of the 2022 Conference on Empirical Methods in Natural Language Processing*, pages 4393–4479.

Lili Yao, Nanyun Peng, Ralph Weischedel, Kevin Knight, Dongyan Zhao, and Rui Yan. 2019. Plan-and-write: towards better automatic storytelling. In *Proceedings of the Thirty-Third AAAI Conference on Artificial Intelligence and Thirty-First Innovative Applications of Artificial Intelligence Conference and Ninth AAAI Symposium on Educational Advances in Artificial Intelligence*, AAAI'19/IAAI'19/EAAI'19.

Tianyi Zhang*, Varsha Kishore*, Felix Wu*, Kilian Q. Weinberger, and Yoav Artzi. 2020. Bertscore: Evaluating text generation with bert. In *Proceedings of the International Conference on Learning Representations*.

Hanlin Zhu, Andrew Cohen, Danqing Wang, Kevin Yang, Xiaomeng Yang, Jiantao Jiao, and Yuandong Tian. 2023. End-to-end story plot generator. *Preprint*, arXiv:2310.08796.

A Appendix

> Could you, using the following format:
> {outline}
>
> please generate an outline for a short story with the following writing prompt:
> '{prompt}'
>
> The outline should have at most 8 nodes.
>
> Outline:

Figure A.1: Prompt for generating outline. Here, {outline} is replaced with an example outline in the required format and {prompt} is replaced with the story prompt that we want to use to generate the outline.

> **Premise:** A humble cheesemaker, renowned for making the best cheese in town, embarks on a daring adventure to slay a fearsome dragon that threatens the kingdom
> **Setting:** A quaint village surrounded by rolling hills and dense forests, within a kingdom plagued by a dragon.
> **Entities and Characters:**
>
> - **Milo:** Milo is the best cheesemaker in the village, known for his delicious and unique cheeses
>
>   ⋮
>
> **Outline:**
>
> 1. **Event:** The village is terrorized by a dragon.
>   **Characters:** Milo, King Aldric
>   **Setting:** Milo's cheese shop.
>
>   (a) **Event:** King Aldric issues a decree.
>   **Characters:** King Aldric
>   **Setting:** The King's castle.
>
>   ⋮
>
> 2. **Event:** Milo prepares for the journey.
>   **Characters:** Milo, Fiona
>   **Setting:** Milo's home.
>
>   ⋮

Figure A.2: Example outline for input to the generation framework.

<table>
<tr><th colspan="2">Example Survey</th></tr>
<tr><td colspan="2">Instructions
• You will be presented with three stories in this document.
• After each story, you will find a set of questions related to that story.
• At the end, there will be a final question asking you to compare all three stories.
Please carefully read all stories and questions. Write your answers in the designated highlighted spaces. Also be sure to highlight the story when instructed to. Important: Answer all questions.</td></tr>
<tr><td>Story 1</td><td>Jake Hunter was known for his lightning-fast reflexes and uncanny ability to anticipate his opponents' moves ...</td></tr>
<tr><td>How coherent was the story (how clear and sensible is it and how well does it flow logically together)? (1-5)</td><td>(1) Not at all coherent (The entire story is unclear, doesn't make sense at all and is inconsistent throughout).
(2) It is logically inconsistent or doesn't make sense for most of the story.
(3) The story is logically consistent and makes sense overall, but has some inconsistencies or parts that don't make sense.
(4) The story is coherent but it has one or two inconsistencies or incoherences.
(5) The story is entirely coherent - there are no inconsistencies and it makes sense.</td></tr>
<tr><td>2. How well did you understand the character's emotions? (1-5)</td><td>(1) The characters seemed apathetic to you.
(2) At least one character slightly related to you on an emotional level.
(3) You recognized specific, but not necessarily strong, emotions (e.g. sadness, joy, fear. . .) in at least one character.
(4) At least one character emotionally involved you, but minor details prevented you from completely relating to them.
(5) At least one character completely involved you on an emotional level.</td></tr>
<tr><td>The following is a bullet point story outline used to generate this story. First, highlight the text in the story that corresponds to each outline point using the specified color for each point (for example the first outline point is yellow, the second is green, etc.). Then answer the question below.</td><td>• Introduction to Jake's unique ability and career
– EVENT:Jake's latest victory showcasing...
SETTING:The boxing ring
CHARACTERS:Jake Hunter, Coach Reynolds
– EVENT:Coach Reynolds discusses Jake's ...
• ...</td></tr>
</table>

(Continued)	
How well do you feel like this text captures each outline point? How well are the characters, scene and event represented in each passage? (1-5)	(1) The text has no relationship with the outline points at all. (2) The text only has a weak relationship with the outline points. (3) The text roughly follows the outline points. (4) The text follows the outline points, except for one or two small aspects. (5) The text follows the outline point exactly.
Story 2	...
Story 3	...
For the following question, place your ranking for each story inside the highlighted brackets.	
Rank the three stories based on how likely you would be to purchase them, assuming you were given the money to do so. Assign a rank of 1 to the story you are most likely to buy, 2 to the next, and 3 to the least likely. Each rank must be assigned to only one story.	() Story 1 () Story 2 () Story 3
Why did you prefer the story you did? Please explain your preferences in 1-3 sentences below.	

Table A.1: An example survey given to participants in the human study. Participants are given the same questions for each story and then asked to rank their preference between stories. The order of the stories is changed for each survey. Each story in the survey is generated from the same outline.

Author Index

Alhafni, Bashar, 11
Anantha Ramakrishnan, Aashish, 74
Arnold, Kenneth C., 62, 69
August, Tal, 47

Briscoe, Ted, 11

Chen, Xiang, 69
Chirkunov, Kirill, 11

Deering, Megan, 109

Habash, Nizar, 11
Hsu, Ting-Yao, 1
Huang, Ting-Hao Kenneth, 1

Jung, Hyunggu, 1

Kim, Jiho, 62, 69
Kim, Sungchul, 1
Kondoro, Alfred Malengo, 37

Laban, Philippe, 69
Lee, Dongwon, 74
Li, Lingxi, 19
Liu, Yijun, 47

Min, Jiyoo, 1

Ng, Ho Yin Sam, 1

Penn, Gerald, 87, 109

Qwaider, Chatrine, 11

Ramakrishnan, Aadarsh Anantha, 74
Rossi, Ryan A., 1

Shi, Ken, 87

Tran, Hieu, 19

Yao, Zonghai, 19
yu, Hong, 19
Yu, Tian, 87
Yu, Tong, 1

Zhao, Zixin, 87

Association for Computational Linguistics
209 N. Eighth Street
Stroudsburg, Pennsylvania 18360

CURRAN ASSOCIATES INC.
proceedings.com

ISBN 979-8-3313-1918-2